Marshall McLuhan

Marshall McLuhan

Cosmic Media

Janine Marchessault

SAGE Publications
London • Thousand Oaks • New Delhi

SAGE Publications Ltd
1 Oliver's Yard
55 City Road
London EC1Y 1SP

SAGE Publications Inc.
2455 Teller Road
Thousand Oaks, California 91320

SAGE Publications India Pvt Ltd
B-42, Panchsheel Enclave
Post Box 4109
New Delhi 110 017

British Library Cataloguing in Publication data

A catalogue record for this book is available
from the British Library

ISBN 0 7619 5264 0
ISBN 0 7619 5265 9

Library of Congress Control Number available

Typeset by C&M Digitals (P) Ltd., Chennai, India
Printed and bound in Great Britain by Athenaeum Press, Gateshead

302.23 MAR 2005 Marchessault, Janine. Marshall McLuhan : cosmic media.

Contents

Acknowledgements

I would like to thank the Social Sciences and Humanities Research Council of Canada for a grant in support of this project as well as the Department of English at McGill University and the Department of Film and Video at York University, for generous administrative and research support. This manuscript was a long time in the making and during that time I have benefited from the intellectual companionship of many groups: colleagues who are part of the Culture of Cities Project in Canada as well as my long-time friends who have kept the Public Access Collective vibrant and connected to public art in Toronto.

I am particularly indebted to Christine Davis and Susan Lord for the sustained intellectual and creative conversations on matters McLuhan. I would like to thank my colleagues at McGill who encouraged the project in its initial stages, most especially Will Straw. I would also like to thank Chantal Kudzi-Zadeh for initial research and Nancy Shaw for inspiring conversations that helped me to understand language poetry. At York University, I am grateful to my colleagues Brenda Longfellow and Evan Cameron for continued encouragement; I would like to thank Theresa Scandiffio, Jen Vanderburgh, and Malve Petersman for help with research; Ken Alan, Julie DiCresce, and Karyn Sandlos for their insightful comments on earlier drafts; Brian Hotson for his work on the index; and Richard Kerr for letting us use an image from his video McLuhan (1993) for the cover; Lorraine Hardie for just being there. I would like to thank Chris Rojek for encouraging this project and for his patience over the years, as well as Kay

Bridger, Ian Antcliff and Susan Dunsmore for bringing the book to completion.

Finally, my deepest gratitude goes to my partner Philip Hoffman for his unfailing support and love and to Jessie, my daughter who, on the brink of adolescence, has helped me to see computer galaxies in an entirely new light – I dedicate this book to her.

Abbreviations

Introduction

McLuhan's Project

> I feel that we're standing on the threshold of a liberating and exhilarating world in which the human tribe can become truly one family and man's consciousness can be freed from the shackles of mechanical culture and enabled to roam the cosmos. I have a deep and abiding belief in man's potential to grow and learn, to plumb the depths of his own being and to learn the secret songs that orchestrate the universe. We live in a transitional era of profound pain and tragic identity quest, but the agony of our age is the labor pain of rebirth.
>
> I expect to see the coming decades transform the planet into an art form; the new man, linked in a cosmic harmony that transcends time and space, will sensuously caress and mold and pattern every facet of the terrestrial artifact as if it were a work of art, and man himself will become an organic art form. There is a long road ahead, and the stars are only way stations, but we have begun the journey. (McLuhan, *Playboy* interview, 1969/1995: 268)

Marshall McLuhan's theories of media, art and culture are being re-examined in the context of new digital cultures and globalization. This book provides a close reading of some of his key texts to discern the contribution his thinking can make to our understanding of the present condition of convergent and yet unstable media cultures. Throughout McLuhan's wide-ranging writings on the media, his central contribution to communication and cultural studies does not consist in any one theoretical insight. Rather, McLuhan's writings over a 40-year period from the 1940s on to his death in 1980 are consistently concerned with understanding the contemporary media as a problem of method. The key to any analysis of the media, which for McLuhan was always connected to the spaces and temporalities of the lifeworld, is a reflexive field approach. Oriented around the archival, encyclopedic, and artifactual surfaces but also 'haptic harmonies' and ruptures, this method draws out patterns that render ground assumptions and matrices discernible. This was encapsulated in his most famous neologism, 'the medium is the message'. McLuhan drew his insights from philosophers of language and modernity: the Cambridge New Critics (Leavis and Richards especially) who were his teachers, along with Nietzsche, Bergson, and Heidegger – all-important influences on his experimental pedagogy.

McLuhan's career encompasses the multiple meanings of the word project: the process of creating, an oral performance, refracted light, psychological transference, a forward moving action, a community in the making. While this book will seek to situate a number of influences and people that informed this project, it is crucial to place McLuhan's engagement within a Catholic intellectual tradition that encompasses Aristotle, Augustine, and Aquinas. We see this reflected in his belief that human cognition and perception are 'miracles' ('Catholic Humanism': 80) that make possible a shared experience of the everyday. Hence all scholarship is essentially research and exploration, it is a dialogue with others. This belief that our engagement with the world will always be a transformative and creative one will drive McLuhan's inquiry into the fundamental process and value of human communication throughout his career – from his doctoral dissertation on *Thomas Nashe and the Learning of His Time* to his posthumously published *Laws of Media*. The humanist ecumenical tradition highlights the importance McLuhan placed on interdisciplinary models of pedagogy and on the significance of a field of study that engages with contemporary culture.

McLuhan's contribution to the study of communication is distinguished by an approach that is aesthetically based, highly performative and historically grounded. Utilizing formal techniques drawn from the Symbolists and twentieth-century avant-garde forms (James Joyce in particular), McLuhan's experimental writings and literacy projects presented a cognitive function for art. His many collaborations with graphic artists, along with his belief that we would all be artists by the twenty-first century, anticipated the central place of interactivity and design in the new information environments of our century.

A public intellectual and media commentator, famous for a brief time, McLuhan, along with his long time collaborator, the radical anthropologist, Edmund Carpenter, organized one of the first truly interdisciplinary research projects in North America. This endeavor was accompanied by several interdisciplinary journals (*Explorations* being the most famous) and the establishment of the Centre for Culture and Technology at the University of Toronto. It is this interdisciplinary experience in the early 1950s fuelled by a desire to create a new field of communications study, that would have a decisive impact on the development of McLuhan's most productive and lasting formulations: the medium is the message, centre-without-margins, acoustic space, non-linear space, prosthetic memory, the global village, hot and cool media among others.

Throughout the 1940s, McLuhan's approach to analyzing culture was cinematic. It was based on a theory of aesthetic arrest and retracing drawn from the Symbolist poets and expressed by film artists such as Sergei Eisenstein and Cesare Zavattini. He saw the cinema and certain forms of poetry as the reproduction of human cognition. In these aesthetic techniques, he saw possibilities for new interdisciplinary and aesthetically based methodologies that would stimulate ideas and insights in the present situation which is difficult to discern since we are in it. In the 1950s and with his colleagues in Toronto, McLuhan developed a phenomenological understanding of culture that was inspired by the oral cultural traditions that Carpenter and Harvard anthropologist Dorothy Lee were studying. We can note that McLuhan moves from a notion of culture as landscape to one of environment, from spectatorship to immersion, and from the cinematic as an analogy for human cognition to television as the new reality and a new methodology.

If there is something truly unique and original in McLuhan's inquiry, and I believe there is, it is not only that he brings aesthetics to communication studies but that his project is marked by the meeting of television and anthropology. McLuhan looked to anthropology for clues to comprehend electric culture in terms of a new construction of space–time relations, new ways of being in the world. McLuhan's project provides a pedagogical imperative for the interdisciplinary study of living cultures as forms of mediation. This book argues that McLuhan's experimental writings can help us to formulate new methodologies for a politically conscious and phenomenologically sensitive humanist scholarship. His commitment to historicizing knowledge as an expression of mentalities does so by breaking down the boundaries between disciplines across the arts and sciences, between nations and cultures, between corporealities and technologies while recognizing and juxtaposing differences. Across McLuhan's explorations of the electric galaxy, he discerns a reconfiguration and increased significance of locality and difference in the face of the globalizing and homogenizing forces of modernity. As national boundaries become more porous and new information technologies enable and create the need for greater collaborations (both economic and culture, both equitable and imperialistic), he discerns a shift in the experience of the margins. He would call this an experience of the 'centre without margins'. In effect, he develops a methodology that enacts this new consciousness that he believes is a direct consequence of technology.

Relations

McLuhan is concerned with the relations between things, both with how consciousness produces relations in order to make meaning and how seemingly unrelated things – the telegraph and the Civil War, or the chorus line and print culture – when taken as contiguous reveal structural homologies. In his world, everything is related and interconnected as it was in the medieval Cosmos. It is the task of the researcher to materialize the web of human relations. McLuhan is not interested in simple connections, however. For it is not the connection between things that will reveal underlying structures, rather, it is in exploring the intervals, oppositions and interfaces between things, the historical shifts and breakages that mark the emergence of new civilizations, that will enable us to grasp an underlying unity. What is often not understood about McLuhan's methodology is that it is historical, and inspired by the anonymous histories of Siegfried Gideon, Wyndham Lewis, Erwin Panofsky, Lewis Mumford and Harold Innis – and more fundamentally by Vico. McLuhan's project grows out of a periodization of communication technologies that is not linear but cyclical. Moving from orality to literacy and back to orality again, McLuhan describes the emergence of new tribal cultures produced by electric media. While these are oral, they do not represent a return to older forms but are a new cultural manifestation that we can decipher through older non-western cultural formations.

Thus, McLuhan's periodization resists the interpretation of electric cultures as a simple return to an archaic consciousness. Yet his cyclical view of history is nevertheless teteological and infused by the conjunction of electricity and spirit. This romantic and mystical association, not uncommon among the French artists and intellectuals who so influenced him (from Mallarmé to de Chardin), produces the kabalistic paradox, which is the relatedness of multiplicity and unity, of the one and the many. This simultaneous experience of unity and multiplicity enabled by the electronic media represents a kind of cosmic consciousness that McLuhan never defines but which is akin to Jung's collective unconscious. There is a dialectic at play in McLuhan's work between the historical materiality of language as cultural artifact and the transcendental aspects of his Thomistic views. *Cosmic Media* seeks to highlight this tension by maintaining Catholic humanism as an ever-present framework in his thinking.

Fame

We can divide McLuhan's career into two periods, essentially before and after fame (the fame itself was short-lived, only about five years from 1966 to 1971). His rise to becoming a clichéd figure in the electric galaxy he sought to analyze was highly orchestrated. It was a marketing experiment carried out by

Howard Gossage and Gerald Feigen and supported by Gossage's San Francisco advertising firm. For McLuhan it was a pedagogical experiment with form (using the media to create awareness of the media) that he believed to have been miraculously successful (Marchand, 1989: 172–3). It was perhaps this success that eventually proved to be his downfall – he was pressed, consumed and forgotten. There is something tragic in McLuhan's absorption and then hostile rejection by the media, which several films have sought to underscore (most recently *McLuhan's Wake* (2003) by Kevin McMahon.) David Cronenberg's *Videodrome* (1983) dramatized this tragic end to perfection with Professor Brian Oblivion dying of a brain tumor and immortalizing himself on television as a religious leader. The truth is stranger. Not only did McLuhan have a brain tumor removed on the eve of his rise to global stardom but also the surgery left him with large memory gaps (he had to reread many books), with hypersensitive audition and a new-found love of singing. A decade or so later, he had stroke which left him with aphasia. McLuhan, who had always stressed the haptic aspects of communication, was left with a dramatic incapacity to speak or to write (Marchand, 1989: 270–7).

When I began research for this book in 1995, the McLuhan renaissance was just beginning. I was swept up in an onslaught of new books, newspaper articles, documentaries and intellectual biographies all geared towards juxtaposing McLuhan with the rise of a radically transformed information society in the West that was being created by the Internet, wireless communication, digital technologies, CNN, etc. While McLuhan's writings do provide insights into the networked society, I have all too often found them misquoted or over-simplified. In discussing McLuhan with colleagues who teach communication studies, I have become increasingly suspicious that nobody reads McLuhan. Rather what is left of his ideas are the superficial clichés and neologisms taken out of context that were part of his later collage books. Thus, *Cosmic Media* reads McLuhan closely in order to consider some of his most fruitful methodologies and to situate his intellectual contribution within a history of ideas.

McLuhan produced eight books and over a thousand articles. I have chosen to examine three of his principle works – *Mechanical*

Bride (MB), *Gutenberg Galaxy* (GG) and *Understanding Media* (UM). Not only are these his only single authored books but they grew out of collaborative research projects in the 1950s and early 1960s that I believe represent his most complex research. I also examine some of his early literary essays collected in *Interior Landscape* (IL) and other works from the innovative journal *Explorations*. McLuhan's letters are a rich source of information, connecting his overall intellectual and creative life to his deep faith which he chose to keep private but which nevertheless was always present in his thinking. I have found a great deal of value in McLuhan's media guides, *Report on Project in Understanding New Media*, *The City as Classroom* (CC), and *Laws of Media* (LM). These texts are geared towards teaching and exploring the media and they continue to be very productive pedagogical devices. The oral aspects of McLuhan's œuvre are also a significant part of his project: lectures, thousands of talks and seminars reflect his commitment both to dialogue, and to media studies as performance.

Cosmic Media

It is sometimes difficult to justify a linear book about an author committed to non-linear, aphoristic modes of thinking. However, I have written this book in the hopes of drawing out and clarifying some of the concepts that could be usefully considered in the present context of global media. Moreover, the oppositions between linearity and non-linearity were exaggerated by McLuhan because these concepts served as schematic tools to make sense of cultural formations. In reality, such oppositions, like the central one in McLuhan's work between orality and literacy, are not mutually exclusive. In oral cultures we find forms of writing, and literacy contains oral dimensions. Moreover, not all linear forms of exposition are simply a straight line, and some forms of collage invite linear interpretations.

Despite his commitment to the rhetorical tradition, McLuhan was a dialectical and an historical thinker. For this reason I have chosen to maintain a chronological form in the presentation of some of his most important ideas. Although time and space have been transformed by technologies, the arrow of time has not, and this ontological dimension of experience was always a central one for McLuhan. This is why McLuhan's work is distinguished by an interest in the corporeal aspects of communication. He was just as interested in poetry as he was in consciousness, perception and the cognitive sciences. In fact, aesthetics, rhetorical form and perception are inseparable in any examination of the media. For this reason, experimental art as a laboratory of perception was a significant research tool for McLuhan, generating 'anti-environments' through reflexive experiments with technology.

McLuhan proposes a methodology for studying living cultures that is televisual. Inspired by early television's ontology, the methodology McLuhan proposed was process-oriented and open-ended. This aesthetic and experimental approach to media study might explain why McLuhan has had a much stronger influence on artists (Fluxus media and performance artists, sound poets, graphic designers, etc.) than on academics. Régis Debray puts it nicely:

> Was McLuhan's name too often in the newspapers for him to be taken seriously by the academy? The proper name's transfiguration into logo, trademark and cliché (a match in acoustic space to the Marlboro man, Chaplin's cane or Marilyn's flared-out skirts) did nothing to facilitate the esteem; and most of us are familiar with the superior tone, somewhere between irritation and playfully mocking, that in the right circles is elicited by this impostor-prophet, this garish and muddled showman, whose buzzwords are every man-in-the-street's common coin – Gutenberg galaxy, 'hot' and 'cold' media, message and massage, etc. – and whom no hard science type grants any seriousness or intellectual dignity. (1996: 69–70)

This lack of 'intellectual dignity' continues to accompany the name of McLuhan but in my experience it seems to be generational. Isabelle Stengers has commented that it is not that academic trends and attitudes change but that people die (2000). I will say no more except that a new generation, which has grown up with television and lives with computers, is more open to McLuhan's experimental techniques and metaphors.

We should never lose sight of the fact that McLuhan was playing a game, writing satire, punning, using rhetorical devices borrowed from advertising to capture his audience's attention. Media studies, whether written or oral, are always performative because these must engage with living cultures. This lack of seriousness frustrated his critics no end precisely because McLuhan refused to defend his own ideas. His game was an endless and sometimes reckless speculation about the present moment, the one that had just passed. The challenge to deal with the present was the one he posed to the academy.

McLuhan's ideas remain most vivid when connected to an historical and social context. *Cosmic Media* is divided into three parts which seek to situate them spatially: Cambridge, America and the Global Village. These geographies are virtual and part of McLuhan's cosmic consciousness. For a young man living in Manitoba, Canada, Cambridge and America were mythological spaces of great intellectual and imperial power. Later McLuhan came to focus more strictly on the Global Village as a stage (still imperial and American) through which the events of the world were narrated for North American and Western European audiences. Despite the rhetoric of cosmic connections, there is in McLuhan's writings, especially throughout the 1950s, a highly developed awareness of the inequitable distribution of wealth and technology in the world. His writings disclose a sensitivity to multicultural and gender differences which I believe reflects the very important collaborations with Edmund Carpenter.

Although McLuhan wrote much about the electronic media, he was essentially a man of letters. While a great deal of his work was committed to non-linear and experimental forms of writing and thinking, this work grew out of a life that moved forward with tremendous intentionality and energy. It was directed by an ecumenical project that was remarkably consistent from beginning to end, and its goal was to spread the word and raise consciousness.

Cosmic Media does not spend much time defending McLuhan against his detractors. The criticisms are many and should be taken seriously: he ignores the content of the media at his peril; his oppositions, while heuristic, are nevertheless too rigid; he has no analysis of the political economy of technologies; there is an underlying mysticism in his thought that accounts for some of his most ahistorical statements; his formalism occludes any account of power; he romanticizes oral traditions often in overtly Orientalist ways. We cannot ignore these issues. However, I also hope, by focusing on McLuhan's methodology, to highlight what I consider to be some of his most sensible and original contributions.

McLuhan does not answer questions so much as raise them. We can read him as an artist who creates tools that foreground the ethics of reflexive methodologies. Yet to distinguish McLuhan as a Romantic artist as does George Steiner when he compares him to Blake *(McLuhan Hot and Cool,* 1967: 239) is to misrepresent his project. McLuhan is a creative researcher and an interdisciplinary thinker who is deeply connected to the Romantic tradition. He does not make art so much as recognize the value of art as a means to discern the production of mediated forms of consciousness. We should bear in mind that McLuhan never claimed to be anything more than 'a student' immersed in the new interdisciplinary field of Media Studies that his work helped to inaugurate.

PART I

Cambridge

1

Romantic Art

Marshall McLuhan should be considered to have been first and foremost an English professor. His intellectual formation in English Studies at Cambridge University deeply influenced his methodological approaches to the media. To begin a study on McLuhan it is crucial to understand that his concept of the media, a term he made famous, starts with an awareness of the materiality of language, with language as *techne*. This awareness stems initially from his love of poetry. It is this passion for the beauty and organic existence of language, both written and oral, that sets McLuhan's writings on the media apart from the more empirically driven approaches that came to characterize the North American social sciences in the 1950s and 1960s. McLuhan's distinctive interdisciplinary style of writing aligns him with a post-war generation of cultural theorists – Raymond Williams, Roland Barthes, Umberto Eco and, most especially, with Harold Innis. While these thinkers did not always share McLuhan's views of the media – Williams and Eco were sometimes his staunchest critics – like him, their theories exceed academically defined norms of writing and disciplinary boundaries. All of them addressed the lived context of everyday culture, those things that make up ordinary perceptions and experiences, and always placed their insights within an historical framework. In their writings, culture becomes so familiar that it ceases to be noticed: it is an environment, a whole way of life, a mythos.

These conceptualizations have helped define some of the most productive questions for media studies and have served to lay the foundations for the development of cultural studies in a variety of national contexts from the 1950s onward.

In order to trace McLuhan's contribution to media and cultural studies, this first chapter will focus on the importance of literary theory, specifically New Criticism, to McLuhan's formalist analysis of media technologies. It is without doubt that McLuhan's studies at Cambridge exerted a formative and lasting influence on his scholarship. Like other cultural theorists of his generation who went to Cambridge, McLuhan would adopt Cambridge's (or Leavis's) commitment to criticism and to a programme of English literacy and pedagogy. Much later, McLuhan sought to establish a Media Studies program at the University of Toronto in addition to initiating several journals and magazines. His aim was to create an intellectual and creative context for the study of communications media that was process-oriented and historically minded, interdisciplinary, and research-based.

Outsider

It is appropriate to situate McLuhan's work within a biographical context since his writings were concerned with the historical sphere in which meaning is made. Throughout his career, McLuhan maintained that growing up on the Canadian prairies had, early on, given him an important perspective on Western civilization. The agrarian culture of the prairies served as a 'counter-environment' to the great centres of culture, providing him with a detached view of the world. In fact, according to McLuhan, this is the position that all Canadians hold *vis-à-vis* culture (Marchand, 1989: 5). Being a former colony of England and France, as well as being neighbour to a more recent empire, the United States, provides Canadians with a unique perspective on both high culture and the mass media. In particular, its peculiar distance from and proximity to the USA have meant that Canada functions as 'an early warning system', providing a model for anticipating future events.

Many have speculated that this position explains why Canada has produced so many of North America's finest satirists and comedians. According to McLuhan, a sense of humour grows out of not belonging. Canadians watch a lot of American television, but rarely see themselves represented. As comedian Mike Myers would explain on an American talk show after the release of the film *Austin Powers*, 'we Canadians watch you on our television and think your culture is strange. Our humour comes from watching television'. Jokes are an important 'anti-environmental tool' that 'do not deal in theory, but in immediate experience, and are often the best guide to changing perceptions' (*The Medium is the Massage*, CBS Records, 1967). McLuhan told jokes and collected funny stories throughout his life because he believed that these were 'indexes of public grievance' (Marchand, 1989: 367). Moreover, comedy rather than tragedy provides a distance from events. Humour and satire are principal features of McLuhan's overall approach to the media and to the academy, which is perhaps why so many communications scholars have refused to take him seriously.

This, however, never stopped McLuhan from taking himself seriously. Not only was McLuhan an outsider by 'birth, nationality, and later by religion and an unconventional style' but he was a 'superior outsider' (Jeffrey, 1989: 7). This attitude is a very conscious critical strategy on McLuhan's part: 'The road to understanding media effects begins with arrogant superiority. If one lacked this sense of superiority, this detachment, it would be quite impossible to write about them. It would be like an octopus attacking the great pyramids' (Stearn, 1967: 284).

McLuhan's sense of his own outsider status must also be understood in relation to his conversion to Roman Catholicism in 1936, which is the definitive aspect of his sense of separation from the material world. Indeed, while McLuhan never comes out as a Catholic, he writes of the analytic detachment enabled by Catholicism:

> Long accustomed to a defensive position behind a minority culture, English and American Catholics have developed multiple mental squints. Involuntarily their sensibilities have been nourished and ordered by a century or more of an alien literary and artistic activity which faute de mieux, they still approach askance. (*IL*: 21)

McLuhan believes in avoiding the singular point of view. Being both a Canadian and a Catholic contributed to his rejection of the fixed point of view as with fixed identity. Canada is a multicultural nation made up of unique and sometimes conflicting provinces, regions and cultures, and this has been of assistance in enabling individuals to offset the single point of view. Indeed, the heterogeneity which defines Canadian culture as a 'cultural mosaic' (that liberal expression made famous by McLuhan's long-time friend Prime Minister Pierre Trudeau) would foster the idea and the very possibility of those multiple 'mental squints'.

Paradoxically, this detachment from the single point of view brings McLuhan closer to an objectivity or an empiricism in which the surfaces of things are juxtaposed. One finds in so many of McLuhan's interviews a heroic sense of being 'in the know', of being closer to the source of truth than anyone else. In an insightful and humorous essay on McLuhan, Marjorie Ferguson has commented on the characteristic 'solipsistic certitude' found in McLuhan's often self-righteous proclamations: 'I am the only one who knows what the hell is going on'; or 'I seem to be the only one who understands what is happening'. I would add to this McLuhan's delight in simply telling people they are wrong: 'There's a new book on the telephone that's just come out. It's a very bad book ... The writers don't know what they're talking about' (*Understanding McLuhan*, CD-ROM). As Ferguson underlines, it is not difficult to see why McLuhan inspired both 'veneration and venom' (1991: 71). Poet, humorist, critic, and above all, Catholic, McLuhan's outsider position reflects a sensibility and a methodology influenced by the modernist writers he admired throughout his life: Eliot, Pound, Joyce, and Lewis, for whom language – the language needed to confront modernity and the forces of modernization – could only be a foreign land.

Raised in a middle-class home on the Canadian prairies, McLuhan was not deprived of 'culture'. From the earliest age his mother introduced him to English poetry and the elocutionary arts. Elsie McLuhan taught public reading and had a successful career touring Canada as a professional monologist. McLuhan was familiar with all the great English poets, and one can just imagine an earnest McLuhan at 18 committing himself to memorizing Milton's

Paradise Lost in order to come to terms with the essence of poetic genius, something he felt eluded him (Marchand, 1989: 9). This is an important biographical detail not only because we can see how McLuhan was groomed by his mother to be an orator from an early age (his brother became a minister), but more importantly it gives some background to the way he viewed language as a sensuous activity. The orality of poetry, the relation between orality and literacy, the spoken word's relation to the body, to temporality and to performance, are all central to McLuhan's first encounters with language as art. When McLuhan turns his sights towards technology, it is not as something that is foreign to bodies but, rather, functions as 'extensions' of them. While the idea of extension comes to him from several sources: Lewis Mumford, I.A. Richards, and later from the anthropologist Edward Hall, it is an idea that at its root comes from his encounter with elocutionary art.

At the University of Manitoba, McLuhan first studied engineering, then transferred to English and History receiving an undergraduate and a Master's degree. His Master's thesis was on the neglected nineteenth-century poet and novelist, George Meredith, but Meredith had little lasting influence on his ideas. The Victorian writers that he encountered along the way did, however, and he would come to know them more profoundly during his years at Cambridge. Although McLuhan rejected the Romantic critique of industrialization, which he understood to support a simple binary opposition between nature and culture, his first book, *The Mechanical Bride: Folklore of Industrial Man*, is written with the tools of this intellectual heritage. I want to turn to examine this tradition and McLuhan's encounter with English Studies at Cambridge where many of his central ideas began to take shape.

Criticism and Pedagogy

McLuhan spent two years in England, and had a nine-year relationship with Cambridge, which was without doubt the place where his sense of being an outsider was first most pronounced.

There was none of the personal sense of superiority discussed above. Instead, upon arriving at Cambridge he immediately felt the need to learn everything over again (Fitzgerald, 2001: 29–30). Rather than beginning a PhD, he began an undergraduate degree and studied with I.A. Richards and F.R. Leavis. Cambridge was where his aesthetic approach to criticism and the media would find its first expression. Although not from a working-class background, McLuhan, like Williams, was on a scholarship and had a sense of not speaking the language, of not belonging, and of being an outsider to the high culture celebrated at Cambridge. It is perhaps this experience of being disconnected from both high culture and from any sense of a distinct Canadian culture (unlike Williams who would come to value his own Welsh roots), that would push McLuhan to search for an integrated aesthetic conceptually bound to both English literature and American popular culture. This would foster key insights on the importance of including popular culture in the study of English.

Contrary to the dominant view in the nineteenth century that industrialization meant progress, writers like Coleridge, Ruskin, and Morris believed that industrialization was leading to a moral, cultural, and social decline in standards of life and culture. Their distrust of the machine age and mass-produced objects would lead each to valorize things made by human hands, embracing the ideals and traditional ways of life associated with the medieval crafts. It is in the nineteenth century and with the Romantics that literature becomes 'literature', an object esteemed for its aesthetic dimension and for its incarnation of human creativity and perception. Various treatises of the time sought to outline the function of poetry, from Percy Shelley's *A Defence of Poetry* (1821) to Matthew Arnold's *The Study of Poetry* (1880).

Literature in both instances is a means of resisting a society that devastates the individual psyche as it colonizes the natural world, where imagination and emotion play a part. Poetry is to serve a political function by resisting instrumental rationalizations and elevating the imagination or the passions above all else. Art exists in an autonomous space that is separate from the rest of the social world and is disinterested. Its purpose, as Kant put it, is purposelessness or as T.S. Eliot would later describe it, 'autotelic' – it exists simply for itself. Literature is valued above, and defined in opposition to, factual writing, and this distinguishes poetry from science. This tradition, in which the artist's imagination creates a purified landscape, is best exemplified by Wordsworth, who was critical of Coleridge's more intellectual and urban enterprise. Poetry is thus transposed into the privileged realm of art, touched by life, being often a passionate mediation of the senses, but nevertheless remaining separate from it.

The Romantic challenge to the forces of modernization, especially in the work of Arnold, Pope, and Blake, but also in the philosophy of Nietzsche, was absolutely central to McLuhan's early conceptualization of literature as resistance. He saw in their transcendental and materialist project an opposition that came in the form of an epistemological project, and indeed such a project would lead to what he believed to be the most important work of art in the twentieth century, James Joyce's *Finnegans Wake*. As he would outline in *The Gutenberg Galaxy*, the Romantic project was based on an internal contradiction, one that has been definitive for the historical avant-garde's mission to do away with art by means of art. It was only by being at war with literature, that is, with itself, that the English Romantics could have any hope of reconfiguring the Gutenberg Galaxy of which they were a product. This 'dilemma' leads to different inflections within Romanticism's various undertakings, which McLuhan discerns as a separation between literary 'vision' and its 'expression':

> For the matter of literary vision will be collective and mythic, while the forms of literary expression and communication will be individualist, segmental, and mechanical. The vision will be tribal and collective, the expression private and marketable. This dilemma continues to the present to rend the individual Western consciousness. Western man knows that his values and modalities are the product of literacy. Yet the very means of extending those values, technologically, seem to deny and reverse them. Whereas Pope fully faced up to this dilemma in *The Dunciad*, Blake and the Romantics tended to devote themselves to one side of it, the mythic and collective. J.S. Mill, Matthew Arnold, and a great many others devoted themselves to the other side of the dilemma, the problem of individual culture and liberty in an age of mass-culture. But neither side has its meaning alone, nor can the causes of the dilemma be found anywhere but in the total galaxy of events that constitute literacy and Gutenberg technology. (*Gutenberg Galaxy*: 269)

Indeed, McLuhan argues that the English Romantics are the first to understand that the rise of mass commercial culture is a product of 'the total galaxy of events that constitute literacy' (*GG*: 269). The notion of a 'total galaxy' avoids a simple determinism and includes everything from the Enlightenment to the most oppressive forms of capitalist culture. It is not surprising to find that the Romantics would have an important influence on McLuhan's thinking, due to the well-known link between the Romantic socialist pro-gramme and the formation of British Cultural Studies, especially that aspect of it referred to as 'culturalism'. Both Williams and E.P. Thompson produced works on Morris as well as Blake (Williams, 1958; Thompson, 1977, 1993, 1966; cf. Black, 2002). Although McLuhan identified himself with Blake on numerous occasions, he was on the whole less concerned with the visionary than with its more pragmatic material expression and grammar. McLuhan's reading of the Romantics led him to Cambridge, but his introduc-tion to Romanticism as a way of knowing and as a political project came to him from New Criticism. It is to the work of Matthew Arnold that I now turn to understand the emergence of a specifi-cally argued pedagogical enterprise and a new kind of cultural criticism.

Arnold, 'The Function of Criticism'

One problem the Romantic project faced was how to discern between what is and is not great poetry by devising a system of value through which not only to interpret the meanings of culture, but also to protect them and make certain that they prevail. John Ruskin would set out to develop a critical discourse for evaluating the function of painting and architecture in culture, and Matthew Arnold set out to justify the development of a criti-cism that was fundamentally pedagogical, but both believed that all art should aim 'to show things as they really are'.

Arnold's writings mark an important moment in the history of art's response to the Industrial Revolution. His thinking inaugu-rates a tradition in critical theory that recast many of the Romantic axioms that have been variously characterized as 'the culture and civilization' or 'culture and society' tradition. The main thread of Arnold's argument is that culture and civilization are oppositional terms. Culture, generally high culture, must be protected from the so-called forces of progress. We will find that some of Arnold's ideas are surprisingly well preserved in the work of the New Critics at Cambridge and in the southern USA, and most centrally in McLuhan's early writings. Under the influence of Coleridge, Arnold rationally and forcefully made the case for the study of literature, arguing that the welfare of culture depends on two things: criticism and education. In his famous treatise, *Culture and Anarchy* (1867–9), Arnold delineates culture in opposition to anarchy by defining it in a now famous phrase as 'the best that can be thought and said in the world'. The ultimate goal of culture is perfection: 'culture which believes in making reason and the will of God prevail, believes in perfection, is the study and pursuit of perfection' (1993: 61). Culture is not 'a having and a resting but a growing and a becoming'; it is not a thing but a process of becoming (ibid.: 62). This particular definition of culture as an 'atmosphere' that is always changing, that encompasses thinking, study, the exchange of ideas, the pursuit of perfection – culture as a movement rather than as an object – brought a new complexity to its meaning.

Culture for Arnold is first and foremost literary culture. In 'The function of criticism at the present time' (1864), Arnold explains that he is interested in literature above other forms of culture because in it 'the elements with which the creative power works are ideas'. Ideas are what make art possible (1993: 28). Great literature is produced in an 'atmosphere' rich with 'fresh and new ideas' (ibid.: 29). Romantic poetry of the first quarter of the nineteenth century, according to Arnold, 'did not know enough'. By contrast, Sophocles and Shakespeare, while not men of books, produced great art because they 'lived in a current of ideas in the highest degree animating and nourishing to the creative power' (ibid.: 30). Like so many literary critics after him (T.S. Eliot and F.R. Leavis in particular), Arnold saw Elizabethan England as the great creative period in the history of English literature, a period where ideas were rich and plentiful and where the place of culture was a natural part of the social fabric. In Arnold's time, with the rise of industrial arts and the great exhibitions, which mixed art and industry, this place was anything but assured. Arnold believed that the function of criticism was to produce new knowledge to nurture the production of great art, to encourage a modern way of thinking to match the massive social and democratic transformations during this period of industrial and economic expansion. Criticism must precede art, and only when criticism has done its job, can great art be produced.

Thus, Arnold gives us a very broad definition of criticism, one that exceeds the boundaries of art objects and is perhaps best characterized as social criticism. He distinguishes between the world of ideas to which criticism belongs and the world of practice to which art belongs. While criticism concerns judgement – establishing an author's relation to a central standard or the application of principles – its aims are not practical, but ideal. Criticism will contribute to the progress of mankind toward perfection only if it is not subject to the practical interests of the political, social and humanitarian sphere, which is historical and changing. Instead, criticism should help us to 'dwell upon what is excellent in itself, and the absolute beauty and fitness of things'. It is only by keeping to 'the pure intellectual sphere' of disinterested 'curiosity', by exercising the 'Indian virtue of detachment' that we may achieve a 'more free speculative treatment of things' and 'see things as they are' (ibid.: 41). Like the modern technologies of transportation, the mind must be free to wander, to be guided by curiosity alone, to create juxtapositions in order to challenge the one-sidedness of practical men. Idealism must replace the relativism of utilitarian society in order to 'nourish us in growth towards perfection' (ibid.: 51).

As much as he argued for disinterestedness, Arnold nevertheless reflected the ideas that were emerging around him in Victorian society. His characterization of ideas and culture in terms of a drive toward perfection has both religious and scientific connotations that must be understood in relation to Victorian and evolutionist views of progress and human development – culture and thought being the highest manifestation of humanity's evolution. Arnold's concept of history was influenced by his father, Thomas Arnold, whose Liberal Anglican view of history supported the belief in the inevitability of Aryan or

Teutonic supremacy, moving closer and closer to 'perfection' with the rise and fall of empires. As Peter Bowler points out, Arnold saw his role as 'softening the puritanical element in Victorian culture without opening the floodgates of anarchy' by providing a balance between the Hellenistic and Hebraistic forces of civilization, and clearly valuing the first over the second (1989: 59). Moreover, as has often been remarked, his conceptualization of culture in *Culture and Anarchy* grows directly out of the context of the suffrage protests of 1866–7, the year that Arnold's considerations on culture came together most forcefully. The 1867 Reform Bill brought about significant political changes that extended the right to vote to large numbers of urban working-class men, many of whom could read but not write. While the means of distribution were increasing, the means of expression and the development of an easy-to-read common grammar were worrisome to Arnold.

With the coming to power of the 'raw and unkindled masses of humanity' (1993: 79), the search for perfection was coming to a halt. A debasement of cultural ideals and a loss of standards for judging culture could only lead to political chaos, confusion and anarchy. Dividing social classes into three categories, Barbarians (aristocracy), Philistines (middle class) and Populace (working class), Arnold does not blame the 'masses' for the decline in standards, but rather the English middle class. The cult of the machine is fuelled by the narrow and inadequate ideals that have belonged to Puritanism, Hebraism, and the commercial interests of the English middle class since the beginning of the seventeenth century. This drab and unimaginative sensibility is responsible for London, 'our city ... with its unutterable external hideousness, and with its internal canker of *publice egestas, privatim opulentia*' ('public poverty and private opulence') (ibid.: 71). Left to its own devices the middle class would turn the Populace into Philistines interested only in the 'blessedness of the franchise ... or the wonderfulness of its own industrial performances'. The way to challenge this decline is a broadly based education in high culture. Culture is the opposite of anarchy, and its function is moral – to touch people with the ideals of perfection, with 'the will of God' (ibid.: 76).

For Arnold, literature and religion share in the same process of making the true ideals of perfection prevail. But each needs the other. Without religion, the profound aspects of the spiritual (which for Arnold are really aesthetic), and the perfection expressed through poetry, will not be recognized. Perhaps more importantly for Arnold's purposes, without poetry, religion produces a narrow and inadequate morality – that is, Puritanism as a product of the Hebraic spirit:

> the English reliance on our religious organizations and on their ideas of human perfection just as they stand, is like our reliance on freedom, on muscular Christianity, on population, on coal, on wealth – mere belief in machinery, and unfruitful; ... it is wholesomely counteracted by culture, bent on seeing things as they are, and on drawing the human race onwards to a more complete, a harmonious perfection. (ibid.: 71)

Culture brings another dimension to the ideals of human perfection, fostered for the most part by organized religion. Against the '*laissez-faire*' attitudes and 'mere belief in machinery' of middle-class liberalism, Arnold argues for a centralized educational system to guide the 'masses' toward perfection. As the highest expression of 'the nation in its collective and corporate character' (Burke), the state must implement within the nation's social institutions the finest ideals of reason and human perfection:

> Plenty of people will try to give the masses, as they call them, an intellectual food prepared and adapted in the way they think proper for the actual condition of the masses. The ordinary popular literature is an example of this way of working on the masses. Plenty of people will try to indoctrinate the masses with the set of ideas and judgments constituting the creed of their own profession or party ... culture works differently. It does not try to teach down to the level of inferior classes; it does not try to win them for this or that sect of its own, with ready-made judgments and watchwords. It seeks to do away with classes; to make the best that has been thought and known in the world current everywhere; to make all men live in an atmosphere of sweetness and light, where they may use ideas, as it uses them itself, freely, – nourished and not bound by them. (ibid.: 79)

Arnold is trying to clear the way not for a popular culture but for a common culture, a disinterested pursuit of 'sweetness and light' that will be disseminated to as many people as possible. But again, culture is high culture, and the common culture envisaged by Arnold will have nothing common about it. The study of literature, as it develops from Arnold, provides a new kind of social cohesion that promises to transcend differences between people. Yet despite his internationalist discourse, there is a patriotic tone to his project of knowing and studying perfection. Ultimately, teaching literature is a national project that is directed towards making England and the English more perfect. Although Arnold sees democracy and the breaking down of class distinctions as part of the natural evolution of society, he nevertheless quotes Ernest Renan approvingly:

> the sound instruction of the people is an effect of the high culture of certain classes. *The countries which, like the United States, have created a considerable popular instruction without any serious higher instruction, will long have to expiate this fault by their intellectual mediocrity, their vulgarity of manners, their superficial spirit, their lack of general intelligence.* (1993: 197)

In order to avoid 'Americanizing' culture, Arnold recommends that 'men of culture' be responsible for elevating the 'inferior classes' through educational programmes specially devised. These 'true apostles of equality' (ibid.: 79) are able to humanize knowledge, to make it accessible to the many. They and the culture they inspire will lead the way 'not only to perfection, but even to safety' (ibid.: 180).

Raymond Williams has pointed out that the hostility to the word culture in English appears around the time of Arnold's work. It is there that culture becomes associated with high culture, or 'culchah', that it becomes something to which people aspire and which, although meant to equalize, also marks out class differences. Arnold's ideas present one of the most sustained arguments for the value of teaching literature, of having literature replace the moral function of religion, and for undertaking criticism. Indeed, T.S. Eliot would maintain that Arnold was not so much a critic as a propagandist for criticism (1950: 1). Importantly for our purposes, Arnold's work is central to the development and moral imperatives of English studies at Cambridge in the 1930s, which, in turn, was an important influence on McLuhan's early moral theories of the media. McLuhan would describe the Cambridge years, or at least his first encounters at Cambridge as a 'shock':

In the summer of 1932 I walked and biked through most of England carrying a copy of Palgrave's *Golden Treasury* … Every Poem in that book seemed written to enhance my pilgrimage: 'Yes, there is holy pleasure in thine eye!/The lovely cottage in the guardian nook/Hath stirr'd thee deeply' … After a conventional and devoted initiation to poetry as a romantic rebellion against mechanical industry and bureaucratic stupidity, Cambridge was a shock. Richards, Leavis, Eliot, and Pound and Joyce in a few weeks opened the doors of perception on the poetic process, and its role in adjusting the reader to the contemporary world. My study of media began and remains rooted in the work of these men … The effects of new media on our sensory lives are similar to the effects of new poetry. They change not our thoughts but the structure of our world. (*IL*: xiii–xiv)

McLuhan is first enticed not simply by Romantic poetry, but by the Romantic view of poetry as a language of beauty, which resists utilitarian culture when cut off from the world and hidden away in the 'nook'. When he arrives at Cambridge, however, these views change, and poetry becomes something not simply cut off from the world, but an object and a process that 'adjusts' the reader to the contemporary world – something which is a guide to living, as Arnold believed poetry to be. McLuhan's understanding of the poetic process derives from New Criticism, an approach to literature and culture made popular by T.S. Eliot as well as McLuhan's teachers at Cambridge – I.A. Richards, and F.R. Leavis among others. Indeed, as a methodology, New Criticism was absolutely essential to McLuhan's analysis of the media (Marchand, 1989: 34). In many ways, McLuhan went on to analyze the media and communications technology in the same way that the New Critics sought to analyze a poem: they focused on intrinsic meanings in terms of the formal aspects of a text, and they sought to understand the encounter between human consciousness and the work of art.

2

New Criticism

The twentieth century, and in particular the First World War, only increased the sense of urgency expressed by Arnold's critique of utilitarian culture and liberal relativism. Like the Romantics before them, the New Critics set out to critique standardization, instrumental reason, and rampant capitalism; as a solution, they stressed the autonomy and the specificity of the individual and artwork. However, unlike the Romantics, whose works they felt were too absorbed by the individual author (Eliot would advocate a return to seventeenth-century metaphysical poets), they sought to understand the function of literature in society. While Arnold had emphasized the function of criticism as a discourse that created an atmosphere conducive to great art, T.S. Eliot, I.A. Richards and F.R. Leavis sought to practise an interpretive criticism that engaged directly with the art.

Eliot: Sense Impressions

In 'The perfect critic', Eliot takes Arnold to task for separating poetry and criticism as being two historically distinct forms of writing, and for emphasizing the idealist rather than the aesthetic aspects of criticism. While the two are different kinds of writing, history has shown that artists often make the best critics – as

Eliot the poet critic should well know. According to Eliot, the art of criticism since Arnold has developed in two directions: one emotional, the other intellectual. Neither is satisfactory. The first is an impressionistic criticism that is ruled by personal emotions that may have nothing to do with the work of art, though it may produce interpretations and translations that creates something new. In this instance, the impressionistic critic becomes an artist, creating new meanings and readings that were not present in the original artwork, and which is thereby lost in the process. Artists often make the best critics because they do not need to use critical writing as a creative outlet and are more able to engage with the work on its own terms.

Like impressionistic criticism, intellectual criticism also loses sight of its object but by imposing abstract philosophical or political interests on the artwork. This abstraction defines the modern world's vast accumulation of information, which dislocates thought from the senses and fragments knowledge so that we know a little about a lot and not much of anything. What is missing in both impressionistic and intellectual approaches is perception. Not surprisingly, Aristotle is the exemplary figure in Eliot's Arnoldian search for perfect criticism. Aristotle, who always engaged with the concrete object directly, exemplifies the disinterested and general intelligence of the truly scientific mind, 'swiftly operating the analysis of sensation to the point of principle and definition' (1950: 11). This intelligence and sensibility, this ability to fully appreciate the object for what it is, defines the practice of criticism that Eliot seeks to promote. The critic should not judge or legislate, but should elucidate: it is up to the reader to judge for him or herself. In order to see the object as it really is, a literary critic should have no emotions beyond that combination of feeling and thought produced by the work of art itself. This immediate impression thus comes to modify the old impressions of objects already known. The interaction creates a dynamic system of impressions that allows for Eliot to make a generalized statement of literary beauty: 'the true generalization is not something superposed upon an accumulation of perceptions, the perceptions do not, in a really appreciative mind, accumulate as a mass, but form themselves as a structure; and criticism is the statement in language of this structure; it is a development of sensibility' (ibid.: 15).

It is important to differentiate this approach from the structuralism that would come into vogue as a methodology in the humanistic sciences largely through the cultural anthropology of Claude Lévi-Strauss three decades later. This will help us to distinguish between the close textual readings of cultural artefacts carried out in the 1950s by Roland Barthes in *Mythologies* from those that we find several years earlier in McLuhan's *The Mechanical Bride*. Like Lévi-Strauss, Barthes' methodology derives from Ferdinand de Saussure's semiology. McLuhan derives his emphasis on structure from the New Critics and from semantics, which will be discussed later. For the moment it is important to keep in mind that the New Critics examine structures that are grounded in the senses rather than in human organizations. The structure that Eliot refers us to stems directly from the sense impressions of the reader. These form structures, which are always mediated by human sensoria, are always in the process of changing as new perceptions come to interact with those already established. For Eliot, the role of the critic is to minimize this fact of mediation, to engage directly with the art object, to 'see it as it really is' by leaving one's personal emotions, and thus history, by the wayside. Eliot does not propose that criticism become a scientific positivism which leads merely to an accumulation of information (the waste land), but rather that the critic develop a scientific mind, sensibility and intelligence as represented by Aristotle. Richards developed this idea into a methodology that, in his desire for precision, would approximate a science.

Richards: Art as Communication

It is surprising that the originality of Richards's ideas have been so little recognized in media and communication studies, given that the central premise of his major work, *Principles of Literary Criticism* (1925), is that art is the communication of experience:

> The two pillars upon which a theory of criticism must rest are an account of value and an account of communication. We do not suffi-ciently realize how great a part of our experience takes the form it does, because we are social beings and accustomed to communication from infancy ... A large part of the distinctive features of the mind are due to its being an instrument for communication. An experience has to be formed, no doubt, before it is communicated, but it takes the form it does largely because it may have to be communicated. (1925: 25)

We find here a tension between experience and language. Their interrelation is part of the complexity of art as something con-sciously made. Art is the record of human experience at its best, since artists, in Richards's view, are the most sensitive and exceptional people – they represent the point of growth, the most advanced expression of a society. Art, as a record of the experiences of exceptional people, provides a body of evidence: 'data' through which to gauge what experiences are of value, and contribute to the general 'health' of a society. This is Richards's theory of value – art is of value for what it can tell us about our-selves, and it is a kind of diagnostic tool. Like Arnold, Richards sees art as a 'criticism of life', and criticism is about judging the moral values of art, what it has to teach us. This is how the teach-ing of literature might replace religion, as it deals inherently with human values and morality. Criticism is to serve a political function. Richards, under the influence of the newly configured School of Philosophy at Cambridge (which included Bertrand Russell, G.E. Moore, and their brilliant student Ludwig Wittgenstein), was centrally concerned with human communica-tion and wanted to place the study of literature within a larger philosophical and epistemological framework. McLuhan would later take this idea and extend it to theorize a special function for art as a 'probe'. Artists, McLuhan believed, could transform things like language or technological media into anti-environments, making us aware of the way a medium of communication acts upon the content of what is communicated. This would lead to his most famous paradox 'the medium is the message'.

McLuhan's love of language play, his use of puns and irony, and especially his insistence on paradox as a way of getting to truth, come to him from New Criticism. Richards does not deal with the popular media but with language as a medium or vehicle for the communication of ideas and experiences. Richards, and his student William Empson, stress ambiguity and multiple meanings as central features of all good literature. The greater the communication of experience, the greater the ambiguity. To draw this insight out, Richards distinguishes between the scientific and the literary uses of language. Scientific language must necessarily reduce the number of possible interpretations: its cognitive aspects and its truth require a language where all ambiguity, paradox, metaphor and word play are eliminated. Literary language explores the richness of meaning, the full ambiguity and multiple dimensions of language. Each furnishes a different kind of knowledge. On the one hand, scientific language deals with empirical reality, playing a cognitive function in society. Literature and the arts, on the other, engage with the rich density of details that are beyond the general empirical description, that exist in the realm of the emotions, of human experience: 'The distinction once clearly grasped is simple. We may either use words for the sake of the references they promote, or we may use them for the sake of the attitudes and emotions which ensue' (ibid.: 267).

While many of the Romantics, such as Shelley or Keats, had made the distinction between poetry and science, Richards's differentiation is guided by Wittgenstein's philosophy of language. Indeed, *The Meaning of Meaning*, co-authored with William Ogden, was intended to provide 'a causal solution to the problems of meaning' addressed in Wittgenstein's *Tractatus*. For his part, Wittgenstein was not impressed and described *The Meaning of Meaning* as 'a miserable' and 'foolish' book (Monk, 1991: 214). Richards would drop the causal solution in his own work and looked instead to the effects and context of language use rather than the author's intentions. Science and art are very different contexts in which language functions to reveal very different things. Literary uses of language draw on the inherent ambiguities of words, their capacity to transform the meanings of other words in juxtaposition, and to open language up to a multiplicity of meanings through metaphor, for example, rather than reducing words to singular references. As different kinds of productions, science leaves little room for interpretation; it is intended to be universal and absolute. Literature, on the other hand, demands an active reader and leaves much more room for interpretation. John Crowe Ransom, one of the most important American New Critics, extended Richards's insights to assert that a poem is 'a democratic state' because it allows its citizens to retain their personalities. A scientific discourse is a 'totalitarian state', because citizens have no rights or interests beyond that of the discourse (Ransom, 1941: 43–4).

Richards sets out to understand this 'democratic state'. He sees the meanings of a literary text as being relative and historical. According to Richards, it is the critic's task to understand how art communicates and how meaning is made through this ambiguity. He breaks meaning down into four categories: 'sense' (meaning), 'feeling' (the emotion that is imparted), 'tone' (how the poem addresses the reader) and 'intention' (what is the desired outcome). Of all of these, feeling is the most difficult to ascertain. Richards's concern is to theorize 'the meaning of meaning', the process by which humans come to understand each other, and the manner in which a poem makes it possible to translate emotion into language. *Practical Criticism* (1929, 1962) is made up of close readings of readings of poetry, many of which are drawn from student assignments. It was Richards's practice to give them unsigned poems to analyze. Some of the poems were canonical, while others were by unknowns. Richards asks, how can we distinguish a good poem from a bad one? He never answers this entirely, except to say that it is all in the reading.

In the Arnoldian tradition, Richards is very much concerned with pedagogy and with teaching students the basic principles of interpretation – not in terms of general laws of meaning, but rather in terms of the process by which a reader will find meaning in a poem. Richards proposes a psychological theory of value that focuses on the meanings of a text as read through the response. His work presents a methodology not for the reading of poetry, but for the interpretation of poetry. He is not concerned with the psychological structure of the stimulating object, the art object, but with the response (1962: 248). He feels that by looking at the way poems are read, and by looking at the history of response to them, there will be an interrelation of both the meanings of the text and the historical meanings of the reader's response; that is, the context in which it is read.

Richards elucidates the human response to art into a scientific methodology that features *gestalt* psychology and the theory of rhetoric. As a starting point for understanding communication, both theories deal with the ambiguous nature of language, the way that meanings depend on context, and how the presence of an active reader produces meaning. This is where we can locate Richards's central influence on McLuhan. By bringing a psychological theory to bear on the making of meaning and by employing a philosophical methodology, Richards's theory of communication directed McLuhan towards language as form and perception. *Gestalt*, a German word that may be translated as 'form', 'figure', and/or 'configuration', is ubiquitous throughout McLuhan's discourse on media and is intended to emphasize the ways in which perceptions are formed and determined by context, configuration, and meaning rather than by the accumulation of sensory elements alone.

Shortly before the First World War, the chief exponents of *gestalt*, Kurt Koffka, Wolfgang Köhler, and Max Wertheimer began to study perception and suggested that it is subject to laws of primitive organization such as proximity, contrast, similarity, and contiguity, which in turn result in a configurational patterning of parts into a unitary whole. *Gestalt* is a phenomenological mode of analysis that does not seek to parse and fragment but to maintain the unitary quality of that which is undergoing analysis (Chaplin, 1975: 216–17). In short, *gestalt* psychology maintains that the human mind will create unity from disparate parts, meaning that the reader fills in the gaps to create a dynamic interaction between parts. Just as language is contingent upon context (the meaning of the word can change over time as it can change in juxtaposition with other words), the meanings of a text are also contingent upon the reader. Perception, like language, is not static; language acts upon the reader as a stimulus, and the reader acts upon language to find meaning in the rich juxtapositions of parts. In *Coleridge on Imagination*, Richards writes: 'it is the number of connections between the many, and the relations between these connections, that give the unity – in brief, that the co-adunation is the inter-relationship of the parts' (1950: 84–5). Poetry, in other words, occurs in the reader's mind.

Richards returns to the trivium, the old university disciplines as defined by the Stoic logos of Grammar (*logos spermatikos*, formal principles of organization), Logic (*logos hendiathetos*, dialectic, reasoning) and Rhetoric (*logos prophorikos*, speech). McLuhan is interested in Rhetoric because this ancient art seeks to overcome, yet never abolish, the ambiguity of language by fostering clear and eloquent exposition aimed at persuasion. Rhetoric necessitates the principles of psychology, because as a speech act, it exists for others, it exists to communicate with others. More than the art of rhetoric, however, McLuhan looked to the science of words, Grammatica, developed by the Stoics. The ancient grammarians believed that Logos was Divine, that human language corresponded closely to the order of reality, and that the essence of things was contained in words. Walter Benjamin shared a similar belief in the power of language and of words. This tradition held an attraction for McLuhan because of his own Catholicism, and also because it was a view held by one of the Catholic thinkers he most admired, Thomas Aquinas, whom he later read at St Louis University in Missouri.

All of these elements combine to give New Criticism an historicity and objectivity that had previously been lacking in criticism, as metaphysical aesthetics, impressionistic review or appreciation. McLuhan is influenced by Richards's historical approach to meaning and to context, and to his approach of placing an object (figure) in relation to a context (ground) in order to analyze social change. The ground comes through the figure; or the figure comes through the ground, a process of 'light through' that is phenomenological in character. McLuhan would develop an historical approach to studying the media in terms of transitions: from tribal to global cultures, from oral to literate forms, from eye to ear, from mechanical to electric technology, and so on, in tandem with the phenomenological idea that behind every situation, there is another situation that peeps through; 'And that peeping through is phenomenology' (*Understanding McLuhan*, CD-ROM, McLuhan Live: Interview with Louis Forsdale, 17 July 1978).

On the cusp of his conversion to Catholicism, McLuhan was somewhat dubious about the relativism underlying Richards's methods. Of their first encounters in 1935 he would write:

> There are no permanent, ultimate, qualities such as Good, Love, Hope etc., and yet he wishes to discover objective, ultimate permanent standards of criticisms. He wants to discover those standards (what a hope!) in order to establish intellectualist culture as the only religion worthy a rational being and in proportion of their taste for which all people are 'full sensitive, harmonious personalities' or 'disorganized, debased fragments of unrealized potentiality'. When I see how people swallow such ghastly atheistic nonsense, I could join a bomb-hurling Society. (*Letters*: 50)

Yet McLuhan would become convinced by Richards's approach to the study of literature, even if it was existential and agnostic. He had a great respect for Richards's methodology of reading and for the combination of rhetoric, psychology and anthropology that he employed. McLuhan would teach a course on practical criticism using Richards's methodologies at St Louis University, a Catholic institution, a few years later. He adopted the techniques that made Richards always stress the effect of a text rather than its author's intention. Studying effects rather than causes would be a key strategy in all of McLuhan's writings.

While teaching at St Louis, McLuhan continued his studies and received his PhD from Cambridge in 1943. Following Richards, he would look to the trivium to analyze the rhetorical strategies found in the satire and the journalism of the Elizabethan writer, Thomas Nashe. In his PhD thesis *The Place of Thomas Nashe in the Learning of His Time*, McLuhan came to understand that the history of ideas could be analyzed in terms of the on-going quarrels between the Platonic logicians and the Sophistic rhetoricians. Indeed, the history of Western civilization could not be understood without taking into account the shifting relations between the branches of the trivium. The opposition between a mechanical and organic culture would come to inform much of McLuhan's early writing on culture. He addresses this in two early essays: 'Edgar Poe's tradition' and 'An ancient quarrel in modern America', in which he locates the differences between northern and southern US sensibilities in terms of their divergent intellectual traditions, the grammatical/rhetorical and dialectical/logical methods. The South, in McLuhan's view, was agrarian and continued to uphold the organic ideals of community, while the North was concerned solely with industry: 'the North wants horse power, while the South wants the horse too'.

Since Newton, the modern world had been colonized by abstract logic and equated with the modern world. McLuhan was critical of the logicians because they let thought dominate the world. He would reject all forms of dialectical reasoning because it reduced the complexity of the world to two poles of abstraction, which were reconciled into a false unity. While he was fond of writing in paradoxes, this came out of the desire to show that reality and language were multidimensional rather than arising from the search for some truthful synthesis. Dialectical thinking was far too instrumental for McLuhan. It was a theoretical simplification of a world that was too complex to be so directly apprehended. His approach was rhetorical rather than dialectical, faithful to 'the Ciceronian ideal' because 'Cicero gave it to St Augustine and St Jerome who in turn saw to it that it has never ceased to influence Western Society' ('Edgar Poe's tradition': 26).

In his essay on Poe, whose criticism and prose would provide important insights for McLuhan in his understanding of communication, he explains the reason that Poe felt so alienated from New England:

> the theocratic founders of Harvard and rules of New England were Calvinist divines, fully trained in the speculative theology which had arisen for the first time in the twelfth century – the product of that dialectical method in theology which is rightly associated with Peter Abelard. Unlike Luther and many English Protestants, Calvin and his followers were schoolmen, opposed to the old theology of the Fathers which Erasmus and the humanist Ciceronians had brought back to general attention after the continuous predominance of scholastic theology since the twelfth century. To the humanists nobody could be an interpreter of Scripture, a true exponent of the *philosophi Christi*, who had not had a full classical training. So Catholic and Protestant schoolmen alike, were, for these men, the 'barbarians', the 'Goths of the Sorbonne', corrupting with 'modernistic trash' ... the eloquent piety and wisdom of the Fathers' ('... ancients' or *antiqui theologi*). (ibid.: 26–7)

So it is that the radically opposed intellectual traditions 'which have been warring since Socrates turned dialectics against the rhetoric of his Sophist teachers'. McLuhan asks, 'what of Poe's affinities with France' (ibid.: 29), which we could also understand later as McLuhan's affinities with France. He finds the affinity between the American South and France in the Ciceronian ideal of a highly 'practical and gentlemanly ideal in which knowledge and action are subordinated to a political good'. As with McLuhan's notion that all good artists are Catholic, so too is it no coincidence that the creative political figures of American life were moulded by the South. Whether one considers Jefferson or Lincoln, one is confronted with a mind that is 'aristocratic, legalistic, encyclopedic, forensic habitually expressing itself in the mode of an eloquent wisdom' (ibid.: 26). Thus, this eloquent wisdom will be valued above all, in all of McLuhan's evaluations of thinkers and their place in the world.

I.A. Richards provided McLuhan with some of the analytical tools and psychological theories for analyzing the human response to art, but it is perhaps for this reason that McLuhan owes his deepest debt to Leavis. Although it is Richards who compared the critic to a doctor, it is truly Leavis who sets out to diagnose the general health of the society in which he lives. McLuhan would maintain the important function of media literacy to produce a diagnosis of the society in which it takes place, but the McLuhan of the 1940s and early 1950s would also see criticism as providing a moral yardstick.

Leavis: Moral Literacy

In 'Poetic vs rhetorical exegesis: the case for Leavis against Richards and Empson', published in the *Sewanee Review* (1944), McLuhan made it clear that he felt Leavis and not Richards was the more important thinker. In McLuhan's early writings and his first book, *The Mechanical Bride*, the influence of Leavis's agrarian sensibility and moral criticism is more evident than is Richards's scientific approach to interpretation. McLuhan argues that Leavis goes much further than Richards and Empson in terms of criticism because he looks not only at how a poem functions but at 'the function of poetry in society'. While the works of Richards and Empson provide a useful method for understanding the mechanics of a poem, their scientific approach is unable to answer the question, 'Is it a poem?' In contrast, Leavis's criticism is exemplary because it is evaluative. His work continues the project proposed but never fulfilled by Eliot so greatly admired by both McLuhan and Leavis, which was to evaluate 'the intensity of the artistic process' ('Poetic versus rhetorical exegesis': 269). In Leavis's thinking, poetry is 'a means of extending and refining moral perception or dramatic awareness', and it is 'the education or nourishment of the affections'. McLuhan claims that Richards and Empson leave us at the 'halfway house' because they refuse to theorize the moral implications of literature, neglecting critical judgment itself, and crucially, evaluation (ibid.: 276). Richards is so concerned with the mechanics of analyzing the response, with the meaning of meaning, that the moral implications of a work become irrelevant or simply relative, which amounts to the same thing.

McLuhan's work throughout the 1940s and early 1950s would embrace criticism as critique, and would consistently return to Leavis's favoured themes: the longing for a lost community with its living cultures, the debasement of culture by the processes and technologies of modernization, the moral critique of industrial culture, and the modernism of Eliot, Pound, Yeats and Joyce. Ever present in all of McLuhan's writings is the idea inherited from both Leavis and Richards, and ultimately from Arnold, that education can challenge the numbing effects of commercial culture. McLuhan conceptualized culture as 'landscape', as 'environment', as 'ground', as 'galaxy' – in short, as space.

McLuhan's notion of culture can be understood in relation to Leavis's work and most certainly to his *Culture and Environment* (1933). Co-authored with Denys Thompson, one of the co-editors of the journal *Scrutiny*, the book extends Richards's practical criticism to advertisements, journals, popular fiction, and films. Close analysis of mass culture, according to the authors, is necessary to counter its pervasive effects: 'Many teachers of English who have become interested in the possibilities of training taste and sensibility must have been troubled by accompanying doubts. What effect can such training have against the multitudinous counter-influences – films, newspapers, advertising – indeed, the whole world outside the classroom' (Leavis and Thompson, 1933: 1). In the tradition of *Scrutiny*, the journal that distributed Leavisian criticism to a larger world outside of Cambridge, Thompson and Leavis analyze modern textual artefacts from the 'world outside', presenting case studies and providing study questions geared toward sensitizing students to the ideologies of consumption and the class biases embedded in commercial culture.

While the questions posed in *Culture and Environment* continue to be instructive and even useful for 'training critical awareness', they are far from the objective prose that we have come to expect from educational texts. For example:

> Explain and illustrate the use of valets, butlers and 'superior'-looking manservants in advertisements. [...] (ibid.: 111)
>
> Work out the life of a person who responds to the advertisements he or she reads. Compare it with the lives of the Villagers in *Change in the Village* and of the Dodsons in *The Mill and the Floss*. [...] (ibid.: 113)
>
> Broadcasting, like the films, is in practice mainly a means of passive diversion, and it tends to make active recreation, especially active use of the mind, more difficult'. How far in your observation is this so, and how far need it be so? (ibid.: 115)

Each of the examples presented in the book makes it clear that there can be nothing redeeming about popular culture. Instead the writers wish to make us aware of the class biases and debasement of aesthetic forms that consumer culture has brought about. It is easy to see how *Culture and Environment* belongs to the cultural tradition that Arnold's thinking helped to establish. For Leavis, the permeation of mass culture into all facets of everyday life must be countered by literary education. Very much in the Arnoldian spirit, Leavis's *Mass Civilization and Minority Culture* (1930) maintained that it was up to the enlightened minority to educate the masses and to protect culture from modern civilization. A world filled with discontinuity must be connected to the continuity of those traditions contained in and represented by literary works. The opposition between culture and everyday life, as well as between culture and society, did not always exist. Instead, Leavis tells us that this separation is a product of the forces of modernization and mass culture.

In all of his writings, but most explicitly in *Culture and Environment*, Leavis looks back to a time when cultures were 'living' and 'organic', connected to the environment, and to a time when the environment was natural – 'an art of life, a way of living, ordered and patterned, involving social arts, codes of intercourse and a responsive adjustment growing out of immemorial experience, to the natural environment and the rhythm of the year' (1933: 1–2). Culture, according to this thinking, grows quite literally out of the environment. When the environment lived in was natural, so was culture. Now that many people's living environments are urban or suburban, culture takes on the mechanical alienated character of the environment that produces it. The clock, for example, becomes the time-keeper rather than the sun.

Culture and Environment presents a collage of quotations drawn from the critical works that Leavis admires most, and from the ads and journals that he detests. The book seeks to break down the division between the classroom and the outside world, and to assert, as so much of Leavis's later writing on education and the university would do (e.g., *How to Teach Reading: A Primer for Ezra Pound* (1932), *Education and the University* (1943), *English Literature in Our Time and the University* (1967)), that educational institutions can present a resistance to mass culture. Leavis and Thompson propose ways to combine the study of cultural history, such as folk songs and advertising, with the study of literary texts. They seek to understand historically the eroding processes of civilization as well as the relation between culture and environment at the present time. Cultural ideals have been lost but remain preserved in the works of pre-industrial England, roughly the sixteenth and seventeenth centuries. There is a resulting sense of cultural crisis and a deep pessimism in Leavis's views of mass culture.

Such a pessimistic and negative stance toward mass culture, especially American mass culture, is one that Leavis would share with other European theorists of the 1930s and 1940s. Most notably the Frankfurt School theorists, T.W. Adorno and Max Horkheimer would coin the term 'culture industry' and characterize mass culture in terms of a 'dialectic of enlightenment' a few years later while living in exile in New York. But unlike the Frankfurt School theorists, Leavis was not a Marxist. His critique of mass culture idealized and mythologized an organic pre-industrial community of the past. Anne Samson has argued that Leavis makes organic community into a kind of Utopia at the expense of the material reality and 'living culture' he was so intent on defending (1992: 53). Ultimately, *Culture and Environment* is built upon a temporal opposition that derives from Arnold and that is very limiting and ahistorical: pre-industrial culture versus industrial culture, modernism versus mass culture, culture versus civilization.

While they were influenced by Leavis, a post-war generation of cultural theorists, including McLuhan, would reject his elitist and nostalgic approach to the study of culture. The same year that he made a case for Leavis against Richards and Empson, McLuhan would also write to his student Walter Ong that:

> the trouble with Leavis is that his passion for important work forbids him to look for the sun in the egg-tarnished spoons of the daily table. In other words, his failure to grasp current society in its intellectual modes (say in the style of [Lewis's] *Time and Western Man* or Giedion's *Space, Time and Architecture*) cuts him off from relevant pablum. (*Letters*: 166)

Indeed, both Lewis's and Giedion's books would provide important epistemological models for examining the 'pablum' that McLuhan would analyze in *The Mechanical Bride*. Leavis's moral denunciation of mass culture as being valueless reduced the complexity of his analysis and of his historical account of culture.

The Cambridge New Critics had stressed the active role of the reader in making meaning, but this response was seen as simply uniform in the face of mass culture. Cultural theorists of the 1950s – McLuhan, Barthes, Williams, and Hoggart, and later those critics (Paul Willis and Stuart Hall) who formed the Birmingham Centre for Contemporary Cultural Studies, developed ethnographic and often autobiographical approaches to analyzing the cultural experiences of mass culture.

Like McLuhan, Williams was critical of Leavis's elitist approach to culture. Yet he was also aware of the important contributions that Cambridge English Studies had made to the development of an intellectual sensibility that would bring about new forms of cultural analysis. In an essay called 'The future of cultural studies', Williams speaks to this past, and it is to Leavis and the Adult Education movement of the late nineteenth century that he calls attention. Cultural studies, according to Williams's genealogy, grows out of the democratic impetus to make the study of English relevant to the experiences of its students, many of them women who were frozen out of higher education (1989: 152). Leavis's contribution, and the contribution of the Adult Education movement, to the study of culture are the emphasis on the present, on that which is contemporaneous with the experiences of students outside the classroom. Although Leavis's thinking upheld the division between art and popular culture, as well as an elitist view of education (believing that only a small minority could be educated), he sought to problematize both the division between reader and text (New Criticism's general contribution) and most importantly, according to Williams, between the classroom and the world outside (ibid.: 153).[1]

All of McLuhan's writings, from the publication of his first book, *The Mechanical Bride*, to his last *The Laws of Media*, were concerned with creating a media literacy based upon the 'analysis of the present time' (*Letters*: 157). McLuhan's media studies texts, *The Mechanical Bride* (1951), *Understanding Media* (1964), *The City as Classroom* (1977) and *Laws of Media* (1988), were all designed to be popular guides that aimed to give students the analytic tools to understand the culture that is everywhere around them. The anthropological approach that would lead Williams to define culture as 'relations in a whole way of life' and McLuhan to understand it in terms of landscape and environment, bears the mark of the Leavisian project. Leavis's stress on an organic past, on a culture connected to nature, while holding up a Utopian vision of the past that is ultimately reactionary, also gives rise to a methodology and an ethic that engages with 'living' culture – an ethic that seeks to understand culture in the context of the present in order to assess it. Media literacy for

Leavis was a way of countering the menace to literacy posed by popular culture.

McLuhan would draw from Leavis and from the Romantics a recognition that literacy is the key to social and political emancipation. The creation of a popular literacy aimed at 'seeing things as they really are' is central to understanding McLuhan's work in terms of a *project*. This project also accounts for his status as a public intellectual and his drive in the 1960s to use the media not so much to convey his message but to inhabit it, to demand of those viewers watching him on television, for example, an awareness of the technology and its effects on their perceptions as well as on their fundamental experience of the world. New Criticism can be understood as a reaction against the teaching of literature in terms of the extrinsic aspects of literature; the historical conditions, social context and author's biography that led to the creation of a poem. Eliot, Richards and Empson believed these had no place in the study of literature. Instead, they, and later the New Critics in the USA such as John Crowe Ransom and Cleanth Brooks advocated specific methodologies for close readings of texts. New Criticism is frequently viewed as being a highly formalistic approach to literature, a universal aesthetics applied to all literature, regardless of genre or origin. It is often seen as merely the technique for close reading to discover coherence and paradoxical unity of opposing meanings that came to dominate how English undergraduate literature was taught in universities.

However, it is important to stress that the Cambridge New Critics were seeking to challenge certain orthodoxies in the study of English by counterposing aesthetics and dealing with the object itself. From I.A. Richards's *Principles* and *Practical Criticism*, William Empson's *Seven Types of Ambiguity*, T.S. Eliot's *Selected Essays*, Leavis's *Reevaluation* and C.S. Lewis's *The Allegory of Love*, the British New Critics brought criticism into the forefront. When these ideas crossed the ocean to the southern US they evolved into another form of criticism that was deeply conservative and a critical orthodoxy that was ahistorical. Yet as these ideas moved to Chicago and came to influence critics like Maud Bodkin, Francis Ferguson and Northrop Frye (McLuhan's long-time colleague at the University of Toronto);

they also forged a rich assortment of approaches to textual analysis that, according to M.H. Abrams, has never been matched in English Studies since. Post-structuralist theory (via the deconstruction of Derrida) and critical theory (via feminist theory) challenged many of the universalist foundations of New Criticism's aesthetic formalism, its separation of text from social and political context. Yet as Abrams points out, the influence of New Criticism on those more theoretical approaches to the analysis of texts (deconstruction, discourse analysis) is still evident in the way the text becomes the location where hidden desires or motives are uncovered (1997: 120–21).

Note

1 Williams argues that Leavis's minoritarian view of education presents a fundamental contradiction for English Studies and its roots in the Adult Education Movement (1989: 153).

3

Catholicism

In order to understand the centrality of pedagogy in McLuhan's enterprise, we need to uncover the tension in his intellectual formation between the historical sense inherited from the New Critics and Catholicism. That is, between the materiality of language and perception, and the transcendentalism of Catholicism. Let me conclude Part I by turning to McLuhan's conversion, which brings to all his writings an underlying coherence, thematic unity and, most certainly, direction.

While McLuhan's religious devotion was never a part of his public persona and was never revealed in his cultural theories, it was deeply present in his thinking. McLuhan's mind and thought are without doubt one of 'the best syntheses yet achieved of the Catholic legacy as this was developed in Aquinas, Joyce, and Eliot' (Kroker, 1984: 68). His views of modern communications technologies changed over the years, becoming less pessimistic and more 'probing', but his epistemological strategy remained constant from his work on Nashe and his trivium studies to his conceptualization of media laws. This is because throughout his life McLuhan was a Thomist.

In 'Catholic humanism', McLuhan explains: 'Knowledge of the creative process in art, science, and cognition shows the way to earthly paradise, or complete madness: the abyss or the top of mount purgatory' (1954: 75). For McLuhan, the Catholic intellectual tradition, reared as it was on Aristotle and Aquinas, provided the most convincing account of human potential. This potentiality is evident in the modern landscape, which is not a passive but an active process that has potential but not fully determinable effects. It is one that is continuously moving forward in terms of the manner in which the newly produced 'organ' pushes aside that which it replaces, adds to, enhances, and/or changes it in some manner. McLuhan is optimistic about such changes because it is less a matter of technology transforming humanity into something it is not, than it is simply the actualization of a potentiality: it is truly 'organic'.

This is an example of the influence of the work of Aquinas, who applied the Aristotelian distinction between actuality and potentiality to a variety of matter. Any substance, such as a piece of wood, will have a set of qualities that are true of it at one moment in time, and another set of qualities that are true of it at another moment in time: the formerly invisible environment becomes the figure that stands out from the ground. Our piece of wood, for example, is a cold and solid mass at one point, but after the application of heat it can be hot and ultimately scatter as ash. In the Aristotelian sense the piece of wood is a parcel of 'matter' that has the capacity for 'substantial change' in its transformation from one form (wood) to another (ash) (Flew, 1984: 5).

While Aquinas did not believe that the creation of beings could be regarded as an actualization of latent essences waiting to be discovered, his statement that the 'senses delight in things duly proportioned as in something akin to them; for, the sense, too, is a kind of reason as is every cognitive power' (ibid.)[1] permits the imagination to be a form of interior sense, which facilitated the intellect's representation, contemplation and modification of objects. What is interesting here is the idea that the imagination is involved in the retrieval and modification of objects, and that this does not result in completely individualistic and discrete ideas or representations. Instead they exhibit a rational order: a pattern that is deeply historical, like language. McLuhan would stress the creative configurational process of perception in all of his writings. This is why he, like the New Critics, would highlight the role of the artist in providing knowledge of the world around us. Art as 'a criticism of life', as an expression of heightened perception that permits the teasing out of existing patterns of existence could lead the way to paradise on earth. Catholicism was not only part of a conscious intellectual strategy for McLuhan, but was also for him a general culture.

Indeed, the relationship between religion and culture is central to McLuhan's understanding of the relationship between culture and environment. Writing to his mother in 1935, McLuhan would try to explain his desire to convert to Catholicism as originating in his search for culture during his early years in Canada:

Catholic culture produced Chaucer and his merry story-telling Canterbury pilgrims. Licentious enthusiasm produced the lonely despair of Christian in Pilgrim's Progress – what a different sort of pilgrim! Catholic culture produced Don Quixote and St Francis and Rabelais. What I wish to emphasize about them is there [sic] various and rich-hearted humanity. I need scarcely indicate that everything that is especially hateful and devilish and inhuman about the conditions and strains of modern industrial society is not only Protestant in origin, but it is their boast (!) to have originated it. ... You see my 'religion hunting' began with a rather priggish 'culture hunting'. I simply couldn't believe that men had to live in the mean and mechanical joyless rootless fashion that I saw in Winnipeg. And when I began to read English Literature I knew that it was quite unnecessary for them so to live ... It was a long time before I finally perceived that the character of every society, its food, clothing, arts, and amusements are ultimately determined by its religion ... (*Letters*: 73)

All of these ideas gelled for McLuhan when he read the Victorian writer G.K. Chesterton. McLuhan stumbled upon his collection of short essays devoted to explicating *What's Wrong with the World* quite by accident while at Cambridge (Marchand: 23). In the tradition of the Victorians, this book railed against industrialization, utilitarian values and capitalist over-development. What is wrong with the world, according to Chesterton, is that we do not ask what is right. For Chesterton, 'practical man' was part of a paltry utilitarian culture that would ultimately lead to the debasement of man through abstraction. Not unlike Arnold, Chesterton maintains that what is needed to combat all the misery of modernization is an understanding of those universal and unchanging notions of human ideals and perfection that ultimately are an expression of God. While we might well agree on what is wrong, Chesterton feels that we won't agree on what is right – which is what is wrong with the world (a kind of postmodern conundrum!).

Just as Arnold had feared the voting power of working-class men, so does Chesterton fear Suffragettes and attempts to engage directly with women's rights or, as he puts it, 'the sex question'. For Chesterton, the answer is not literature, as it was for the Romantics, but property: 'the art of democracy' (Chesterton, 1910: 47). He believes that 'every man should have something that he can shape in his own image, as he is shaped in the image of Heaven' – every man is literal here, as women were not to be property owners. He is not advocating capitalism, which involves the usurpation of other people's property, and he does not understand the limits of creativity, but rather distributionism – the equal distribution of property as the basis of any free culture.

Chesterton would espouse many of the values that McLuhan held, a belief in universal reason and Christian values, 'a deep affinity with medieval Christianity', the family and personal liberty. Chesterton had converted to Roman Catholicism and McLuhan wrote a short article on him in 1936, the year of his own conversion, entitled 'G.K. Chesterton: A Practical Mystic'. This article celebrates the joy of Chesterton's prose and poems; for instance, the 'green hair' on the hills, or the 'smell of Sunday morning' (1936: 455). McLuhan admired Chesterton so much that he joined the Distributist League and subscribed to Chesterton's newsletter *G.K. Weekly*, the movement's official organ. This is as far as McLuhan's direct involvement in politics ever went.

McLuhan not only admired Chesterton's prose but his general approach to ideas – relying on percepts instead of concepts, ideas rather than facts. In his social prose, Chesterton reveals the mysteries of the everyday, 'the miracles of sense and consciousness' (ibid.). He rejects the 'clear' realities of popular science and 'Anglo-Saxon superiority' because the 'real world is full of bracing bewilderments and brutal surprises'. In effect, writes McLuhan, 'All profound truth, philosophical or spiritual, makes game with appearances, yet without really contradicting common sense'. He would comment approvingly in a letter to his parents that Chesterton's *Short History of England* contained not one single date (*Letters*: 11). Chesterton writes history and learns from what never happened or, more precisely, from what was never allowed to happen – 'the principle of the guild was a sound principle; and it was the principle and not only the practice that was trampled under foot' (1936: 459). This is an approach to history as structure rather than dates that McLuhan would emulate, the rhetorical world 'rigid with thought and brilliant with color', a world that is 'the very anti-thesis of the pale-pink lullaby land of popular science'. The difference that Chesterton's vivid prose made was between 'a cathedral window and blank infinity' (ibid.: 457). This cathedral metaphor underlined Chesterton's practice of Thomistic analog-ical thinking. And indeed, like St Thomas, he is able 'to focus a vast range of material into narrow compass; and his books though very numerous are extremely condensed' (ibid.: 462). We can see in McLuhan's praise for Chesterton's style, which brings together a vast assortment of details which 'bristle with con-temporary meaning', a premonition of McLuhan's own mosaic method, one that he would also recognize in Harold Innis's his-torical imagination.

Chesterton is involved in a project of 'synthesis and recon-struction' of medieval history and tradition because he is con-cerned with the present. Like Ruskin, Rossetti and Morris, he is interested in the great architecture and art of the Middle Ages, but, more so than they, he is concerned with the theological origins of that period (the life of St Francis and the thought of Aquinas) to ensure that 'future steps' not be 'blindly mistaken' (ibid.: 462). He is committed to the ordinary man. It is expressly because Chesterton is concerned with maintaining the social fabric and in establishing some objective sense of equality that his political programme calls for a return to the land, a connection to both geography and to history as a basis for common under-standing of justice and shared meaning. McLuhan's endorsement of this programme foregrounds his naïveté, but also what would become a central concern with space and its relation to history, as we see most especially in his work on 'interior landscape poetry' and the theory of the arrested moment, which he locates in Coleridge's poetry, a central influence on the Symbolists who came to develop the discovery more fully.

Cinema

McLuhan's writings must be framed by the Catholic intellectual tradition, which combines Aristotle, Augustine and Aquinas to give the human senses a central place in the drama of human cognition. McLuhan pairs Aquinas with *gestalt* psychology, compares human cognition to the poetic process and the detective fiction to understand that all forms of inquiry must be essentially a matter of perception and memory. Apprehension of reality itself is the incarnation of the exterior world, involving the creative engagement of human imagination. This intellectual tradition represents an approach that stresses the creative in the act not of decoding but of deciphering (Peirce instead of de Saussure). In McLuhan's work, grammar (Divine Logos) is never separate from meaning; he associates writing with the rise of cities. Like Henri Bergson (also influenced by Augustine), McLuhan sees the cinematic apparatus as the mechanization and distortion of the process of apprehension:

> In ordinary perception men perform the miracle of recreating within themselves – in their interior faculties – the exterior world. This miracle is the work of the *nous poietikos* or the agent of the intellect – that is the poetic or creative process. The exterior world in every instant of perception is interiorized and recreated in a new matter. Ourselves. And in this creative work that is perception and cognition, we experience immediately that dance of Being within our faculties which provides the incessant intuition of Being. I can only regard the movie as the mechanization and distortion of this cognitive miracle by which we recreate within ourselves the exterior world. But whereas cognition provides that dance of the intellect which is the analogical sense of Being, the mechanical medium has tended to provide merely a dream world which is a substitute for reality rather than a means of proving reality. ('Catholic humanism': 80)

Like Bergson, McLuhan differentiates between 'the miracle of cognition' which essentially concerns the materialization of reality, and the representation of reality in the cinema, which is a 'dream world'. Yet where Bergson can see nothing of use in the movie, McLuhan will find that it can in fact 'offer quite different effects'. Turning to a long quotation from the Italian Neorealist screenwriter and film-maker Cesare Zavattini, McLuhan foregrounds precisely Zavattini's approach to the everyday that so attracted the Christian phenomenologist and realist critic André Bazin. This is Zavattini speaking but it could just as well be McLuhan:

> While the cinema used to make one situation produce another situation, and another, and another again and again, and each scene was thought out immediately related to the next (the natural result of a mistrust of reality), today, when we have thought out a scene, we feel the need to 'remain' in it, because the single scene itself can contain so many echoes and reverberations, can even contain all the situations we may need. ...

> We have passed from an unconsciously rooted mistrust of reality, an illusory and equivocal evasion, to an unlimited trust in things, facts and people. Such a position requires us, in effect to excavate reality, to give it a power, a communication, a series of reflexes, which until recently we had never thought it had. It requires, too, a true and real interest in what is happening, a search for the most deeply hidden human values; which is why we feel that the cinema must recruit not only intelligent people, but, above all, 'living' souls, the morally richest people. ('Zavattini quoted in Catholic humanism': 80–1)

It is the emphasis on the spatio-temporal integrity of the singular situation in all 'its echoes and reverberations' rather than a series of situations aligned in a sequence of events that will create an understanding of life. For as Zavattini explains, to 'understand it [life] involves a minute, unrelenting and patient search' (ibid.: 82). This search drove McLuhan's project which, while emphasizing the very modernist dictum that the 'medium is the message', is also fundamentally realist.

Note

1 In a letter to Walter Ong (31 May 1953), McLuhan encourages him to develop a Thomist Theory of Communication: 'Reading St, Thos De Trinitata Q VI a2 objection one and reply there to, a very Ramistic text, whether in spec. on divine things imagination must be altogether relinquished: "It may be answered: sacred scripture does not propose to us divine truths under the figure of sensible things in order that our intellect should remain there, but that from these things it should mount up to such as are invisible."' Thomas Aquinas (1225–75) commentary on the "De Trinitate" of Boethius, Question VI, Article 2, Objection one and reply thereto'. (Letters: 237)

PART II
America

4

Early Media Studies and Mama's Boys

As an undergraduate studying communications in Canada in the late 1970s, I was told to stay away from McLuhan. *The Gutenberg Galaxy* was said to be nonsense, *Understanding Media* was all wrong, and the later McLuhan essays were bad art. McLuhan's first book, *The Mechanical Bride* was never mentioned. I found the book quite by accident when I was teaching a media literacy course to teenage girls at a Catholic high school. Given that the book had originated while McLuhan worked in a Catholic institution, one could suppose that it was collected by the school to support an anti-modern mission to see through the media in order to recover values for better living. As for myself, I was looking for something modern and challenging that would introduce young women to the idea that technologies are gendered, that culture is everywhere, and that language is political. The book engages in an analysis of modern domestic life in the United States through a form that utilizes advertisements as rhetorical analogies for capitalist modernity.

The text and image collages of *The Mechanical Bride* grew out of the 'Culture and Environment' courses that McLuhan taught throughout the 1940s at St Louis University in Missouri and as such they are designed as pedagogical tools. Indeed, Walter Ong, who was a student of McLuhan's at the university, maintains that the book, and McLuhan's interest in knowledge formation and language, was fuelled by the Catholic institution's milieu. St Louis University had a relationship to Cambridge English Studies, and housed several other Cambridge PhDs. McLuhan brought New Criticism to the curriculum by developing courses on 'Rhetoric and Interpretation' that combined literary history and criticism. McLuhan's courses and his research were influenced by St Louis University's particular brand of Thomism, which was characterized by a return to the original texts. The city of St Louis, one of the places where jazz and the blues were formed, also influenced his thinking as it had earlier stirred Eliot: 'The city of St Louis, with its origin via the French fur traders who opened up the entire North American continent, is a meeting-point of East and West and South by virtue of its two great rivers, the Missouri and the Mississippi' (*Letters*: 485). It is 'the strategic location' of St Louis, historically on the frontiers of metropolitan and agrarian life, that was later transformed into a central trope in his thinking about Canada's location in between Europe and the United States. From the very start there was an awareness of geography and culture, an awareness that culture was tied to geographic location and was therefore, profoundly anthropological. Thus, there is in McLuhan's first book an ironic and empirical anthropological dimension that treated urban and suburban culture in terms of 'industrial folklore'.

The Mechanical Bride was a long time in the making and was a project variously called *Guide to Chaos* and *Sixty Million Mama's Boys*. *The Gutenberg Galaxy* took the form it did, filled with scholarly quotation rather than ads, because McLuhan saw *The Mechanical Bride* as a failure; while it was positively reviewed, by Walter Ong among others, it only sold several hundred copies when it was first published (Marchand, 1989: 110). Unlike most academic books, *The Mechanical Bride* was written to reach a wide audience beyond the academy. Despite McLuhan's claims to the contrary, *The Mechanical Bride* displays an overt moral concern with the content and the marketing rhetoric of everyday commodity culture. His 'exhibits' function to generate discussion and to incite further exploration of everyday urban artefacts.[1] The book does not feel dated because the artefacts are drawn from that period directly after the Second World War when North American consumer culture, driven by the market's need to find domestic uses for wartime technologies, was always already kitsch. This new world of purposeless commodities is 'the folklore of industrial man'. McLuhan would write to Ezra Pound, with whom he maintained a long-standing correspondence: 'Looks like Vanguard Press will finally let my *Folklore of Industrial Man* out of five year cold storage this Fall. Shall see about further essays in that direction after that. It is a book which would do well in France or Italy. *Neurotica* magazine has published some of it' (*Letters*: 229). McLuhan's work has always done better in European countries, Latin America and some parts of Asia than in Anglo-American contexts.

It is in *The Mechanical Bride* that McLuhan begins to search for the deeper structures shaping the apparently empty meanings of post-war American culture. While *The Mechanical Bride* is marked by literary studies, it is in fact an early cultural studies text whose strategy is to discern unconscious cultural patterns and desires by displacing a variety of seemingly unrelated cultural artefacts drawn from newspapers and magazines. *The Mechanical Bride* should be read as a pedagogical project that first introduces us to the importance McLuhan places on media literacy. We can attribute the driving force behind his critical writings over three decades to a deep pedagogical commitment to a programme of media study. The desire to raise consciousness is no doubt inflected by his Catholicism and the literacy project formulated by the New Critics. In fact, the mandate of Cambridge English Studies, and in particular the work of F.R. Leavis, was transposed on to McLuhan's early vision of media studies as a 'guide to living' and a way of resisting the flood of capitalist culture.

McLuhan takes Leavis's concept of living culture to heart in *The Mechanical Bride* by 'showing the community in action'. Following Leavis, he makes a case for a new kind of media education. Against the *Great Books of the Western World* series organized by Mortimer Adler in the late 1940s, he directs attention to 'the unofficial instruction carried on by commerce through the press, radio, movies'. The *Great Books* project seeks to counter this unofficial instruction with grand ideas but in fact merely represents 'an unintentional reflection of the technological world' (*MB*: 43). The media cultures have come to be 'the only native and spontaneous culture in our industrial world' (ibid.: 44). For McLuhan it is by going through the popular cultures of the present, with 'the particulars of contemporary existence' that one can converse with the great minds of the past. Thus he calls for 'a part-time program of uninhibited inspection of popular and commercial culture' that, until the present, has been entirely ignored in the schools and colleges. Finally, 'the study of the great books would then be pursued with a fuller sense of the particularity of cultural conditions, past and present, without which there is no understanding either of art, philosophy, or society' (ibid.: 45).

While McLuhan does not wish to celebrate popular culture (on the contrary), he recognizes that without placing ideas in the historical and social context through which they continue to survive, they will have no effect on, or meaning in, the present. Like the adult literacy movement of the previous century that laid the foundations for English Studies, McLuhan wishes to engage with readers and invite them to analyze the culture in which they are immersed on a daily basis.

Barthes and Early Media Studies

In Anglo-American countries, Roland Barthes' *Mythologies* continues to be one of the founding texts used to introduce students to the semiology of popular culture (soap ads, popular rituals, wrestling, the face of Garbo) and to a form of writing that mirrors the fragmented culture it is analyzing. *The Mechanical Bride* precedes Barthes' book by five years and arguably has a far greater critical range. While intellectual fashion and the economics of publishing may well account for the absence of *The Mechanical Bride* on critical bibliographies, this absence also speaks to a general, mostly unspoken assumption that has underscored the way McLuhan's writings have been consistently overlooked. In the

1967 Preface to the English translation of Barthes' first book, *Writing Degree Zero*, Susan Sontag encapsulates this. She compares Barthes' 'original sensibility' to Karl Krauss, T.W. Adorno and Kenneth Burke, who all belong to 'that rare breed of intellectual virtuoso' unlike McLuhan who 'suggests the risks of radical unevenness of quality and judgement incurred with this magnitude of intellectual appetite and ambition' (ibid.: vii). That McLuhan is made to represent the risks involved in interdisciplinary thought or 'a radical unevenness' is not inappropriate. How can one engage in critical thinking without risk? The element of risk differentiates original thinkers from pedestrian theorists and certainly Krauss, Adorno, Burke and Sontag have taken risks by producing works that follow lines of thought that seem unclear or wrongheaded but lead to fruitful investigations at some future time and take on meaning for a new generation. Both Barthes and McLuhan engage in a criticism concerned with everyday life that expresses 'the intoxication of the mind' as Barthes would put it, a thinking, a writing, that surpasses the boundaries of pleasure circumscribed by desire, a writing that is also paradoxically distanced from itself through a profound self-reflexivity. This is what makes reading them always exciting, evocative and surprising.

McLuhan is not so attached to ideas as he is to a process of thinking through ideas as he would confess in the Preface to *The Mechanical Bride*:

The various ideas and concepts introduced in the commentaries are intended to provide positions from which to examine the exhibits. They are not conclusions in which anybody is expected to rest but are intended merely as points of departure. This is an approach which it is hard to make clear at a time when most books offer a single idea as a means of unifying a troup of observations. Concepts are provisional affairs for apprehending reality; their value is in the grip they provide. This book, therefore, tries to present at once representative aspects of the reality and a wide range of ideas for taking hold of it. (*MB*: vi)

We can see how McLuhan envisions Media Studies in terms of a laboratory, open to experiment, thought and dialogue. Concepts and ideas are tools for making sense of the world in its fleeting and multiple modalities. It is this speculative and largely open approach to studying culture that can be interpreted as lacking in the academic rigour of more traditional forms of disciplinary scholarship. This openness, however, is what makes *The Mechanical Bride* such a valuable pedagogical tool. Not only does it provide some wonderful concepts through which to grab hold of specific tendencies in the culture under analysis, but also it introduces the phenomenological aspects of cultural studies – the difficulties inherent in studying living processes. The sub-title of the book, 'The folklore of industrial man', while ironic (very much in the tradition of the Vorticists), highlights the anthropological and ethnographic aspects of McLuhan's project which is to devise a framework through which to observe the rhetorical forces of the modern world.

One of the reasons that I have assigned *Mythologies* to my undergraduate students, over the years, is its theoretical framework, which is consciously absent from all of McLuhan's writings. Barthes describes this as a 'double-theoretical frame':

> on the one hand, an ideological critique bearing on the language of so-called mass-culture; on the other, a first attempt to analyse semiologically the mechanics of this language. I had just read Saussure and as a result acquired the conviction that by treating 'collective representations' as sign-systems, one might hope to go further than the pious show of unmasking them and account in detail for mystification which transforms petit-bourgeois culture into a universal nature. (1970: 9)

Yet despite this framework, the essays in *Mythologies* are not terribly systematic and they do not reveal the 'mechanics' of myth in a precise way. For as Barthes notes, semiological analysis is initiated only in last essay of the book (ibid.: 9).

Barthes anticipates the problem of a lack of theory when he asserts that his ideology critique reflects neither the subjective freedom of the critic nor the objective vocation of the scientist. While he never explains precisely how he avoids the simple dichotomy, demystification is 'not an Olympian operation'. In other words, uncovering 'bourgeois norms' in the myths that we encounter everyday is not a difficult task. Rather, it is a question of seeing through what seems obvious, the well-known translation of which is the 'what-goes-without saying' (ibid.: 11–12). McLuhan would write that he has chosen objects for their familiar quality, these 'represent a world of social myths', they speak a language we both know and do not know' (*MB*: vi) Both McLuhan and Barthes are concerned with the commonsensical meanings of popular rhetoric as these are disseminated in advertising and media.

In a letter to the Canadian journalist Robert Fulford, who referred to Barthes as 'France's Marshall McLuhan', McLuhan would point to their similarities and differences. He saw in Barthes' writing a method that, like his own, examines effects rather than causes, studies patterns without overarching theories. He would explain that his own writings depend entirely on perceptions and not ideas:

> the untrained intellectual deals only with concepts and theories, and has little skill in the study of effects and consequences ... As for Barthes, he is a 'phenomenologist' – that is, one who tries to see the patterns in things while also playing along with the dominant theory of his world. Personally, I prefer to study the pattern minus the theory. (*Letters*: 540)

McLuhan has often claimed to be untheoretical, a claim that is substantially true. However, his methodology is certainly predicated on theories and cultural histories. While both McLuhan and Barthes were concerned with structures, it is important to keep in mind the differences between Saussurean semiotics and New Criticism. One important distinction lies in the realm of the reader, and the social space and context of language use. For McLuhan, Q.D. Leavis's study of *Fiction and the Reading Public* created an uproar because she claimed that 'highly literate people could lead moronic lives through most of their waking hours'. This study was unusual for the way it brought in context (a reading public) to analyze objects (literature), what McLuhan would later call 'figure/ground' relations (ibid.: 467). The New Critic's model of communication reached its most sophisticated conjugation in Richards's work. His concern with the psychological processes of interpretation introduced a cognitive dimension to English Studies that we do not find in French semiotics. In his last book, *Laws of Media*, co-written with his son Eric, McLuhan was critical of Saussure's model of language; the distinction between 'langue' and 'parole' was far too linear and reductive (*LM*: 111). It is the psychological and contextual aspect of

New Criticism that, as I argued in Part I, can help account for McLuhan's sustained interest in the psychological and physiological aspects of perception.

Barthes was more concerned with discourse than science. In fact, a sense of history and of the heterogeneous materialities of everyday life would lead Barthes away from the science of signs. He would indicate in his famous autobiography that the separation between sign and signified falls apart with the subject. Barthes' *bête noire* is analogy because it implies an 'effect of Nature'. Homology 'stands as beneficent opposition to perfidious Analogy'. Homology is 'simply structural correspondence' (1977: 44). It is a form of creative structuralism.

Although McLuhan's thinking is informed by Thomism and analogical thinking, his work also depends on the uncovering of homologies and correspondences. McLuhan's book grew out of years of teaching 'Culture and Environment' courses, using slides of popular artifacts as objects of analysis. Barthes' book is similarly heterogeneous, made up of short essays that were originally a series of feature articles written over a two-year period for *Les lettres nouvelles*. Both books explore a variety of objects – ads, comics, photographs, encyclopaedias, newspapers and more – chosen for their everyday familiarity, and to some degree, according to the interests of the authors. Famously, both authors choose to analyze soap detergents, perhaps the icon *par excellence* of modernity's lack of history. Each was influenced by modernist literature, in particular the Symbolist poets (Poe, Flaubert, Mallarmé, Baudelaire), who understood language as structure. Non-linear and non-sequential, McLuhan's and Barthes' works express on-going processes of analysis. McLuhan makes a point of this, as Barthes would in *Lover's Discourse*, when he remarks in the Preface to *The Mechanical Bride* that his book can be opened randomly, according to the interests of readers: 'Because of the circulating point of view in this book, there is no need for it to be read in any special order. Any part of the book provides one or more views of the same social landscape' (*MB*: vi).

It is this non-linearity that makes both McLuhan and Barthes' experimental texts readily understandable to a new generation raised on computer games and digital media. Along with *Culture and Environment*, and Wyndham Lewis's *The Doom of Youth*, which includes a discussion of advertising in a section called 'Gallery of exhibits', both *The Mechanical Bride* and *Mythologies* exemplify the critical impulses behind post-war media literacy. The new literacy is presented as a political practice, informed by modernist aesthetics aimed at making visible the subliminal ideologies hidden in the artifacts of modern capitalist cultures. What differentiates Barthes and McLuhan from Leavis and Lewis is that they are able to see the workings of ideology in popular culture and in high art. In other words, high culture is not exempt from capitalism. Moreover, they seek to communicate with a larger audience by utilizing the popular cultural forms they are analyzing: 'Why not use the new commercial education as a means to enlightening its intended prey?' writes McLuhan (*MB*: v).

Both McLuhan and Barthes practise a form of criticism that breaks down the boundary between poetic and critical writing. While the British New Critics like Eliot and most especially Richards wrote poetry and criticism, they were clear to separate one from the other – literature from science, for example – as being different genres with unique epistemological and grammatical rules. *The Mechanical Bride* and *Mythologies* do not compartmentalize criticism, creative interpretation and popular advertisements as distinct forms of writing. In fact, both McLuhan and Barthes have been taken to task for their writing styles which blur the boundaries between fiction and creative interpretation and scholarship (Curtis, 1978).

James Carey has complained about McLuhan's 'exploratory' approach:

> McLuhan is beyond criticism not only because he defines such activity as illegitimate but also because his work does not lend itself to critical commentary. It is a mixture of whimsy, pun and innuendo. These things are all right in themselves, but unfortunately one cannot tell what he is serious about and what is mere whimsy. His sentences are not observations as assertions but, in his own language, 'probes'. (1968, 291)

In a similar vein, Raymond Picard has written of Barthes:

> [His] work disregards elementary rules of scientific, or quite simply articulate, thought. On almost every page, in the frenzy of its headlong

systematizing, the part is given for the whole, an instance of two for the universal, the hypothetical for the categorical; the law of contradiction is flouted; accident is taken for essence; chance for law. (In Curtis, 1978: 139)

No doubt, it is the poetic and sometimes wildly speculative nature of their writing styles that irked the critics. In fact, McLuhan would refer somewhat ironically to his first book as 'a new form of science fiction, with ads and comics cast as characters'. He goes on: 'Since my object is to show the community in action rather than prove anything, it can indeed be regarded as a new kind of novel' (*Letters*: 217). A strong indication of McLuhan's debt to the Symbolists is the notion that his book is a 'landscape', a reconstructed social space that has been 'arrested' for the reader.

Barthes claims a comparable approach to his cultural criticism: 'In daily life, I feel for things I see and hear a sort of curiosity, almost an intellectual affection, which is of a novelistic order' (1981: 192). Famously, in his autobiography, he makes reference to himself in the third person, opening with the directive, 'It must all be considered as if spoken by a character in a novel'. Whether it is 'a new kind of novel' or 'a novelistic order', both authors read the life-world as if it were a text, a novel, and their descriptions of daily life reflect this equalization of reality (the news) and fiction (novels) as discourse and for McLuhan a new form of experimental ethnography that he would develop throughout the 1950s. Although 'The Folklore of Industrial Man' is the sub-title of *The Mechanical Bride*, it could just as well apply to *Mythologies*. Both books analyze discourses that stem from the laboratory, the studio, and the advertising agency. Furthermore, this folklore is presented in a deeply sarcastic (Flaubertian) manner. 'To live to the full the contradictions of my time,' writes Barthes at the end of *Mythologies*, 'may well make sarcasm the condition of truth' (1970: 12). To one of his detractors who found his descriptions overly dramatic, McLuhan retorted that he was very consciously attempting to write using the form of Mannipean Satire (*Letters*: 236). McLuhan states in the Preface that his tone of amusement should not be confused with mere indifference. Rather, readers should understand that 'moral indignation' is no longer an adequate response. Instead, he offers the detached viewpoint that comes with humour.

Recognizing the similarities in their practice, Barthes is said to have invited McLuhan to collaborate on a book (*Letters*: 539). While this never happened, it is clear that both authors espouse the same mission: to wake up the reading public, to make conscious those operations which are unconscious in everyday life. Despite the similarities between the two books, McLuhan's book is much more consciously a work of collage and juxtaposition with its 59 visual/textual artifacts. But the central difference between the two books is more fundamental. It concerns identity construction in relation to capitalism. Barthes' *Mythologies* seeks to undo bourgeois ideology by examining class-bound epistemologies, while McLuhan's book takes gender as a central organizing category for consumption. This is because, essentially, Barthes and McLuhan were seeking to awaken the minds of citizens living in different societies – France and North America. Barthes draws on myths that may well be American in origin, however, their context of reception is France. McLuhan, on the other hand, is engaging first and foremost with the utopian tenets of the American dream, with social rather than economic class, within the context of the United States.

The Mechanical Bride

The American dream that is central to the premise of *The Mechanical Bride*, in McLuhan's interpretation, is mediated through patriarchal capitalism, and built upon an oedipal scenario. The choice of the book's title, which was to have been *Sixty Million Mama's Boys* or *Guide to Chaos* but ended up being *The Mechanical Bride*, speaks to an instrumental culture unable to break free of its origins and unable to build meaningful relationships. Thus, the image of America that McLuhan discerns across so many ornamental surfaces is promulgated on a death drive, a technological construction and marketing of boundaries extended beyond bodies. Essentially caught between past and present, America is a nation that sees itself as the world. It is no surprise, then, that the two studies featured throughout the book are Alfred Toynbee's study of civilizations[2] and Margaret Mead's *Male and Female: A Study of the Sexes in a Changing World*. While Toynbee brings the past into the present 'as a working model for present political experiment', Mead's work functions to set different unrelated societies side by side 'to provide a greatly enriched image of human potentialities' that challenged normative gender roles. Such an 'image of the planet as city' reveals both the universal fabric and the singularity of differences across many worlds (ibid.: 3). These enable a detached viewpoint by displaying differences across space and time; they present a model of scholarship that McLuhan likens to cubism and to the heterogeneous form of the newspaper itself.

While it is the search for 'cosmic harmonies' (ibid.: 4) and insights derived from correspondences that will fuel McLuhan's methodology in this and all his subsequent writings, it is first and foremost a symptomatic reading of consumer ideologies that guides his book. In a culture geared toward 'comfort and thrills', these ideologies are all strangely discarnate:

> Know-how is so eager and powerful an ally of human needs that it is not easily controlled or kept in a subordinate role, even when directed by spectacular wisdom. Harnessed merely to a variety of blind appetites for power and success, it draws us swiftly into that labyrinth at the end of which waits the minotaur. So it is in this period of passionate acceleration that the world of machines begins to assume the threatening and unfriendly countenance of an inhuman wilderness even less manageable than that which once confronted prehistoric man. Reason is then swiftly subdued by panic desires to acquire protective coloration. As terrified men once got ritually and psychologically into animal skins, so we already have gone far to assume and to propagate the behavior mechanisms of the machines that frighten and overpower us. (ibid.: 34)

Although 'the pocketbook is the gland in the new body politic that permits the flood of goods' (ibid.: 88), *The Mechanical Bride* depends on the opposition between machines and humans. This relation would become increasingly complicated in McLuhan's later writings where he would see technology as extensions of bodies. In *The Mechanical Bride*, however, he still sees 'the dream of technology' in terms of an 'inhuman wilderness' and the 'know-how' of the marketplace. If men assume the guise of technologies, it is out of fear and panic – a way of mastering technology rather than, as he would later posit, because technologies are amplifications of human sensoria. The 'passionate acceleration', which McLuhan will later locate in electric media, leads to a state of 'panic' that ignites the conjunction of sex, death and technology.

Sex Machines

One might consider the relevance that *The Mechanical Bride* has for gender and feminist media studies as a media literacy project. While McLuhan was not a feminist, his work is significant for early feminist thought. The 'glamour cake' femininity remarked upon in *The Mechanical Bride* is, along with Betty Friedan's work, one of the first commentaries on images of women in the North American media. One of the most significant aspects of *The Mechanical Bride* is the degree to which gender forms the central category in his critique of post-war America and its conflation of knowledge with new forms of consumer culture. His early analysis of American popular culture discerns patterns of gender construction organized along the lines of consumption. He is particularly sensitive to the way women's bodies are not simply objectified but instrumentalized and rationalized to mirror 'the dynamo of abstract finance and engineering' (*MB*: 96). The merger of science and capitalism defines the utopian blueprint of America as a disembodied space untouched by history, yet fully automated. The design of a 'technological wilderness' features models of femininity and masculinity that depend on the triad of sex, technology and death.

It is women's experiences that have disappeared in what McLuhan identifies as a drive to push the boundaries of physical experience beyond the body. Women's bodies are the primary and original commodity. In post-war America, these bodies are advertised through 'glamour cake' postures and highly charged displays of affect and melodrama. Through rhetorical ploy, 'moving emotion and merchandise', subjectivities are invited to obey the law of numbers figured not by the folk but rather in the laboratory, the studio and advertising agency. Although the selection of materials in *The Mechanical Bride* seems random and heterogeneous, McLuhan finds a unity and cohesion of narrative structures underpinning advertising rhetoric across a wide spectrum of commodities from pulp fiction to life insurance: 'This consistency is not conscious in origin or effect and seems to arise from a sort of collective dream' (ibid.: v). Thus McLuhan is not simply proposing a conspiracy imposed on the minds of innocent citizens. Rather, he is concerned to understand these ads as public displays, models of behaviour and social situations that will tell us something profound about the society from which they emerge.

McLuhan explores the mechanized dream filled with the desire for speed expressed through the conflation of women and cars: 'Can the feminine body keep pace with the demands of the textile industry?' (ibid.: 93). Statistical curves and female curves lead to 'the interfusion of sex and technology' (ibid.: 94). Tied to symbolic orders and shared meanings of a culture, these images of mechanical dolls speak to a desire to expand the sexual domain and to 'possess machines':

> The visual and not particularly voluptuous character of commercially sponsored glamour is perhaps what gives it so heavy a narcissistic quality. The brittle, self-conscious pose of the mannequin suggests the activities of competitive display rather than spontaneous sensuality. And the smartly turned-out girl walks and behaves like a being who *sees* herself as a slick object rather than is aware of herself as a person. 'Ever see a dream walking?' asks a glamour ad. The Hiroshima bomb was named 'Gilda' in honor of Rita Hayworth. (ibid.: 99)

The Mechanical Bride is not Duchamp's 'Bride Stripped Bare by her Bachelors Even' – she is all dressed up and like all bachelor machines she is not a woman: she is a date, a 36–24–36, a hot number. The clockwork precision of scholastic method has been secularized and applied to modern business. Now finance rather than God instils a religious intensity and moral duty in the new cultural landscape of capitalism. Women's bodies and sex have been technologized and pushed to a final limit 'in an effort to pass the frontiers of sex' to be touched 'metaphysically' by crossing the final and ultimate sensory boundary, death:

Perhaps that is what the public wants when it reaches out for the inside story smoking hot from the entrails of vice or innocence. That may well be what draws people to the death shows of the speedways and fills the press and magazines with close-ups of executions, suicides, and smashed bodies. A metaphysical hunger to experience everything sexually, to pluck out the heart of the mystery for a super-thrill. (ibid.: 95)

This drive for extreme sensation, for the real thing, the bang of 'history in the making' finds expression in the wide occurrence of cluster images of sex, technology and death which constitute the 'mystery of the mechanical bride'. McLuhan well knows that Freud theorized this intersection of sex and death as 'death-drive', part of a primordial wish for origin and completion in *Beyond the Pleasure Principle* (1961: 174). The notion that citizens wish to be touched 'metaphysically' is never fully elaborated except that it belongs to a collective dream or unconscious. The 'mystery of the mechanical bride' is as fundamental to modernity as the serpent's coil or the death of God, as Nietzsche propounded. De Sade, of course, is another source for this intersection of sex and death in the famous statement that Georges Bataille drew upon to explore the parameters of eroticism, 'There is no better way to know death than to link it with a licentious image' (1986: 11). McLuhan is more concerned with the dream effects, with the manner in which collective desires find articulation in the rhetorical ploys that are capable of inducing a consumer 'trance'. How (not why) are consumers induced into specific kinds of consumption?

Masculinity is manned by self-centred 'mama's boys', eroding those family and communal values so dear to McLuhan and, importantly, any notion of the common good. The central problem for McLuhan is that Science has been reduced by the market to become applied science that, without a war to advance it, has but one purpose which is to feed the death-drive through chorus lines, girdles, nylons, nuclear manners, and household cleaners. The orchestration of puffball emotions takes its cue from one moral centre: financial success. 'Know-how' books abound, which is why McLuhan sees instruction and socialization being carried out in significant ways through the media; an idea that provides ample justification for a programme of media analysis that is both sociological and aesthetic.

The interfusion of sex and the mechanisms of the market is supported by ad agencies and Hollywood who, as they 'watch, anticipate, and control events on the inner, invisible stage of the collective dream have unwittingly become the collective novelist – producing the intimate revelations of the passions of the age'. The present environment, is a 'huge collective novel', that can be read only by those 'trained to use their eyes and ears, and in detachment from the visceral riot that this sensational fare tends produce'. The humorous tone of *The Mechanical Bride* calls upon the 'detaching power of wild laughter' (MB: 97) as well as the formal discoveries of the historical avant-garde.

Montage and Modernity

It is not only the content of *The Mechanical Bride* that is innovative but also inseparable from the content, it is its methodology. This methodology, which we find throughout all of McLuhan's works, stresses the political imperative to 'see things as they really are' with all the attendant difficulties such a task entails. Like English Studies in the previous century, McLuhan's interdisciplinary and probing media studies is a political activity that demands rational detachment. For this, McLuhan develops an aesthetic approach to analysis as he would later recall in the famous *Playboy* interview in 1969:

> For many years, until I wrote my first book, *Mechanical Bride*, I adopted an extremely moralistic approach to all environmental technology. I loathed machinery. I abominated cities. I equated the Industrial Revolution with original sin and the mass media with the Fall. In short, I rejected almost every element of modern life in favour of a Rousseauvian utopianism. But gradually I perceived how sterile and useless this attitude was, and I began to realize that the greatest artists of the 20th century – Yeats, Pound, Joyce, Eliot – had discovered a totally different approach, based on the identity of the processes of cognition and creation. I realized that artistic creation is the playback of ordinary experience – from trash to treasures. I ceased being a moralist and became a student. (*EM*: 265)

Bear in mind that despite claims to the contrary, McLuhan's prose in this first book is filled with critical judgements on the modern world. There are few treasures and much trash among the folklore of modern man and Leavisian utopianism is alive and well here. What he begins to develop quite apart from Leavis's critical literacy, is a methodology drawn from the art practices of the previous century. McLuhan sees the artistic process in the tradition of Symbolist poetry as a form of 'playback' – as a retracing of ordinary experience. This retracing is central to his layout of found materials.

The method for his book is inspired by Poe's 'A descent into the maelstrom' as he states in the opening passages: 'Poe's sailor says that when locked in by the whirling walls and the numerous objects which floated in the environment: "I *must* have been delirious, for I even sought *amusement* in speculating upon the relative velocities of their several descents toward the foam below"' (*MB*: v). The 'whirling phantasmagoria' is studied by arresting its action for 'contemplation' so that its usual participants are released from their habitual somnambulism. Unity is not imposed on diverse objects, rather, these heterogenous surfaces are 'dislocated' to reveal dynamic patterns that shed light on a 'complex situation' (ibid.: vi). *The Mechanical Bride* was intended as a popular form and borrows the structure of newspaper. While Poe is an important literary influence on McLuhan throughout his career, it is to Charles Dickens that credit must go for recognizing the technological format of the press as an expression of modernity. In his wonderfully evocative essay, 'Joyce, Mallarmé, and the press,' McLuhan writes:

> The networks of news, trade, and transport were one. And the newspapermen like Dickens who had no stake in established literary decorum were quick to adapt the technology of print to art and entertainment. Well before the French impressionists and symbolists had discovered the bearings for art of modern technology, Dickens had switched the picturesque perspectives of the eighteenth-century novel to the representation of the new industrial slums. Neurotic eccentricity in the sub-world of the metropolis he proved to be a much richer source for the rendering of mania and manic states of mind than the crofters of Scott or the yokels of Wordsworth. And Dostoevsky mined from Dickens freely, as G.B. Shaw did later still. But just how valid

were the impressionist techniques of the picturesque kind familiar to the news reporter appears in the notably essay of Eisenstein in *Film Form* where he shows the impact of Dickens on the art of D.W. Griffith. (*EM*: 64)

McLuhan did not fail to note that Dickens like Poe, was a 'newspaper man' and his methodology was the result of a new awareness of simultaneity brought about through the press. This recognition of the importance of Dickens and the newspaper is reflected in the first exhibit in *The Mechanical Bride*, which is none other than the front page of the *New York Times*. McLuhan foregrounds a continuity between modern art and the modern newspaper, between high art and popular commercial culture in the 'industrial imagination'. To those who decry the intellectual decline brought about through the popular press, he calls attention to the technical form rather than the message of modern newsgathering. It is the form of the newspaper layout, the heterogeneous clash of views that the Symbolists recognized and utilized as a new art form:

> the French Symbolists, followed by James Joyce in *Ulysses*, saw that there was a new art form of universal scope present in the technical layout of the modern newspaper. Here is a major instance of how a by-product of industrial imagination, a genuine agency of contemporary folklore, led to radical artistic developments. To the alerted eye, the front page of a newspaper is a superficial chaos, which can lead the mind to attend to cosmic harmonies of a very high order. (*MB*: 4)

The front page of the newspaper with its juxtapositions and simultaneous realities was the model for the Victorian novel, which the Symbolists (Poe and Mallarmé in particular) appropriated. Dickens's observational techniques correspond to the methodologies put forward by the English Empiricists where singularities of characteristics take precedence over an approach to observation based in assumptions. McLuhan's methodology is very similar; working without assumptions and suppositions, he will seek to foreground characteristics in order to discern patterns. As noted earlier, he refers to his book somewhat audaciously as a novel rather than a theoretical study. But what of the connection between disparate textual objects in *The Mechanical Bride*? How are the rhetorical fragments and disjointed images of McLuhan's text interrelated?

Sergei Eisenstein's newly translated writings, which were written under the sway of Symbolist aesthetics, James Joyce and Marx, provided another important influence on the overall montage aesthetic of *The Mechanical Bride* (*MB*: vi). Although McLuhan would reject dialectics, it is not surprising that he would find Eisenstein so inspiring. Eisenstein's belief in the possibility of a new epistemology that brings together aesthetics, sensuality and Science offered an avant-garde methodology premised on montage for analyzing the life-world within an historical framework.

According to Eisenstein, the 'extraordinary plasticity' of the Dickensian universe can be attributed to the creation of 'atmosphere' (1949a: 198). For Eisenstein the connection of narrative details, which produce a feeling of atmosphere becomes for Dickens, and later Griffith, the very basis of narrative structure. Fragmentation as an aesthetic of reality, like the exteriorization of interiority (stream of consciousness revealing hidden thoughts and memory fragments) that McLuhan described as 'interior landscape', depends on lack. As Dickens advocates: pleasure and suspense are derived through a withholding of information, through the 'regular alternation' of the comic and the tragic, through the 'dilemmas in which [the author] leaves his characters at the end of every chapter' (ibid.: 223). Fragmentation as a principle of narrative exposition functions to construct an inherent potentiality within the narrative, a promise to reveal the whole spatio-temporal picture, thus healing the wound it inflicted in the first place. For the literary critic Georg Lukács, this wound reflects the oppressive fragmentation inflicted by a class society. The driving force behind realist aesthetics is (proletarian) humanism, which aims 'to reconstruct the complete human personality and free it from the distortion and dismemberment to which it has been subjected in a class society' (1972: 5). Thus, the objectifying forces of class society are subjected to an objectification, which mirrors and heals suffering through 'organic totality' – the sublation of abstraction.

If we try to understand McLuhan through this lens, then we should distinguish between remembrance (the realist novel described by Lukács) and retracing or reconstruction. In other words, the aesthetic practice that interests the avant-garde poets, Eisenstein and McLuhan is the juxtaposition of heterogeneous fragments which the newspaper as form and practice represents, as a means to reconstruct experience. McLuhan likens this technique of reconstruction theorized most consciously by Poe and later Eisenstein to the detective story:

> Holmes remarks: 'In solving a problem of this sort, the grand thing is to be able to reason backwards'. A generation earlier, Edgar Allan Poe hit upon this principle of 'reconstruction', or reasoning backwards, and made of it the basic technique of crime fiction and symbolist poetry alike. Instead of developing a narrative straight forward, inventing scenes, characters, and description as he proceeded, in the Sir Walter Scott manner, Poe said: 'I prefer commencing with the consideration of an effect'. (*MB*: 106)

As we have seen, studying effects rather than causes was McLuhan's starting point. The first step in the reconstruction of the scene of the crime is to proceed from the effects and to move backwards to the crime – the reconstruction of the scene is not a linear affair but is bound to an aesthetic of simultaneity. McLuhan would explain this relation in a short manifesto published in *Explorations* a few years after *The Mechanical Bride* was published:

> About 1830 Lamartine pointed to the newspaper as the end of book culture. At the same time Dickens used the press as base for a new impressionist art which D.W. Griffith and Sergei Eisenstein studied in 1920 as the foundation of movie art. Robert Browning took the newspaper as art model for his impressionist epic *The Ring and the Book*; Mallarmé did the same in *Un coup de dés*. Edgar Poe, a press man and, like Shelley, a science fictioneer, correctly analysed the poetic process. Conditions of the newspaper serial publication led both him and Dickens to the process of writing backwards. This means simultaneity of all parts of composition. Simultaneity compels sharp focus on *effect* of the thing made. Simultaneity is the form of the press in dealing with Earth City. Simultaneity is formula for the writing of both detective story and symbolist poem. These are derivatives (one 'low' and one 'high') of the new technological culture. Simultaneity is related to the telegraph as the telegraph to math and physics. (*EM*: 201)

While the naturalist paradigm will reconcile the disparate elements to solve the mystery, Eisenstein (and so does McLuhan) advocates no such reconciliation. As is well known, D.W. Griffith's film, *Intolerance* (1916) was revered by the Russian Constructivists for its fragmentation of space and time. The film failed to reconcile its parts to a totality because the cross-cutting between four historical narratives (biblical story, modern story, St Bartholomew Day plot and Babylonian narrative) could never belong to the same universe. For the Russians, and Eisenstein in particular, this film gave birth to a new form of film construction: intellectual montage. Eisenstein would write in 'A dialectical approach to film form':

> I would not attempt to deny that *this form is most suitable for the expression of ideologically pointed theses* ... we have taken the first embryonic steps towards a new form of film expression. Towards a purely intellectual film, freed from traditional limitations, achieving direct forms for ideas, systems, and concepts, without any need for transitions and paraphrases. We may yet have a *synthesis of art and science*. (1949b: 63)

While the intellectual film is a writing that encompasses art and science, it is not a shorthand to reality. Indeed, intellectual montage foregrounds the very conditions of narrative meaning by drawing upon the Hegelian model of dialectical thinking to direct the mechanism of cutting, and in so doing it brings the spectator into the process of making history. Thus, Eisenstein maintains that the Soviet cinema, with its founding paradigm in montage, contributed to the aesthetic and political growth of the cinema, to the movement from the *'cinematographic eye* to the *image of an embodied viewpoint on phenomena'* (1949b: 233). This movement is essential and stands in opposition to the historical condition of cinematography as technological Eye, which is a product of positive science. Eisenstein outlines a Marxist approach to making films, a dialectical materialism that recognizes the image as sign and the cinematographic eye as embodied. Eisenstein, like McLuhan after him, was attracted to hieroglyphs, ideograms and archetypes as forms of writing that collapse sign and signifier. Eisenstein would revise intellectual montage to include more 'sensual' experimental forms of cinema. As with so many thinkers concerned with the somatic (Eco, Derrida, McLuhan), James Joyce is central.

Sensual Thinking

Upon reading *Ulysses*, Eisenstein was immediately struck by Joyce's ability to collapse the subjective and the objective in a process of writing which took the form of interior monologue. Inner monologue, as a structuring principle, could find 'full expression' in the cinema, for 'only the sound film is capable of reconstructing all phases and all specifics of the course of thought' (*Film Sense*, 1969: 105). Eisenstein compared the notion of 'affective logic' associated with spoken (as opposed to written) language, to cinematic montage, which is regulated by similar laws. Through the analogy he discovers a third term:

> montage had to make further serious creative 'cruises' through the 'inner monologue' of Joyce, through the 'inner monologue' as understood in film, and through the so-called 'intellectual cinema', before discovering that a fund of these laws can be found in a third variety of speech – not in written, nor in spoken speech, but in inner speech, where the effective structure functions in an even more full and pure form. But the formation of this inner speech is already inalienable from that which is enriched by sensual thinking. (ibid.: 250–1)

Eisenstein distinguishes the syntax of inner from outer speech: 'How you talk "to yourself" as distinct from "out of yourself"'. Inner speech then implies the incorporation and the internalization of social discourse, which, through this process, is subsequently broken down, condensed and abbreviated.

Eisenstein's exploration of the principles inherent in inner speech coincides with the work of the Formalist critic Boris Eikhenbaum who, in 1927, contended that the cinema did not simply escape the bias of words, but rather constituted their displacement in what he took to be the process of internal speech. Eikhenbaum maintained that theories of montage would have to be constructed to take into account the way in which the viewer 'reads' images: 'He must continually form a chain of film-phrases or else he will not understand anything' (1974–5: 13–14). Eisenstein's concern is to transform this process of 'reading' – a logical and learned process – and restructure it as a sensual activity. Thus, his earlier project to induce abstract and ideological reasoning is forfeited to pure 'sensation'.

> Now the spectator's reaction must not be thought but pathos, 'ecstasy' ... the very concept of montage is overhauled. Since the work of art must map the way we create felt concepts in life, montage's ability to render the dynamic flow of images makes it the sovereign formal principle. (Bordwell, 1974–75: 41)

Eisenstein was striving to formulate a new language derived from the sensual, and his unfinished film *Que Viva Mexico* was to be a testament to this experiment. In light of this, it is interesting that he held a fascination for dream work, for the relationship between words and images, and for secret laws of origin, which he felt could be discerned in ancient languages and primitive rituals. Eisenstein was attempting to translate into film the very sensorial processes of perception – the way 'we create felt concepts'. Eisenstein sought to change social structures by changing consciousness – by releasing it from the social strictures, which lead to its domination. His practices sought to affirm a new ecstatic consciousness not by means of invention of the new but rather by looking to the forms of ancient cultures for what they can reveal about the contemporary moment.

As is well known among film scholars, Eisenstein was accused of abandoning materialist practices in favour of mysticism and orientalism – (something that could be said of McLuhan's overvaluation of orality in relation to aboriginal cultures). However, it could be argued that Eisenstein's practices can be interpreted as materialist imperatives.[3] For example, Paul Willemen has argued that:

> internal speech (thought) can operate with extreme forms of abbreviation, condensations, image equivalents or fragments of image equivalents, extraordinary syntagmatic distortions, and so on. In fact, all the mechanisms which Freud detected to be at play in dream work can be seen at work in internal speech as well. (1981: 61)

The connection that Willemen makes between inner speech and dreams is significant for, as Freud maintained, the dream image can be understood as 'grounded in folklore, popular myths, legends, linguistic idioms, proverbial wisdom and jokes' (Freud,

Interpretation of Dreams, 1999). Moreover, Willemen claims that inner speech is not to be understood as a realm of pure subjectivity but rather as an articulation which is 'lined' with the ideological, that is, grounded in the social.

Thus, we find that this principle, used in accord with montage, can serve to reveal the foundations of epistemological/ideological practices: inner speech can reveal the materialist history of language. At the same time, inner speech can disturb this history by positing heterogeneity – differences in articulation and emphasis. Thus, for McLuhan it is by going *through* the processes of mediation (in collage and montage) that one can come to understand the popular discourses of ads as forms of reality and articulations of the collective dream.

Eisenstein's work (writings and films) presents a pedagogical model of the cinema. It is one that McLuhan would appropriate for a new model of media studies. Here books are not simply transparent objects that comment on another reality, rather, texts are physical forms that induce particular kinds of shock effects and insights.

Conclusion

Stuart Hall has asserted that *The Mechanical Bride* is McLuhan's only political book:

> In fact [McLuhan] referred to this book as 'a civil defense against mass media fallout'. But the disillusionment soon turned into its opposite – celebration, and in his later work, he took a very different position, just lying back and letting the media roll over him; he celebrated the very things he had most bitterly attacked. (1996: 132)

Hall's characterization of McLuhan's later work as simply celebratory has been challenged by a growing body of scholarship (Cavell, 2002; Fekete, 1982; Genosko, 2001; Grosswiler, 1998; Kroker, 1984; Stamps, 1995; Theall, 2001; Wilmott, 1996). McLuhan's methodology and his moral critique of the media, I would argue, remained remarkably consistent throughout his career. The development of heuristic tools that would form the basis of a media studies programme was fuelled by an ethical imperative. The shift that one may detect from this early book to his subsequent writings is one from content analysis to an analysis of structures understood through technology rather than ideology. It was the emphasis on ideology and rhetoric that McLuhan ultimately saw as a failure, because after five years of negotiations the book finally emerged just as television was transforming the face of everyday culture:

> *Mechanical Bride* is a good example of book that was completely negated by TV. All the mechanical assumptions of American life have been shifted since TV; it's become an organic culture. Femininity has moved off the photographic, glamour cake altogether into the all-involving tactile mode. Femininity used to be a mingling of visual things. Now it's almost entirely nonvisual. I happened to observe it when it was reaching the end of its term, just before TV. (*EM*: 267)

The notion that femininity has moved from a photographic space into a post-visual acoustic space is worth noting and will be taken up in greater detail in the next chapter. Throughout the early 1950s, McLuhan worked with the anthropologist Edmund Carpenter to develop the idea of 'acoustic space', which he opposes to visual space. Acoustic space is a decidedly non-commodifiable form, which, according to McLuhan, is feminine in nature. *The Mechanical Bride* also contains many of McLuhan's central ideas in embryonic form: the 'planet as city' created through the press is certainly the hallmark of the 'global village' or, as he wanted to call it after the invention of television, the 'global theatre'. The emphasis on the form of the newspaper rather than the message foretells his neologism 'the medium is the message'. Moreover, these insights into patterns of address and gesture, recurring narratives and characters, are part of a consciousness-raising politic, which he is anxious to connect to a humanist education. It is only through 'rational self-awareness' and dialogue that a change in the market's definition of progress is possible.

The desire for a popular literacy is key to understanding McLuhan's work. Hall's view that the later McLuhan simply lets 'the media roll over him' can be challenged if we foreground McLuhan's pedagogical project, his work on effects as a form of consciousness-raising. Such an emphasis can go some way toward accounting for McLuhan's status as a public intellectual, and his central contribution to the rise of communication studies in Canada, as we explore in the next chapter. But Hall is right to note that there is something singular and distinctive about this first book. Its approach is based on an aesthetic of simultaneity and it is a political project that belongs to a tradition of ideology critique. *The Mechanical Bride* is tied to the world of print, while his work from the 1950s onward was written under the influence of television. The difference is to be found in the particular temporal dimension of the collage. In constructing a textual maelstrom, McLuhan does not so much bring a temporal aspect to his arrested moments as foreground the sedimentations of historical processes somewhat akin to dreamwork or the recollection of a dream.

In 'Cogito interruptus', Umberto Eco has maintained that the technique of radical juxtapositions is a technique common both to the insane and to the authors of a reasoned "illogic" – its prime virtue and difficulty is that it is ineffable' (1986: 222). Books based upon radical montage tend to see the world in terms of symbols and symptoms. For Eco, McLuhan's books are impossible to summarize or to review – as readers we can make our way through one particular line, but, like the Dickensian novel, they exceed their readers by creating atmosphere that defies linear argument. From his early years at Cambridge in the mid-1930s, McLuhan would use the artistic process and the learning process interchangeably. Learning is a creative activity, an act of the imaginative retracing of experience, of making experience visible. McLuhan understood that aphorisms, paradox and collage represent a broken knowledge and, as such, invite further speculation and participation. This is an aspect of McLuhan's work that is often misunderstood. He views knowledge as necessarily always partial and always grounded in the senses and in dialogue with others. As noted earlier, his interpretive methodology grows out of criticism rather than theory because he wishes to address what is contemporary, present and always in process. Theoretical frameworks cannot deal with immediacy but rather must reduce the phenomenal world and particularities to a model; theories answer questions rather than raising them. McLuhan is looking for a method that is open to the ephemeral nature of the world and he finds this method in the poetic experimentations of the historical avant-garde. Avant-garde practices for McLuhan can serve a cognitive function by linking 'the storehouse of achieved values' with new discoveries and forms of awareness.

In his essay, 'McLuhan as teacher', Walter Ong has maintained that McLuhan's 'intellectual synapses leaped wide gaps. Like long sparks on a huge static machine when the charge builds up enough to tear through the resisting air, his formulations crackled, and they set nerves on edge. But a dismaying number of his "generalisations" turned out to be true' (1981: 132). Perhaps most astonishing in reading McLuhan's work so many years later is its prophetic quality. This is because whether dealing with the world of print or of other media, he understood modernity in terms of mediation, and as a fundamental reconfiguration of reality – of subjectivities and bodies – through time and space technologies, or the mechanical bride.

McLuhan was primarily interested in contemporary media. This is not to say that history does not figure in his work as it does with Innis. Rather, as we shall see with *Gutenberg Galaxy*, history is always contemporary.

Notes

1 In his first teaching post at St Louis University, McLuhan began to use advertisements (a strategy Leavis also developed) to study popular rhetoric because a new generation of students refused to read Arnold or to understand the value of romantic rebellion de Kerckhove (de Kerckhove interview, Understanding McLuhan CD ROM, 1996). Yet the Romantics were always present in his thinking.

2 McLuhan would later write quite critically of Toynbee that he is

> like an announcer at a sporting event. He tells a good deal about what is happening. His tone of earnest concern indicates to the reader or listener that the events have some significance. In the same situation Innis would have observed that the form of the sporting event was an interesting model of perception, giving us an immediate image of the motives and patterns of the society that had invented this corporate extension of itself. (Foreword to *Bias*, 1968: x)

We can get a good sense of how McLuhan's concentration has shifted over to form by the early 1950s.

3 In 'Eisenstein's epistemological shift' (1974–75), David Bordwell suggests that Eisenstein's preoccupation with inner speech – which signalled a return to the subject – constituted a break away from his earlier materialist formulations of intellectual montage. Bordwell attributes this shift to the political context of the early 1930s in Russia, that is, to the abolition of the materialist cinema and the new-found allegiance to Socialist Realism. However, Gregory Ulmer in *Applied Grammatology* (1985: 288) maintains that the shift does not imply an abandonment of his earlier formulations but can be seen in fact as an extension of those theoretical experiments. Ulmer points out that Eisenstein's dissatisfaction with the 'intellectual cinema' came with the poor reception accorded *October* (1928) Moreover, this shift in emphasis occurred prior to 1930.

5

Experimental Seminar

My computer was struck by lightning when I began work on this chapter. My logic board and the material on my hard drive disappeared, perhaps appropriately, into the galaxy. Everyone who has ever worked on a computer has experienced this loss of data and wondered where, in the ephemeral world the information has gone. Although these kinds of incidents are common, they nevertheless always remind us of the vulnerability of our information systems. This 'outage', perhaps not entirely the way McLuhan would have meant it, is a fine way to introduce the notion of human memory as it relates to electricity. As if anticipating the two incidents that he would suffer in his life, a brain tumour, which wiped out part of his memory and a stroke, which left him with aphasia, this relation was always central to his theorization of culture. Essentially, McLuhan believed all technologies to be extensions and expressions of our bodies. Thus, for him it would be no accident that our cities resemble computer chips from the air, or that the Internet seems in its form to reproduce the nonlinear patterns of thought processes. These are outerings of our bodily functions.

McLuhan sought to 'probe' the dematerialization of culture that defines the electric period, not as a visual sphere, but as 'acoustic space'. McLuhan's writings after *The Mechanical Bride* engage with the post-visual orality of electric culture where past configurations of culture, from the medieval manuscript to the modern press to the cinema screen, have become visible for us to study as the content of emerging technologies. But it is centrally their effects on our physical and psychic bodies that would always drive McLuhan's investigations into changing perceptions. Technologies, like the language we carry around inside our selves, are 'extensions' of human bodies and McLuhan would refuse the nature/culture divide. Throughout the 1950s, McLuhan develops a sensory theory of communication. This chapter is devoted to the development of this approach, an interdisciplinary and historical method of analyzing everyday life in terms of its communicative processes.

The Gutenberg Galaxy is generally acknowledged to be McLuhan's most important book. It is this book, original in its form and thought, along with the work of George Grant, Harold Innis and Eric Havelock that helped to establish a distinctly Canadian intellectual tradition in cultural and communication studies. This distinct tradition is characterized by 'a discourse on technology' (Kroker, 1984; Charland, 1990), a discourse that sees technology as constitutive of social and psychic space. *The Gutenberg Galaxy* takes a different approach to analyzing the media than does his first book, *The Mechanical Bride*, focusing not on content analysis of popular commercial discourses but on the structure and sensorial experiences of that content, on its conditions of possibility. McLuhan explicates the technological conditions of modernity as first and foremost an experience of visuality. We can locate in McLuhan's work a distinctive shift from content analysis to form in the early 1950s. While *The Gutenberg Galaxy*, like *The Mechanical Bride*, is a non-linear collage of different perspectives, it is distinguished from this earlier work in its radical interdisciplinarity. As I discuss in this chapter, we can see this interdisciplinary approach developing throughout the 1950s in the pages of the journal *Explorations* (1953–59), and through his relationship to the intellectual community known under the rubric of the Culture and Communication Seminar (1952–53) at the University of Toronto. This community and its unique journal were committed to an experimentation founded upon the meeting of disciplines. In particular, two areas of research would exert a tremendous influence: art and architectural history, and anthropology. Interestingly, the meeting of art history and anthropology would lead McLuhan to include examples from diverse national cultures (oral, visual and electronic), lending a distinct multicultural quality to his work on communications, an emphasis on diversity that was undoubtedly influenced by the environment he was working in – Toronto, the location that would evolve into the multicultural city *par excellence*.

The shift from content to structure in McLuhan's research should not be seen as an essential break from the earlier work but rather as a development of his project, very modern in its articulation, of making the invisible visible. There is a fundamental Canadian influence on his work in the richly detailed historical writings of political economist Harold Innis. However, crucial to the arguments presented in this book, McLuhan never relinquishes the critical pedagogical project of Cambridge English Studies, which takes its cue from the English Romantics. As it develops over a 30-year period, from *The Mechanical Bride* on, this project will not distinguish between poetry and criticism but, rather, takes shape at the intersection of disciplines, temporalities and everyday life.

McLuhan's project to understand contemporary experience in terms of its mediations through technology (whether it be the English language or remote sensing technologies) remained more than a persistent theme in all of his writings: it was the intellectual project to which he would devote his life. In this sense, *The Gutenberg Galaxy*, like Chesterton's small book, *What's Wrong with this World*, is a work concerned with culture in its historical dimensions. The comparison is apt, moreover, because McLuhan is not the future-oriented high tech cybertheorist able to prophesy Internet culture, but because he is a Victorian man of letters, a satirist, very much steeped in literary culture. As a conservative satirist, his insights, even at their most radical, derive from a distanced engagement with the present as a landscape to be represented to the public in the most grotesque and humorous of ways. It is because McLuhan is so much a product of literary culture that he is able to discern a shift from mechanical to electric culture. This will bear itself out in the work he develops throughout the post-war period of 1950s' North America. McLuhan is not interested in 'connections' so much as he is in the space between connections, that is, in intervals. This is how he brings a historical perspective to his media studies. He does not focus on continuities so much as on discontinuities and breakages: shifts that he seeks to interpret by way of their spatial and bodily effects.

McLuhan came to teach at the University of Toronto in the late 1940s, and it is worth sketching the activities that occupied him in order to situate the insights he would develop over that decade into a book. Initially called an exploration of the *Gutenberg Era,* he would put the emphasis on space, or temporal space, with the new title *Gutenberg Galaxy* that seeks to understand a central shift from oral culture to writing. We find in *The Gutenberg Galaxy*'s formal enterprise a new stress on structure, specifically those invisible structures which shape human affairs. Intrinsic to this, and fundamental to it is the way in which specific technologies work on sensorial experiences, and the way these technologies privilege certain senses over others. Before discussing McLuhan's analysis of cultural contrasts proper I want to turn to the communal work he carried out with several thinkers whose interdisciplinary approaches were at the heart of *The Gutenberg Galaxy*.

Toronto

Just after the publication of *The Mechanical Bride*, McLuhan discovered a new object, which made his book seem immediately out of date – the 'Electronic Bride' (Marchand, 1989: 110, 288). This bride was, of course, television, entering Canada in 1952 with the establishment of the Canadian Broadcasting Corporation, a government-sponsored public broadcast system whose mission, like that of the National Film Board of Canada (NFB), was to make a modern nation out of Canada, to unify the large unwieldy country by creating a mediated interpretation of the nation. It is not surprising that both Innis and McLuhan would theorize a space-binding role for communications media. Canadians have instant access to all American radio and television which, experienced in the Canadian milieux, 'feeds the philosophic attitude of comparison and contrast and critical judgement' (Canada: the borderline case, 1977: 247). As noted earlier, McLuhan believed that Canadians occupied a special place at the intersection between empires – Britain and the United States. The proximity to the United States, in particular, gave Canadians a unique ability to stand apart from and to judge the technological dynamo. Given the history of Canadian television as a circuit for the importation of American culture, it is also not surprising that television would be seen as dissolving rather than maintaining national boundaries, helping to create a 'global village' or 'earth city'. This is the case not just with television, but with all electronic media. Although *The Gutenberg Galaxy* is a book about the impact of the printing press on forms of life, it can also be seen as one the first theoretical discussions of television's formal properties.

From the late 1940s on, and particularly after his arrival in Toronto, McLuhan was committed to creating a new school and to working within a community of intellectuals. McLuhan's work needs to be understood as arising out of collective engagement, conversations, letters and dialogue. Just as *The Mechanical Bride* grew out of courses he taught at St Louis University, so too did *The Gutenberg Galaxy* grow out of an interdisciplinary confluence of students, scholars, scientists, artists and journalists in Toronto. Moreover, it is important to remember that McLuhan's insights depended on the coming together of different disciplines as well as different cultures that were beginning to populate the city.

One can scarcely imagine a more dismal and bland place than Toronto in the early 1950s. It embodied everything that was mind-numbingly dull about Canada, as McLuhan would write of it in *Counterblast* (1954), his homage to Wyndham Lewis's magazine *Blast* (1914–15): 'In 1954 Wyndham Lewis blasted Toronto in the novel SELF-CONDEMNED. HIS René (reborn) seeking his true spiritual self selects Toronto, Momaco: (Mom & Co.) as a colonial cyclotron in which to annihilate his human ego. He succeeds. … Toronto home of Victorian Panic & Squalor, urgent reminder of the

DESPERATE CONDITION of man; The TELEVISION TOWER on Jarvis St. elegant scoffer at Toronto's architecture' (*Counter Blast*, 1954: npn.). To complement this characterization and to set the scene of the experience of this city, I would like to add the distinguished Canadian artist Joyce Wieland's recollections of walking through Toronto in 1950:

> I could walk with my girlfriend Mary from Broadview and Danforth to Keele St. and we wouldn't see anything. We made suicide pacts. We would say 'This is life and this is what happens to you so you might as well jump off the bridge' (Bloor Viaduct), and we were considering it because there was fuck-all! There was an art gallery and a few people but no feeling. (in John Porter, 1984: 26)

Wieland's sense that she couldn't 'see anything' in Toronto is not entirely without foundation. Throughout the 1950s and well into 1960s, the inner municipality of the city was reconfigured to accommodate an explosive metropolitan growth in which the urban region's population more than doubled. The demolition of historic buildings in the city's old business district, the destruction of older residential pockets within the urban core (displacing some 13,000 people) reflected Toronto's municipal planning policies which favoured development and saw history as an impediment to real modern progress (Caulfield, 1994: 18). This kind of urban renewal was occurring in all the larger metropolitan centres around North America. In Robert Moses' New York, where highways were destroying the rich neighbourhood communities, citizens' groups led by activist Jane Jacobs would challenge this lack of history. Famously, Wieland along with artist Michael Snow and countless other bohemians after them, fled to New York to join the culture scenes there. Toronto got them back along with Jane Jacobs, who relocated in the 1970s. Not surprisingly, McLuhan would later collaborate with Jane Jacobs on a film about saving Toronto neighbourhoods. Throughout the 1950s and 1960s he worked with researchers and activists who were involved in encouraging Toronto's growing heterogeneity, its history, and its lived cultures.

Toronto in the early 1950s began to experience visible changes: a vast influx of immigration brought a multiplicity of races and ethnicities, cultures and languages to the city. McLuhan's long-time collaborator anthropologist Edmund Carpenter would recall, 'BBC directors looking for work, Hollywood writers fleeing McCarthy. But also a technological breakthrough with television, a live medium in 1950' (2001: 250). Indeed, it is the very quality of televised reality, its liveness, that must be seen as a catalyst for many of McLuhan's insights on electronic media as a return to orality, and even his anticipation of the characteristics of the internet. Other portable technologies tied to television, such as the development of lightweight recording technologies and synchronized sound, expressed a new aesthetics of freedom. McLuhan, like André Bazin, saw neo-realism as a fundamental product of the sound cinema and a political drive for freedom, an emphasis on the integrity of space and time, which he did not view as being in opposition to montage. Especially in post-war America, reality was packaged through advertising and the press, and the need to find new domestic applications for technologies developed for war also led to a new explosion of visual styles as he had explored in *The Mechanical Bride*. This is the surrealism that begins to define the American style:

> BLESS USA cornucopia of daily
> *SURREALISM. THE HEARST PRESS*
> locked in the (embrace) of
> intoxicating numbers
> 36 – 21 – 35
> Miss America's split T
> FORMATION
> The practical communism and cosmic con-
> formity achieved by American
> MASS-PRODUCTION. (*CounterBlast*)

This aesthetic of 'cosmic con-formity' developed out of capitalism whose production methods mirrored the lines of the page. Explicating this structural homology would be the subject of *The Gutenberg Galaxy*. America presented the spectacular 'light show' that Torontonians were witnessing from afar, and because of this distance these 'islanders' were given a better understanding of its surrealism. It was precisely the new culture that emerged in post-war America that was of interest; the commodity culture that he had studied in *The Mechanical Bride* had expanded to cover every aspect of lived experience.

Committed to a communal ideal of intellectual exchange, McLuhan was intent on finding a community of thinkers to collaborate and develop interdisciplinary and experimental frameworks for studying contemporary culture. Such a community came together at the University of Toronto under the auspices of the Communication and Culture Seminar funded by the Ford Foundation (1952–53). The research group included: McLuhan, English; Edmund Carpenter, Anthropology; Tom Easterbrook, Economics, Jacqueline Tyrwhitt, Urban Studies; and Carl Williams, Psychology. Communications was in the air. The Korean War had foregrounded the possibilities of brainwashing and the need to study the perceptual processes of the brain. One way to accomplish this study was to understand how communications impact upon perception. Inspired by Innis, this interdisciplinary group examined the bias of communication, with a special emphasis on oral and post-visual cultures.

Communications as a Field of Study

McLuhan's encounter with both art history and anthropology would have a decisive impact on the conceptual frameworks he brought from English Studies, placing an emphasis on both history and geography. A journal called *Explorations* would publish writing by the group along with psychological studies of the media effects, experimental poetry, scientific studies, and urban studies. Founded by Carpenter and co-edited by McLuhan, *Explorations* focused on culture as a landscape. In particular, an 'acoustic landscape' became an important structuring principle that grew out of the seminar. McLuhan seized upon and connected this concept to the writings of T.S. Eliot and Pound. While a study of bias was the central area, the journal was devoted to developing a pedagogical approach to studying contemporary culture. The idea that this was a new field of study, one that required new methodologies, would direct the journal's most creative energies. In the history of Cultural Studies in Canada, this journal is an important starting point for defining the research agenda for the Toronto School of Communication.

Yet, as Carpenter remarks, the school was not formal. Rather, comparing Toronto to an island, he maintains that it was a bunch of islanders simply watching a spectacular light show from afar. This was McLuhan's feeling about Canada, more generally as the *Dew-Line Newsletters* (1968–70) later proposed: Canada provided an early warning system for the United States, located between two empires and yet having a separate identity. Toronto, in particular, housed a coterie of intellectuals and artists that would meet every day at four o'clock at the Royal Ontario Museum coffee shop: McLuhan, Tyrwhitt, Carpenter, Donald Theall, John Irving, sometimes Easterbrook and less often Innis, and often visitors Dorothy Lee, Siegfried Giedion, Ashley Montagu, Karl Polyani, and Roy Campbell (Carpenter, 2001: 251). The novelty of television meant also an openness and access. For example, Carpenter and Tyrwhitt used the media to challenge some of the city's more excessive development projects. This was a period when the arts were developing in Canada and when experimental and documentary film-makers were forming their own communities. There were art scenes in the city in which performance, graphic art, and poetry were a central manifestation of an avant-garde and youth culture. There was a sense of possibility and creativity. Carpenter remembers this period in Toronto's history as 'a remarkable moment'. Toronto, with its ugly architecture and meanness, was also a place that was changing. It was a young city in the process of inventing itself. It was also a period that was completely conducive to a journal like *Explorations*, 'before the net closed, one could explore, speculate' (ibid.: 252). *Explorations* was read in Paris, by such figures as Derrida, Barthes, Lévi-Strauss and Sontag (ibid.: 238). The journal would contribute to the rise of 'MacLuhanism' in France some years later.

Throughout the 1950s Carpenter was McLuhan's closest collaborator. Theall (1971) argues that Carpenter's radical anthropology exemplifies the experimental approaches to culture that served to develop *The Gutenberg Galaxy* as well as McLuhan's later 'concrete essays'. Carpenter went on to set up an anthropology department in Northridge California that was committed to inter-disciplinarity, combining the performing arts with media and perception. Throughout the 1960s, Carpenter's experiments with multi-screen projection and film would be of interest to McLuhan, who would act as consultant on the Imax presentation for Expo '67 in Montréal, as well as pursuing his own film and video experiments. With the Culture and Communication Seminar and the journal, one thing became clear: their methods for studying communications grew out of percepts and experimental techniques that combined experimenting with media, reading across a wide array of disciplines and engaging with everyday culture – rather than using established concepts and theories. The essays published in the journal were later collected in an anthology co-edited by Carpenter and McLuhan. In their Introduction they describe the journal in a way that could serve as an introduction to *The Gutenberg Galaxy*:

> *Explorations* explored the grammars of such languages as print, the newspaper format and television. It is argued that revolutions in the packaging and distribution of ideas and feelings modified not only relations but sensibilities. It is further argued that we are largely ignorant of literacy's role in shaping Western man, and equally unaware of the role of electronic media in shaping modern values. Literacy's vested interests were so deep that literacy itself was never examined ... The aim of this anthology is to develop an awareness about print and the newer technologies of communication so that we can orchestrate them, minimise their mutual frustrations and clashes, and get the best out of each in the educational process. The present conflict leads to the elimination of the motive to learn, to diminution of interest in all previous achievement: it leads to loss of the sense of relevance. Without an understanding of media grammars, we cannot hope to achieve a contemporary awareness of the world in which we live. (1966: 2)

This approach to studying the media as languages, to studying their grammars, was in stark contrast to the general field of communications as it was emerging in the 1950s, which stood between the behavioural sciences of Wilbur Schramm and the structural functionalism identified by Talcott Parsons, Robert Merton, Elihu Katz and Paul Lazarsfield (Carey, 1983: 311). James Carey has suggested a third response to the social 'ferment' of post-war America, beyond behaviouralism or the functionalism that appeared under the banner of mass culture, encompassing effects but also the debates over culture and modernity as well as power and politics. He situates the work of Harold Innis within this category alongside C. Wright Mills, David Riesman, and Kenneth Burke. Such a tradition was developing in a parallel fashion in England under the banner of Cultural Studies around the writings of Raymond Williams, Richard Hoggart and E.P. Thompson. A footnote in Carey's essay situates McLuhan as an eccentric within this configuration:

> The oddest creature of the lot was Marshall McLuhan, who took his literary studies under Raymond Williams's teacher, F.R. Leavis, and took its results to the University of Toronto where he rethought the whole thing under Harold Innis. Of such improbable combination was 'the medium is the message' born. (ibid.: 312)

McLuhan is without doubt the 'oddest creature of the lot', and in later work Carey will chastise him along with 'the medium is the message' for a lack of historical and material rigour (1968, 1981, 1986). McLuhan's work does represent a hybridization of Leavis's criticism and of this third group concerned with mass culture and modernity. In fact, McLuhan admired all three of the thinkers Carey situates in the third tradition. Riesman's work on the consumer mentality is acknowledged in *The Mechanical Bride* as an important influence and McLuhan had published several of his essays in *Explorations*. McLuhan certainly admired Kenneth Burke, whose theory of language revitalized an older tradition of 'inclusive consciousness' (*Letters*: 327). But most especially, McLuhan was very conscious of Innis's historical imagination.

Perhaps one of the many things that distinguishes McLuhan's unconventional approach from the thinkers listed by Carey is his concern with youth culture. It was McLuhan's commitment to understanding the contemporary world that (like the group under Stuart Hall at the University of Birmingham some years later) led him to conceptualize a research programme that would engage directly with the new sensibilities of youth culture. In Toronto, this new sensibility was demonstrating itself at the Ontario College of Art, at Ryerson Polytechnical Institute, and at Central Technical High School, where teenagers were experimenting with media technology, where avant-garde art was being defined through technology and through an engagement with popular culture. The seeds of video art in North America begin with the encounter between high art and television and it is not surprising that McLuhan played such an important role in its formation early on.[1] This relation between the 'industrial imagination' and art practices was not unfamiliar to McLuhan as he long had admired this discursive approach to art making in the historical avant-garde and modernist writers such as Joyce, Lewis and Pound.

Communication and Culture Seminar

McLuhan's formalism, his emphasis on the medium as content, was inspired by another set of thinkers that Cary leaves out, who would play a central role in McLuhan's thinking and introduce an important paradigm into communications research: computers. In 1948, the year that television enters popular culture in the United States, two major publications would hit the emerging field of communication studies: Norbert Wiener's *Cybernetics: Or Control and Communication in the Animal and the Machine* and Claude Shannon and W. Weaver's 'A mathematical theory of communication'. These works impressed McLuhan negatively as they stood very much at the opposite end of the interdisciplinary approach he was seeking to develop. The absence of any consciousness that people would be using computer technologies to produce cultures in the functionalist Shannon–Weaver model and in Wiener's cybernetics stood in stark contrast to the picture he wanted to paint. McLuhan believed that computers and popular culture would be inextricably linked before the end of the century and that any account of these technologies had to include culture. He stressed the need to situate computers within an historical 'galaxy' that includes all other forms of communication. It is this 'publishing event' and the absence of culture as an epistemological term that would directly shape the design of McLuhan's research project into the media throughout the 1950s (Theall, 2001: 7).

In a now famous letter to Harold Innis, McLuhan's colleague at the University of Toronto in 1951, McLuhan would criticize Wiener, and along with him Karl Deutsch, for not recognizing the importance of rhetorical forms and of the 'traditional arts' as 'the essential type of all communication'. McLuhan is critical of an approach to analyzing communications media that is ahistorical and that does not take into account the older forms of communications: 'instead' these offer 'a dialectical approach born of technology and quite unable of itself to see beyond or around technology' (*Letters*: 222). McLuhan was responding to the abstraction of communication from everyday practices and language and, most importantly, from a history of communication. The closed and functionalist viewpoint on technology cannot recognize dynamic systems of reality and the impact of previous historical forms. 'The Medieval Schoolmen ultimately ended up on the same dialectical reef' (*Letters*: 222). As we have seen, McLuhan was critical of dialectics and theoretical frameworks (although he employed both) that isolated objects and processes from dynamic relations in the world i.e., from uses, service industries and effect. The Shannon–Weaver model, the studies of Wiener and Deutsch will have limited use (at least for the humanistic scholars) because of their disconnected and closed approach to studying technology.

In his letter to Innis, McLuhan outlines 'an experiment in communication': an 'esthetic analysis' of the common features found in a variety of specialized fields. This project, he writes, is inspired by Siegfried Giedion's *Space, Time and Architecture*, as well as *Mechanization Takes Command*, and will seek to uncover a hidden ground, the 'underlying unities of form which exist where diversity is all that meets the eye'. The organizing concept is 'Communication Theory and Practice'. For example, the actual techniques of economic study today may be relevant 'to anybody who wishes to grasp the best in current poetry and music. And vice versa'. It is precisely this interdisciplinarity, the connections between movements and systems, that would make McLuhan's thinking and experimental techniques so important to a generation of avant-garde artists in the USA and Canada: John Cage, Merce Cunningham, Robert Wilson, Robert Rauschenberg,

Nam June Paik, B.P. Nichol, Glenn Gould, Michael Snow and Joyce Wieland. Indeed, artists' media experiments in performance, music, and visual arts would in turn exert influence over McLuhan's theorizations regarding the effects of the new media that he would publish in *Understanding Media*. His numerous collaborations with graphic artists like Quentin Fiore and Harley Parker exemplify his belief later on that true learning and insight could only come through an integrated model, that is, one that involves art and science.

In the Communication and Culture Seminar and through the pages of *Explorations*, many of McLuhan's central concepts would be developed: acoustic landscape, non-linear modes of thinking, the notion of secondary orality, global village and the medium is the message – all interrelated ideas that grew fundamentally out of anthropology. The concept of acoustic space grew out of the seminar and its interdisciplinary atmosphere but certainly the idea of an acoustic, cacophonous space had long been on McLuhan's mind especially as connected to the noisy art of the Symbolists and the Vorticists. It was developed in an interdisciplinary context out of the notion of 'audile space' in psychology (Carleton Williams); from literary theory and most forcefully out of anthropology and in particular Carpenter's research into the unique qualities of aboriginal cultures:

> Earlier I'd wondered if Plato's and Aristotle's 'hierarchy of the senses' enjoyed counterparts in tribal societies. Did each culture possess a unique sensory profile? Why was sight so often muted in tribal art and dance? Was non-representational art direct sensory programming? 'Acoustic space' offered a clue. If the ear's 'grammar' could pattern space, could other sensory codes explain silent music, invisible art, motionless dance? Were the senses themselves primary media? (2001: 241)

We can see the way that acoustic space as a concept is very much an anthropological term and one that was fundamental to the seminar. According to Carpenter, it was Dorothy Lee, a radical anthropologist from Harvard, who had a lasting influence on this concept and on the notion that acoustic space is essentially non-linear. I want to turn to her work because it will help to clarify aspects of acoustic space.

Acoustic Space and Non-Linear Forms

McLuhan is often linked to the socio-linguistic Sapir–Whorf theory of language (Carey, 1968: 282) but he should also be linked to work of Dorothy Lee who was developing similar ideas around the same time but with greater nuance. The Sapir–Whorf theory stipulates that language itself alters perception and experience. It postulates that a way to study a culture is to study its languages in detail: temporal structuration and sentence construction, subjective clauses, and so on. While not having read this work on the way that language determines experience in different cultural settings, Dorothy Lee was engaged in carrying out research into similar questions that arguably possessed far greater depth. Lee's work is little known outside of anthropology (and even in anthropology) but to read her essays is to discover a true commitment to humanistic study and a dedication to pedagogical forms bound to the oral tradition within the diversity of cultures around the world. Lee, having resided for a period with Alfred Whitehead, and a friend of Margaret Mead and Gregory Bateson, is the original explorer of the journal *Explorations*. Although originally from Greece, she studied at Vassar on a scholarship and became part of the early American cultural anthropology that included Boas, Henry, Radin and others. Her research is always comparative and her belief is that we can learn about ourselves and the world by studying other cultures – the sub-title of her second book of essays is 'What We Can Learn from Other Cultures'. Her approach was very much in opposition to the general trend developing in anthropology during the 1940s and 1950s, which came to stress the scientific rather than humanistic aspects of anthropology.

The impact of Lee's fieldwork and research is not readily discernible because of her commitment to dialogic forms rather than academic publishing. Having left her position at Harvard because she was dissatisfied with academic life, she moved on to different teaching positions, choosing to teach in home economics[2] as opposed to anthropology, choosing not to publish her ideas but to develop them through workshops and intimate meetings with students where she searched to create pedagogical situations in which her students could develop their own ideas. For several years she worked with Carpenter in the Department of Art and Anthropology he helped to set up in Northridge California. Many of her essays concern education, self and value and are a product of the humanist intellectual tradition.

Lee's essays on value, education and anthropology are collected in two books, *Freedom and Culture* (1959) and *Valuing the Self: What We Can Learn from Other Cultures* (1986). In 'What price literacy?' she asks questions that recall Innis's distrust of the mechanization of knowledge: 'Are we giving up our heritage of wonder, of curiosity, of questioning, of plunging into chaos and creating life out of it? Are we giving up our sense of mystery, the excitement of being lost in ambiguity and building a world out of it?' (1959: 42) The answer is cautionary, an overreliance on books, maps, and labels, as opposed to experience, will create closed systems and put an end to new insights and integrated epistemological frameworks that connect with and help us to understand the life-world. In this short essay, Lee makes reference to a multiplicity of pedagogical situations that are cross-cultural, relating traditional, diasporic and modern learning situations.

For example: An autobiography written by an African schooled in Konakry who gave his father a map to remember a difficult journey; the use of proverbs when teaching children lessons regarding boasting among the Ngoni in East Africa; Louis H. Sullivan, world-renounced architect and teacher, cannot do math as a child because he wants living details; Virginia Woolf writes about readers as accomplices; Charles Eastman, or Ohiyesa, a Dakota brought up by his grandmother was sent out everyday to explore with only the instructions to 'look carefully at everything you see'; and finally, Jewish boys in Eastern Europe who must read commentaries on the Torah and come up with new interpretations, or at least one question never before asked (ibid.: 1959: 43–48).

What these examples illustrate so beautifully is that orality and writing are not simply separate processes but have been and are often inextricably bound together. What she fears is the separation of written forms from context, from living actors and active readers. Her examples reveal the ways in which human plurality is expressed as a relatedness between self and other, self and world in a manner that fundamentally acknowledges differences in the world. Lee's essays are filled with these kinds of cultural singularities that are not just lists of her encounters but a tapestry of voices and cultural experiences. We can see here how she might well have been a central influence on the *Explorations* philosophy and its commitment to understanding rather than explanation, exploring through percepts rather than concepts, through interdisciplinarity and a diversity of cultural experiences.

More than a method, Lee's fieldwork is concerned with the experience of value in and through the structures of culture. For Lee, language is everything, and culture is a symbolic system, which transforms physical reality, 'what is there, into experienced reality'. Lee believes that reality is codified differently by different cultures in the plurality of languages and cultural codes and rituals that populate the world. Reality itself is infinite she argues. Different cultures provide a different perceptual framework through which to judge, experience and, indeed, value things. Each culture has a unique system of codification. Thus, she warns that when the anthropologist-ethnographer has to make her way into another codification of reality, she has to forget habits of fast reading, because the trajectory of a sentence is unpredictable. This is not to say that Lee is a cultural relativist, a position she staunchly rejects (ibid.: 105). The assumption behind her insight is not that reality itself is relative (if it were, the communication between cultures would be impossible) but that codification is differently punctuated and categorized by participants of distinct cultures. Lee is interested in the manner in which social actions within each culturally structured situation relate self or collectivity to the universe (society, nature, reality). She is concerned with how different cultures express this relatedness.

In her fieldwork on the Trobriand Islanders, Lee discerns a codification of reality (reality codified through language and other patterned cultural behaviour) that is different from her own Western framework. In the language of the Trobriand Islanders,

Lee discovers structures that are non-lineal, that may encompass an experience of reality different from hers. As Malinowski had noted, the Trobrianders speak in points rather than connecting lines. Lee develops this observation to consider the differences between thinking through 'the line' versus through the pattern. She argues the Trobrianders think through patterns, they do not think in terms of causality, lineal temporal structures geared towards the future, and they do not value lineality in their cultural behaviours and rituals: 'the validity of a magical spell lay not in its results, not in proof, but in its very being: in the appropriateness of its inheritance, in its place within the patterned activity, in its being performed by the appropriate person, in its realization of its mythical basis' (*ibid.*: 145). Likewise, their relation to time and history. Work 'contains its own satisfaction'; the present is not a means to a future pleasure or reward. Pregnancy is celebrated not as a means to an end but as a state of being. The 'point' itself contains all time but the point about points, as McLuhan would later comment, is that there is no point (*Letters*: 368). Lee concludes by questioning the line as the basic structure of reality, a question that has been raised by those not naïvely 'steeped in their culture – among many of our artists, for example' (1959: 120).[3]

Lee had been developing these ideas since the end of the Second World War through her doctoral research into the linguistic structures of the Wintu. Carpenter and McLuhan would publish her work in *Explorations* alongside essays on the function of tactility in language development, haiku poetry (Suzuki), archetypes (Fry), social kinetics (Birdwhistell), the history of urban planning (Thyrwitt) and speculations about media forms. All these themes were connected in different ways to the Communication and Culture Seminar and participants would make innovative links and epistemological interfaces across disciplines. While simply applying Lee's observations regarding nonlinear codifications of reality to electric media may have seemed intellectually reckless and even imperialistic to some (Ross, 1989; Spivak, 1999), it did yield some extremely fruitful insights. Reading this work some 50 years later, certainly in the context of digital cultures and the popularization of non-linear editing and non-linear narrative forms in television and games culture, the concept of non-linearity seems less strange than it may have at the time.

McLuhan had a part to play in popularizing the very terms of Lee's discussion by translating these into descriptions of the new media. It is from Lee's insights into this spatial differentiation that McLuhan would develop a description of media forms in terms of their linearity. While McLuhan's translation was somewhat crude, the concept provided a way to get at some fundamental differences between writing and the new forms of orality that were coming into being with the electronic media. Moreover, as we shall see in the next chapter, this emphasis on non-Western cultures also reinforced McLuhan's own historical telos of a return to orality. For McLuhan, non-linearity was used to understand the structures of oral cultures and linear thought became a, albeit at times simplistic, shorthand for book culture, the product of literacy.

The concept of acoustic space did not simply originate with one insight or person but was born out of a confluence of ideas: Lee's insights into non-linear patterns of oral cultures were connected, among other things, to some of the ideas generated by the experiments with auditory space being devised by psychologist E.A. Bott at the University of Toronto. Writing many years later, McLuhan explains that Bott discovered that acoustic space is 'a perfect sphere whose centre is everywhere and whose margins are nowhere' (*Letters*: 368). Such a description would no doubt influence his notions that the new media create 'a centre-without-margins'. Across all these conversations and ideas, McLuhan and Carpenter would describe auditory space in the pages of *Explorations*, 7:

> the essential feature of sound is not that it has a location but that it be, that it fill space. Sound is an envelope. No point of focus; no fixed boundaries; space made by the thing itself, not space containing It is not pictorial space but dynamic, always in flux; creating its own dimensions moment by moment. It has no fixed boundaries, is indifferent to background the ear favours sounds from any direction, it can experience things simultaneously. (1957: 4)

While McLuhan's early essays and *The Mechanical Bride* were concerned with visual economies and fragmentation, we can discern in the 1950s essays and books, the development of a new conceptualization of space that is sound-based. McLuhan and Carpenter bring a mythological dimension to their conceptualization of a new space, which is, for McLuhan at least, a theological space.[4] It is also a feminine space for, as Michel Chion has underlined, the acoustic sphere is always feminine because the first voice we all hear is that of the mother (1994: 26). If *The Mechanical Bride* foregrounds the intersection of death and sex as a metaphysical desire for origin, then McLuhan's *Explorations* work will see this return to origin as something that is in process and is manifested through that mythological consciousness T.S. Eliot called 'auditory imagination':

> the feeling for syllable and rhythm, penetrating far below the conscious levels of thought and feeling, invigorating every word; sinking to the most primitive and forgotten, returning to the original and bringing something back, seeking the beginning and the end. It works through meanings, certainly or not without meanings in the ordinary sense, and fuses the old and obliterated and the trite, the current, and the new and surprising, the most ancient and the most civilized mentality. (reprinted in *Explorations*, 4; Eliot, 1955: 118–19)

In this new form of imagination (which we find also described in the stream-of-consciousness writings of Joyce and in Eisenstein's theory of inner speech), McLuhan discerns the 'the new metaphor' because 'we are all deaf-blind mutes in terms of the new situation'. But, McLuhan argues, 'we are back in acoustic space' and we must reconnect with 'the primordial feelings and emotions … from which 3000 years of literacy divorced us'. (*CounterBlast*, 1954: npn.) This new old space is a technological space, 'the city no longer exists', and the new media are nature. The disappearance of the distinction between urban and natural spaces, the emergence of a global metropolis that has transfigured time and space is the result of the television, newspaper and magazine: 'Gutenberg made all history SIMULTANEOUS: the transportable book brought the world of the dead into the space of the gentleman's library; the telegraph brought the entire world of the living to the workman's breakfast table' (ibid.).

McLuhan will take up the possibility that all history is simultaneous in *Gutenberg Galaxy*. While print helped to standardize and linearize all of history, television brings the entire world to the workers' breakfast table. CNN has helped to make this statement, outlandish in 1954, into a norm. It is not only the notion that history is constructed through technology that theorists like Henri Lefebvre, Jean Baudrillard and Paul Virilio would appreciate, but it is McLuhan's insights into the reality-making capabilities of the media. For Baudrillard (1983) in particular, it is McLuhan's great contribution to have anticipated the function that the media would play in mediating and becoming reality. The concept of acoustic space can lead to some dizzying connections and networks of ideas. For our purposes, it is important to understand that McLuhan develops this concept both as an analogy for new media environments and as a methodology to analyze them.

Notes

1 See Richard Cavell's excellent book, *McLuhan in Space: A Cultural Geography* (Toronto: University of Toronto, 2002) which traces the influence that McLuhan exerted on the visual arts and literary communities in North America from the 1950s onward.

2 Dorothy Lee identified herself first as a mother, having raised four children on her own after the sudden death of her husband anthropologist, Otis Lee.

3 See 'Linguistic reflection of Wintu thought' (originally published in 1944 in *International Journal of American Linguistics*, vol. 10, 1944) and 'Lineal and non-lineal codification's of reality' (1950, in *Psychosomatic Medicine*, no. 12) in the anthology edited by Carpenter and McLuhan (1966). Robert Graves would disagree with the characterization of Trobrianders as non-lineal, citing among other things one of the myths recorded by Malinowski. Further, Graves points out that such a pattern of behaviour may be more typical among Mediterranean cultures because the weather conditions allow them to live without planning. In colder countries, agricultural restrictions and fuel issues have meant that cultures must be future-oriented and more lineal in order to plan for the winter. Further, he notes certain non-lineal behaviours in his own English culture, such as aimless wandering. Carpenter and McLuhan would publish their ideas side by side in order to encourage debate. Graves's criticisms highlight the need to develop more complex understandings of orality – namely, that these are different across cultures. His criticism does not, however, discount the category of non-linearity (*Explorations*, 'Comments on lineal and non-lineal codifications of reality').

4 McLuhan would draw attention to François Rabelais's description of 'the intellectual sphere, the centre of which is at all points and the circumference at none, which we call God' (*Pantagruel* V: 47). McLuhan also cites Pascal who describes nature as an 'infinite sphere, the centre of which is everywhere, the circumference nowhere' (*Letters*: 368).

6

Innis, New Media
and the University

There is no study of McLuhan that does not include a discussion of Harold Innis, often to the detriment of McLuhan. Many critics, most notably James Carey in *McLuhan: Pro and Con* (1968), see McLuhan's work as merely building on one of Innis's minor insights regarding the impact of the media on the human sensorium. McLuhan had indeed maintained that *The Gutenberg Galaxy* was 'a footnote to the observations of Innis on the subject of the psychic and social consequences, first of writing and then of printing' (*GG*; 50). It is apparent, however, that he takes the study of communication in a different direction, namely towards a study of aesthetics and human perception. Nevertheless, McLuhan held Innis's scholarship in high esteem and did much to promote his work. In the Preface to *Empire and Communications*, McLuhan writes:

> If Hegel projected an historical pattern of figures minus existential ground, Harold Innis, in the spirit of the new age of information, sought for patterns in the very ground of history and existence. He saw media, old and new, not as mere vortices at which to direct his point of view, but as living vortices of power creating hidden environments that act abrasively and destructively on older forms of culture. (Innis, 1950: vi)

It is the 'living vortices' in Innis's research that held out a great attraction for McLuhan and that no doubt influenced his own thinking on how to conduct research into media effects. This chapter is primarily concerned with the two men's different interpretations of the use of new media in learning situations. The mechanization of learning in the university was a problematic that was central to both Innis's and McLuhan's research agendas, and we can understand their valuation of oral culture in terms of a concern with the standardization of knowledge and the reduction of the epistemological enterprise to static information.

Innis

In the two years before his untimely death, Innis published two books that would form the foundation of communication studies in Canada: *Empire and Communications* (1950) and *The Bias of Communication* (1951). Both works drew upon a vast interdisciplinary literature and historical methodology to consider the manner in which communications technologies create patterns of apprehension and distinct spatio-temporal configurations of social organization. Innis offers a study of institutional structures and power, of centre–margin relations, while McLuhan's aesthetic approach is more concerned with effects on bodies, perceptions, and on new configurations of culture characterized by a 'centre-without-margins'. In Innis, McLuhan was able to recognize a formal approach that he himself had been developing in *The Mechanical Bride*, published the same year as Innis's *The Bias of Communication*. Moreover, just as he had admired in other intellectual projects, from Chesterton's *History of England* to Giedion's history of mechanized culture, Innis provided McLuhan with a model through which to study history, a model tied directly to Canada's geography.

While *The Mechanical Bride* had explored a spatial landscape of commodity production, Innis introduced an historical account that was richly nuanced and grounded in place. Without an understanding of the aesthetic context from which such a methodology was born, Innis was using methods of collage and juxtaposition to create a landscape out of time and historical facts. As McLuhan had done with *The Mechanical Bride*, Innis, in a far more extensive way, presented a history of civilization by creating a dynamic model that would present simultaneous events unfolding in different parts of the world. McLuhan explains in his later Introduction to Innis's book:

> For anyone acquainted with poetry since Baudelaire and with paint-
> ing since Cézanne, the later world of Harold A. Innis is quite readily
> intelligible. He brought their kinds of contemporary awareness of the
> electric age to organise the data of the historian and the social scien-
> tist. Without having studied modern art and poetry, he yet discovered
> how to arrange his insights in patterns that nearly resemble the art
> forms of our time. (Foreword to *Bias*, 1964: vii)

For McLuhan, the 'contemporary awareness of the electric age' in Baudelaire's poetry or Cézanne's painting finds expression in the aesthetic forms of montage as seen in the newspaper or in the cinema. Linear sequences of words are replaced by a dynamic and open field of relationships. McLuhan recognized the impor-
tance and originality of Innis's insights and he made Innis's dense and difficult prose famous. While Innis 'takes much time to read', he also 'saves time' because every 'sentence is a compressed monograph' (something McLuhan praised in Chesterton's writing). *Bias* is filled with a vast assortment of historical references, 'libraries' that cross the civilizations and disciplines of the West (ibid.: ix). A form of presentation that demands the active participation of the reader, Innis's reader will experience not 'a polished essay' or packed information, but instead 'an unremitting appeal to thought' ('Innis and communication': 96). The reader will 'make discovery after discovery that he [Innis] himself has missed'. This intertextual layering is the pedagogical strategy that underlies all of Innis's later writings and certainly all of McLuhan's writings from the 1950s onward: 'Innis is not talking a private or special-
ist language but handing us the keys to understanding technolo-
gies in their psychic and social operation in any time or place' (Foreword to *Empire*, 1972: xii).

According to McLuhan, the radical historian of economics and communication discovered an essential method of using historical situations as a lab in which 'to test the character of technology in the shaping of cultures'. Like a scientist, Innis used the method known in chemistry as the 'interface' and in so doing presented:

> a new world of economic and cultural change by studying the inter-
> play between man's artifacts and the environments created by old and

new technologies. By investigating social effects as contours of changing technology, Innis did what Plato and Aristotle failed to do. He discovered from the alphabet onward the great vortices of power at the interface of cultural frontiers. He recovered for the West the world of entelechies and formal causality long buried by the logicians and teachers of applied knowledge; and he did this by looking carefully at the immediate situation created by staples and the action of the Canadian cultural borderline on which he was located. ('Canada: the borderline case': 222)

While both McLuhan and Innis have been charged with over-emphasizing a 'formal causality' in their work, attributing far too much to the impact of specific technologies of communication, we must bear in mind that the mosaic method works to foreground certain causalities but never in a completely deterministic manner:

> Toward the end of *Empire and Communications*, Innis speeds up his sequence of figure-ground flashes almost to that of a cinematic montage. This acceleration corresponds to the sense of urgency that he felt as one involved in understanding the present. It is certainly crucial for the reader of Innis to recognize his method for presenting the historical process as being inseparable from contemporary reality. (Foreword to *Empire* vii–viii)

Innis pursued his graduate studies in the Department of Economics at the University of Chicago in the 1920s. During this period the School of Sociology, founded by George Herbert Mead, was at its height. While McLuhan believed him to be 'the most eminent' of the Chicago School headed by Robert Park, this has been debated. Apart from the writings of Thorstein Veblen, an early member of the School, Innis's students report that the school, which was by no means a unified entity, went largely unmentioned in seminars and in his published work (Stark, 1994). We do see in Innis, as we do in McLuhan, the influence of a German philosophical tradition concerned with the effects of modernity on everyday life, forms of sociability and organization. While moved by different objects (poetry and social structure), modernity figures centrally in the Chicago School and the Cambridge New Critics. McLuhan saw Innis as building and extending some of Robert Parks's insights regarding the importance of communications technologies and forms of transportation in structuring 'men's habits' (Foreword to *Bias*, xv–xvi), and it is in fact McLuhan who has arguably worked most to build on these insights by focusing on the way media create environments.

Nature and History

Innis first gained recognition for his books on Canadian economic history with studies of the staples industries in Canada. Rather than looking at the abstract system of commodities and exchange value, Innis sought to theorize economics by grounding it in the history of place. Further, he was committed to his own birthplace, Canada. In *Empire and Communications*, Innis studies the character of Canada's political economy by looking at a history of its trade practices. With this in mind, he examines the staples industries that were themselves defined by Canada's extensive waterways and Pre-Cambrian formation. These geographical formations encouraged a concentration on bulk products, which were in turn defined through the cultures of the aborigines (1950: 3). Innis studies the fur trade, lumber industries, and cod fisheries to analyze how, for example, the different colonial powers stake their claims on the land and develop their industries in ways that lead either to monopolies or to decentralization. The character of Continental development moves in the direction of centralization. Innis traces how certain staples industries develop into monopolies (Hudson Bay Company fur trade) while others do not (cod fisheries along the Atlantic Coast line). As monopolies develop around some regions of Canada (fur), others emerge. The French empire's claim to the St. Lawrence river, for example, shifts from fur to the timber trade. Staples leave their mark on things, on culture and on institutions.

Innis's studies of the extract industries in Canada led him to what is known as the staples thesis. The history of Canada can be written in terms of the history of its staples industries, through their connection to an empire that recognized Canada only as a natural resource to be exploited. This is not to say that Canada has no history beyond the empire but rather that the experience, social organization and identity of the Canadian nation are bound to a history of imperialism, resource extraction and consequently of centre–margin relations.

Innis's studies are characterized by thick description or what he called 'dirt research', painstakingly carried out empirical inquiry – famously, he undertook canoe trips to investigate the effects of transportation on the processes of production. The unique traditions, values and character of the peoples of Canada, aborigines in particular, along with the geographic character of the land and waterways, would all contribute to the emergence of specific staples, practices and transportation technologies, which would in turn effect the social organization of trade. Thus, Innis provides an alternative to traditional histories of capitalism and class analysis. This focus on the history of trade practices in Canada can help to account for an entirely different paradigm in the Canadian critique of modernity. Negative dialectics in Innis and McLuhan grows out of a post-colonial consciousness, with a stress on cultural difference and hierarchies, rather than the European critical theory (e.g., Frankfurt School) with its stress on class.[1]

Borderline: Space and Time

Innis, a careful researcher of specific details of economic history, would in the last decade of his life, move on to study the effects of human communication on the social organization of space and power. We can see that his interests in empire, in centre–margin relations and authority, were present from the start. Innis's early studies, as McLuhan recognized, examined the 'immediate situation' of the staples industries, seeing staples' extraction as creating a political and economic landscape, a context of everyday life. Indeed, it was the 'action' of the 'Canadian cultural borderline on which he was located' that allowed Innis to develop specific insights into the relation between technology, time and nation that we find in his last two books.

It was the 'borderline' that McLuhan would develop in his own critical thinking around the sentimentality of the border. His essay, 'Canada: the borderline case', for example, opens with a quote from a Canadian diplomat (drawn from the official

Canadian bicentennial gift to the people of the United States called *Between Friends/Entre Amis*) which is particularly evocative of the interests that borders hold for theorizing culture: 'The boundary between Canada and the United States is a typically human creation; it is physically invisible, geographically illogical, militarily indefensible, and emotionally inescapable' ('Canada: the borderline case': 226). McLuhan tells us that the 'border is not a connection but an interval of resonance' which is a scientific term. Interestingly, and not surprising that McLuhan would pick up on this, it is also a musical expression; it is the thing that allows music to be an expression, the space between sounds that allows us to hear music. The interval is the 'interface' where two objects meet and where identity finds its shape in difference, or *différance* as Derrida would later put it. The interface 'refers to the interaction of substances in a kind of mutual irritation. In art and poetry this is precisely the technique of symbolism (Greek *symballein* to throw together) with its paratactic procedure of juxtaposing without connectives'. Thus, borderline in McLuhan is both aesthetic, epistemological and juridical: Cézanne's 'realization of space by the juxtaposition of areas of pure color' ('Notes on the media as art forms': 9) can be understood alongside the multiple borders of newspaper columns and the borders that divide countries. Similarly, and this is what McLuhan was able to recognize and understand as radical methodology in Innis's work, the borderline is historical, charged with emotional intensities, and in Canada's case is 'porous'. History written from a location along the borderline can reanimate and challenge official history and reassert the effects of time.

Innis was deeply affected, like so many of his generation were, by the First and Second World Wars. Unlike McLuhan, who never went to war, Innis had served for eighteen months in the Canadian Army during the First World War, and he would become more acutely aware of cultural imperialism and domination through this experience (Heyer, 2003: 3–4). Not only would his studies of Canada's economic history and colonial dependence allow him to understand how identities are space bound, but also how localized and specific histories of colonialism are all too often left unwritten or are written by the colonizers. In *Empire and Communications* he writes as 'a citizen of the British Commonwealth of Nations', which has been influenced by the economic development of empires and as one 'obsessed' with the nature of that influence. From the opening pages of his study of the history of communication and empires, Innis acknowledges a biased history. Yet it is his position in Canada that has made him particularly sensitive to certain processes of decentralization and centralization related to empires.

In his earlier study of the staples histories of Canada,[2] Innis had contemplated the effects of the pulp and paper industries on the culture of newsprint and on the shaping of public opinion. His earlier studies had shown the effects of the organization and production of staple materials on empires: 'attempts by France to check the increase of fur production; English Purchasers to "the high price of timber"; the attempt to restrain the sensationalism of the new journalism which followed the availability of cheap newsprint' (*Empire*: 5). His new study would look at the history of the West, divided into writing and printing periods, in terms of communication staples – clay, papyrus, parchment and paper – and their relation to the success and fall of empires. Innis argues that the different stages in the history of Western civilization and its empires could be seen to correspond to the dominance of different media of communication that favour either the church or the state. He surmised that the media employed by different empires, whatever their content, are 'biased' toward either time or space. Time biased media are those that are durable in character such as parchment, clay and stone, which preceded printing. The heavy materials are suited to the development of architecture and sculpture. These media do not travel well because of their mass, but they provide enduring records. They emphasize time and continuity, history and tradition; they are useful for maintaining centralized and hierarchical organizations and religion against secular forms of government. Media that emphasize space are apt to be less durable and are easy to transport across space, such as papyrus and paper. These favour the military, the secular and decentred forms of administration, since large spaces can be controlled from afar. Empires grow through the space-binding media but they truly flourish under conditions 'in which civilization reflects the influence of more than one medium, and in which the bias of one medium towards decentralization is offset by the bias of another medium towards centralization' (ibid.: 5).

With his emphasis on these different media, Innis sees writing as the major technological innovation in his analysis of empires. However, he knows that oral culture is a central aspect of time-biased civilizations. Classical Greece reflects a moment of perfection in Innis's history because of its balance of the technology of the alphabet and oral culture. Some of the most rewarding passages in *Empire and Communications* are those devoted to analyzing the relations between oral and written cultures, namely in the rise of Greek civilization. It is his desire to understand the significance of the spoken word and his recognition that such cultures have 'left little tangible remains' that lead Innis to a fundamental insight regarding history and epistemology:

> The significance of a basic medium to its civilisation is difficult to appraise since the means of appraisal are influenced by the media, and indeed the fact of appraisal appears to be peculiar to certain types of media. A change in the type of medium implies a change in the type of appraisal and hence makes it difficult for one civilization to understand another. (ibid.: 6)

This kind of reflexivity is typical of Innis's writing – and we should read his use of a mosaic approach, his disjointed and sometimes elliptical prose, his tentative lay out of historical causalities, as evidence of his rejection of totalizing theories and views of history. Any accusation of technological determinism must be tempered by an awareness of Innis's mosaic method and the speculative nature of his insights.

Innis believes that media have an 'important influence on the dissemination of knowledge over space and over time' (1951: 33). He does not set up a simple opposition between oral culture and writing but sees writing as having emerged from specific forms of orality in, for example, music and epic poetry: 'Writing enormously enhanced a capacity for abstract thinking which had been evident in the growth of language in the oral tradition' (Innis, 1950: 7). With the increasing reliance on writing to fulfil the function of experience-based memory, memory itself becomes 'transpersonal', individuals must grapple with symbols rather than things, and experience goes beyond the concrete 'into a world of conceptual relations created within an enlarged time and space universe' (ibid.: 7). In short, Innis sees the history of Western civilization in terms of a trajectory from a time-biased culture to one that emphasizes space.

In his famous essay, 'A plea for time', delivered at the 150th anniversary of the University of New Brunswick in 1950, Innis argues that it is only through a renewed emphasis on time to 'check' the effects of space that Western modernity may achieve a balanced ethical system of governance and knowledge. He quotes one of McLuhan's favourite sources, Wyndham Lewis's *Time and Western Man*, and distinguishes his own plea from the time philosophies of phenomenologists like Henri Bergson, for whom the moment is always a 'becoming' and as such carries no absolute value, no state of permanence 'beyond time'. Rather than living in the moment, Innis points us towards the importance of 'individual continuity'. The modern Western world sacrificed sculpture to music, and as such has lost the temporal continuity and permanence that are a product of oral culture and community. The West, with its emphasis on space and its neglect of time, separates 'the sense of sight and touch' and produces 'both subjective disunity and external disunity'. According to Innis, it is the material structures and traces of time that may bring back unity to the world.

This notion would appeal to McLuhan a great deal and he develops it much further, seeking to describe the effects of media on the human sensorium and on the physical environment. We shall see that McLuhan is closer to the philosophers of time and his ideas closer to music, in his exploration of the moment, than to Innis's emphasis on individual continuity and permanence.

Innis's essay culminates in an oft cited appeal to:

> somehow escape on the one hand from our obsession with the moment and on the other hand from our obsession with history. In freeing ourselves from time and attempting a balance between the demands of time and space we can develop conditions favourable to an interest in cultural activity. (Innis, 1951: 89–90)

Though Innis did occasionally join McLuhan's intellectual coterie, they were never friends or even close allies. While they were colleagues at the University of Toronto from 1947 until Innis's death in 1952, their meetings were said to be unspectacular, with the differences between the two becoming immediately apparent. McLuhan's conservative and Catholic politics clashed with Innis's liberalism and Canadian nationalism. McLuhan was always more oriented around popular cultural issues, art and aesthetics, while Innis was more sociological and historical. Other differences were also apparent in their views of America – McLuhan loved America's 'cornucopia of surrealism'; Innis was concerned over its impact on Canadian identity.

Some critics have downplayed the influence of Innis's ideas on McLuhan, claiming that the alliance helped McLuhan gain credibility within the university (Carpenter, 2001: 248). Nonetheless, it is clear from McLuhan's letters and comments that Innis was the 'extra boost' that moved him into studying media technology. Innis, he maintained, was more of a 'freak' than he was: 'How did that hick Baptist ever come up with this amazing method of studying the effects of technology?' (Marchand, 1989: 113). This method of studying the effects of communications technology as well as a formalist view of technology both informed and reinforced several ideas that McLuhan had been developing since his days at Cambridge. The emphasis that Richards and Leavis had put on the formal effects of language had certainly opened his thinking to Innis's proposals concerning communication technology as creating specific kinds of physiological and epistemological biases. The idea that language creates spatial and temporal experiences was part of his thinking since his graduate studies at Cambridge.

Both Innis and McLuhan were utopian thinkers and both valued the oral tradition as a path to community and a just society. For Innis, this path is to be found in Greek antiquity. For McLuhan, oral culture is contemporary, whether it be in the long enduring non-Western cultures or the 'second orality' as Walter Ong would call it of the new media. McLuhan and Innis shared a deep concern with university education and the humanities. They belonged for a short period to the Values Group at the University of Toronto, a group devoted to studying the effects of commodification on curriculum as well as on the humanistic subjects. But perhaps nowhere were their differences more apparent than in their views of the role of new media in education.

New Media and the University

In his report, 'Adult education and universities', Innis explains how the modern idea of education is bound up with a radical democratic project born of the Enlightenment. For Innis, this project was being threatened by the mechanization of learning: 'Education has been largely concerned with the conservation of knowledge, and in turn becomes extremely conservative … This tendency towards conservatism has been enhanced by the mechanization of communication in print, radio, film' (*Bias*: 204). Even before computers entered the classroom, Innis ascertained that instructional technologies could be used to produce 'useless knowledge of useful facts'. The emphasis on factual information and classification rather than ideas – 'abstract ideas are less susceptible to treatment by mechanical devices' (ibid.: 204–205) – was symptomatic of both an obsession with and loss of history. According to Innis, education and information were becoming identical. With the merging of state and university, and the concomitant mechanization of knowledge, pedagogy was being made to conform to the instrumental (i.e., market-driven) concerns of the university, emphasizing vocational training and specialism over the stimulation of thought. While the university was expanding its student body, changing curriculum, and adding courses, Innis believed this to be less a matter of intellectual growth than of economics. Universities should strive to foreground the relation between power and knowledge in order to produce open minds able to question assumptions. Thus, while he held that the university should be 'available to the largest possible number', he also maintained: 'Adult education, appealing to large numbers with limited training, can be disentangled with difficulty from the advertising of large organisations concerned with the development of goodwill' (ibid.: 213).

There is, of course, more than a hint of elitism in Innis's understanding of Canada's 'limited intellectual resources'(ibid.: 207), in his view that universities, having taken on the monopolistic character of the media, were following 'the pattern of advertising', lowering academic standards to 'reach lower levels of intelligence' (ibid: 213). Innis's ideas around the 'information industries', like Adorno and Horkheimer's 'culture industry', are informed by 'the dialectic of enlightenment', by an underlying tension between mass culture and modernism, or centre and margin. This tension enables Innis to clearly discern the ramifications of the mechanization of knowledge: the merging of education and marketing, and the privileging of facts over concepts in learning.

Like Innis, McLuhan is concerned with education, and with the effects of media on education. His approach, however, is different from Innis's, being perhaps more pragmatic but no less idealistic. For him, the mechanization of learning is inevitable, which is why he began to introduce an analysis of advertisements into his classes. The way back to the great works and ideas of the past is through the commodified languages and popular cultures of the present. McLuhan believes that rhetoric has migrated into the realm of commercial culture, so that education, if it is to reach young minds, must be rethought to include the media. Thus, in 1951, McLuhan would write to Innis of a new field of study, one directly inspired by *Empire and Communications* and one that includes new media forms:

> If literature is to survive as a scholastic discipline except for a very few people, it must be by a transfer of its techniques of perception and judgment to these new media. The new media, which are already much more constitutive educationally than those of the class-room, must be inspected and discussed if the class-room is to continue at all except as a place of detention. As a teacher of literature it has long seemed to me that the functions of literature cannot be maintained in present circumstances without radical alteration of the procedures of teaching ... As mechanical media have popularized and enforced the presence of the arts on all people it becomes more and more necessary to make studies of the function and effect of communication on society. (*Letters*: 222)

If *The Mechanical Bride* focused on the corporate executive and the middle-class suburban consumer, then a new object of study emerges for McLuhan in the 1950s that would inform his study of contemporary media. It is to the teenager as a cultural consumer that McLuhan would aim his new research programme as well as his argument for educational reforms and a new interdisciplinary area of study devoted to the media. As an object of study, the young tell us something about the effects of new media on human sensorium and popular culture. For example, the appearance of the comic book is an indication that the age of the book is coming to an end; in its place, 'a nascent pictorial and dramatic form which has sprung from the new stress on visual-auditory communication in the magazines, the radio and television. The young today cannot follow narrative but they are alert to drama. They cannot bear description but they love landscape and action' (*Letters*: 222).

Such statements regarding the character of media forms and the changing sensorium of the TV child are typical of McLuhan's insights which are largely intuitive, deriving less from social scientific research than from his own experiences teaching English. McLuhan would approach the new sensibility of his students as an anthropologist. What is striking to us reading McLuhan's writing on teenagers of the 1950s is his refusal to pronounce moral judgements on popular culture, to insist that such new forms of culture represent a denigration or decay of great literature. In a very Brechtian manner, we find a refusal to maintain an opposition between education and entertainment. Such a refusal was already present in his work leading up to *The Mechanical Bride*, yet it is through his work with the Communication and Culture Seminar as well as his work with Carpenter that strategies for education based on new media forms begin to develop.

This was forcefully outlined in his *Explorations* essays 'Classroom without walls', a play on Malraux's museum without walls as well as 'Notes on the media as art forms', both of which argue for a new pedagogical programme devoted to studying the popular media and advertising as aesthetic forms. For Malraux, the invention of photography had freed the canvas from anecdote and narrative to become 'not a vehicle but sheer expression'. This was the heritage of Cézanne, whose concentration on one formal problem led to a breakthrough as spectacular as that of

Planck and Einstein. But this discovery appeared simultaneously in poetry and music, enabling us to see 'that every channel of expression (press, radio, cinema) awaits a similar day of emancipation. Each medium is in some sense a universal, pressing towards maximal realization ... lead(ing) us to investigate the possibilities of orchestral harmony in the multi-leveled drive towards pure human expressiveness' ('Notes on the media as art forms': 10). Thus, McLuhan will argue for media studies as an interdisciplinary and multidisciplinary investigation. The classroom without walls, like its counterpart in Malraux's museum, is an argument for an education that is connected to rather than separated from the life-world. McLuhan believed that the real education was taking place through the media.

Innis and McLuhan helped to constitute the entity known as the Toronto School of Communication. This was never a formal association or School since Innis died in the early 1950s and never participated in McLuhan and Carpenter's seminar. But they both have left behind a distinctive body of work that asks us to see communications technology as central to any account of the social and cultural infrastructure of societies. While Innis's and McLuhan's approaches are complementary, it is McLuhan's aesthetic approach that offers the most possibilities for thinking about and theorizing new media situations. This is primarily because Innis died just as television was taking hold of North America and because McLuhan was primarily interested in contemporary media. This is not to say that history does not figure in his work as it does in Innis's. Rather, as we shall see with *Gutenberg Galaxy*, history is always contemporary.

Notes

1 See Judith Stamps's innovative philosophical study comparing the critical theory of the Frankfurt School (Adorno and Benjamin) with the Canadian critique carried out by Innis and McLuhan (*Unthinking Modernity: Innis, McLuhan and the Frankfurt School*, 1995).

2 See *Essays in Canadian Economic History* (1956) and *The Fur Trade in Canada* ([1930] 1970).

7

Galaxy

The last word of *The Gutenberg Galaxy: The Making of Typographic Man* is 'time'. There is no other piece of writing in McLuhan's œuvre that is as sensitive to historical shifts and that provides such a rich collage of ideas and patterns of thought. This book, along with *The Mechanical Bride*, are no doubt McLuhan's best works. Both are formal experiments and insightful examinations of modernity. *The Gutenberg Galaxy* is equal in complexity to the works of Siegfried Giedion and Harold Innis, to whom he acknowledges a great debt. But McLuhan's greatest influence in this book is Joyce. Alternate titles of *The Gutenberg Galaxy* were *Gutenberg Era* and *The Road to Finnegans Wake*. Like Joyce's book, it was intended as a history of writing (*Explorations*, 2: 75). The book itself consists of a collection of quotes and ideas gathered over a 20-year period and it was 'packaged' into a book over the course of a summer (Marchand: 154).

The Gutenberg Galaxy is concerned with the fundamental differences between oral culture and literate culture. His study is located at the historical interface between script and print as these have come to define cultural experiences and modes of perception. Following both Innis and Lewis Mumford (whose *Technics and Civilization* was an important if understated influence on his thinking), McLuhan analyzes these technologies in terms of the kinds of spaces and bodies they make. *The Gutenberg Galaxy* is an exceptional book that is sensual in its thinking and full of a radical interdisciplinarity that takes its reader in unexpected directions by juxtaposing thinkers and research projects in exciting and unanticipated ways. It has the kind of depth and density that McLuhan admired in Innis. While McLuhan maintained that he believed it to be simply a footnote to Innis's research on the history of civilization in *Empire and Communications*, it is a wholly different project (*GG*: 50). Although sharing some of the historical periodization of Western civilization understood in terms of communications technology, McLuhan's analysis focuses on a relation between corporeality and technology. While oral and written cultures are important indicators of an historical trajectory in Innis's analysis, McLuhan will understand the present in terms of a new shift forward in a return to orality.

McLuhan has been criticized for his lack of historical substance, especially in his later work, yet we might use *The Gutenberg Galaxy* as a reference point for understanding his commitment to locating phenomena within historical patterns in a way that is highly performative and temporally grounded. There is a new methodology that appears in *The Gutenberg Galaxy* that is significantly different from his previous literary work. This is because *Galaxy* was written in the context of television. If one takes time to read the book, and it is not an easy book to read, then one will find that McLuhan does not set up a simple technological determinism as so many of his detractors have claimed. All of the technologies he discusses are themselves products of cultures and his study is premised on an historical dialectic. It is also highly self-reflexive, probing and exploratory, dialogical and acoustic. For this reason, it is an impossible book to summarize. When one does, the complexity and richness of his arguments are lost precisely because there is less an overall argument than a presentation of interrelated ideas and studies pertaining to Western modernity.

McLuhan utilizes a mosaic method, which is an aesthetic approach to laying out a problematic in a dynamic and musical orchestration of parts in order to find underlying patterns. The use of quotation is a conscious strategy to create an intellectual collage or *essai concrète*, producing a heteroglossia made out of a plurality of perspectives and research projects. By utilizing the interdisciplinary model, that he had been working with in the Communications and Culture Seminar as well as through *Explorations*, there is no one dominant discipline or intellect in his tapestry. Rather, McLuhan juxtaposes a multiplicity of voices around one problematic – the phonetic alphabet and the rise of visual culture in the West. We can compare this approach not only to Roland Barthes' in *A Lover's Discourse*, which collects ideas in no particular order but also to Walter Benjamin's study of passages in Paris of the nineteenth century, published in *The Arcades Project*. The editor of Benjamin's book, Rolf Tiedemann has complained of the project's 'oppressive chunks of quotations', yet as the book's English translators have commented, 'Benjamin's purpose was to document as concretely as possible, and thus lend a "heightened graphicness" to, the scene of the revolutionary change that was the nineteenth century' (Benjamin, 1999). Benjamin and McLuhan have been productively compared (cf. the debate between McCallum (1989) and Stamps (1990)), and I would like to briefly sketch some important similarities and differences between them especially around their methodology.

Benjamin and the Death of Intention

The Surrealist project exerted a profound and contradictory influence on Benjamin's conception of film as a liberating agency, exposing the collective unconscious and emancipating an alternate spatio-temporality: 'Our taverns and our metropolitan streets, our offices and furnished rooms, our railroad stations and our factories appeared to have locked us hopelessly. Then came the film' (1973: 229). For the Surrealists, the metropolis is taken to be part of the natural world filled with cryptic structures waiting to be deciphered through intense confrontation. In his essay on Surrealism, Benjamin points out that the emphasis on 'experience', 'innervation', 'intoxication', and 'pure immediacy' wages an assault against the narrowing of experience in bourgeois society. Profound and meaningful experience is possible, the Surrealists argued, only through intoxication, through a 'loosening of the self'; this separation of self and body leads to a 'profane illumination, a materialistic, anthropological inspiration'. Once this inspiration informs the art work it can 'bring the immense forces of "atmosphere" concealed in [concrete] things to the point of explosion' (1979: 227). In this sense, experience can itself become revelatory and lead to 'collective innervations' and finally, 'revolutionary discharge' (ibid.: 239):

> A constructive case of revelation of an experience. The scene of this revelation is the memory. The related experiences do not constitute, when they occur, revelation, but remain concealed to the one experiencing. They only become revelation when more and more people become conscious of their analogy in retrospect. (Benjamin, trans. in Bürger, 1984: xv)

It is only retrospectively as an image produced through a 'loosening of self' and intentionality that experience can become collective, revelatory and hence revolutionary. Whereas atmosphere in Dickens, for example, is the overall structuring totality of the city, in the Surrealist work, atmosphere (totality) is exploded and fragmented. This does not mean that the notion of totality is absent but, rather, it is present in the form of a lost totality, a utopia that can only ever be recollected in the fragments of memory.

Indeed, Benjamin's attraction to Surrealism and his optimistic appraisal of the revolutionary potential of film must be understood in terms of the theological premise, the Messianic current that runs through all of his writing. The initial draft of what was to become *The Arcades Project*, 'Paris, capital of the nineteenth century', provides a good illustration of how the concept of redemption is transposed onto a notion of historical praxis without recourse to a teleology. The original intention of this project, which Benjamin had discussed with T.W. Adorno, was to uncover the primitive archaisms embedded in the seemingly progressive façade of the modern era. The presence of technological gadgets and innovations, the excess availability of myriad commodities were seen as nothing more than a veil masking the reproduction of 'the always the same' suffering. In the draft sent to Adorno in 1935, this original conception was significantly revised. In *The Arcades Project* the technological *façade* and commodity production are now interpreted in terms of dialectical images:

> Corresponding to the form of the new means of production, which in the beginning is still ruled by the forms of the old (Marx), are

images in the collective consciousness in which the old and the new interpenetrate. These images are wish images; in them the collective seeks both to overcome and to transfigure the immaturity of the social product and the inadequacies of social organization of production. At the same time, what emerges in these wish-images is the resolute effort to distance oneself from all that is antiquated – which includes however, the recent past. These tendencies deflect the imagination (which is given impetus by the new) back on the primal past. In the dream in which each epoch entertains images of its successor, the latter appears wedded to elements of primal history – *Urgeschichte* – that is, to elements of a classless society. And the experiences of such a society – as stored in the unconscious of the collective – engender, through interpenetration with what is new, the utopia that has left its trace in a thousand configurations of life, from enduring edifices to passing fashions. (1999: 4–5)

Adorno would find much to criticize in this passage but, for our purposes, the most important of these criticisms is the conflation of the commodity form with consciousness. The banner of the New, Adorno contends, perpetuates and disguises the traditional (oppressive) relations of production and thus, should be elucidated only in terms of a negative image: Hell. The notion of a collective unconscious (of the collective memory of classlessness) motivating the transformation of capitalist production is completely mythic and nostalgic. Benjamin's formulation suggests that the fetish character of commodity production is a 'fact of consciousness' instead of, as Adorno insists, recognizing it as 'dialectical, in the eminent sense that it produces consciousness' (1969: 111). In short, Adorno points out, a change in consciousness will not simply effect a change in the relations of production – reified experience is not reducible to consciousness but has its basis in a concrete material reality, which Benjamin seems to elide.

One can apply these criticisms to Benjamin's understanding of the cinema: his assertion that film is capable of revealing the unconscious structures of reality – thus producing a revolutionary consciousness – does not take into account the institutional function of cinema as a cultural industry, nor the historical conditions of its development. The notion that the cinema reflects the desire on the part of the 'masses to bring things closer spatially and humanly', a 'perception whose "sense of the universal equality of things" has increased to such a degree' that it seeks to equalize everything through reproduction, is a somewhat

simplistic interpretation (one that Adorno attributed to Brecht).
Explications of this kind bear the mark of the Enlightenment, the
promesse de bonheur of social unity and coherence that justifies
the economic development of all new technologies and serves
commodity production so well (1969: 223).

This utopian/primordial desire underlying the production of
the New was similarly touched upon in McLuhan's analysis of the
American dream in *The Mechanical Bride,* which he locates in
a collective unconscious. For McLuhan, this dream is utopian
and archaic. As both Benjamin and McLuhan well knew, Freud
theorized this utopian aspect as the 'impulse towards perfection'
or the death drive:

> The path … back to complete satisfaction, is as a rule barred by the
> resistances that maintain the repressions, and thus there remains
> nothing for it but to proceed in the other, still unobstructed direction,
> that of development, without, however, any prospect of being able to
> bring the process to a conclusion or to attain the goal. (*Beyond the
> Pleasure Principle,* 1961: 174)

This development is, arguably, the very ontology of the photographic image: the perfect/automatic reduplication of irre-
versible moments and the overcoming of loss through
consumption. In *The Political Unconscious,* Fredric Jameson
makes a case for the relevance of Freud's theory of desire not
as a universal atemporal characteristic of the psyche but as a
product of the psychic fragmentation figured by 'capitalism with
its systematic quantification and rationalisation of experience,
its instrumental reorganisation of the subject as much as of the
outside world' (1981: 152). Within this configuration, we can see
how the 'death drive' is useful for understanding the ideological
operations of different moving image technologies over the past
century, insofar as these exhibit the desire to overcome death,
promising to fulfil a wish for total and unified mastery by *bringing things closer.* McLuhan would articulate this tendency
expressed in the popular media as a desire to get

> the feel of it … Put that sidewalk microphone right up against the
> heart of that school kid who is looking at the Empire State Building
> for the first time. 'Shirley Temple gets her first screen kiss in a picture
> you'll never forget', and so on … In all such situations the role of tech-
> nology in providing ever intenser thrills is evident. (*MB*: 101)

There is in this collective dream a fundamental desire to touch and experience all aspects of the world, and it through technological extensions that such a desire is fulfilled. This is a process described by both Benjamin and McLuhan as the breaking down of distance, and of time – a movement backwards towards origin. For McLuhan in particular, such a return to a unified universe in the electric galaxy, while utopian in its aspiration, is a real possibility.

Nevertheless, like Benjamin, McLuhan is interested in constellations of meaning rather than any finite causalities or unifying framework. Thus, the important renaming of his book *The Gutenberg Galaxy* reflects the development of his method, and the influence of Giedion, an influence – the allegorical possibilities of the fragment – that we find also in Benjamin (Buck-Morss, 1999: 468, n. 45). Both believe that a mosaic method offers the 'only practical means of revealing causal operations in history' (*The Gutenberg Galaxy*) and the media are fundamental to any description of modernity as reification.

This said, one of the differences between the two can be found around the issue of historical material determination. In Benjamin, the forces of history are at times essentialized as spontaneous reflex on the part of the working classes or as a collective unconscious. While we find very similar notions at work in McLuhan's early writing, these are absent in *The Gutenberg Galaxy*. In this book causal operations remain unspecified. For Innis, the impetus behind various changes in technology is tied to government management and administrative power, but in *The Gutenberg Galaxy* this power structure is obscure. Technologies are the results of other technologies and of cultures; they in turn affect the way we experience everyday life – the way forms of life are practised and oriented. The causes for the mutation in technologies, for the obsolescence of one technology or the invention of another, for the transition from oral culture to scribal culture, are never addressed. Historical changes occur and it is up to the analyst to 'describe and diagnose before valuation and therapy' the present situation. McLuhan's voice does not so much frame the quotations as provide an interface between the different cultural commentaries, creating a network of insights, in a 'crisp simultaneity'. As we examined in the last chapter, the mosaic construction is acoustic, and as a methodology it reveals the 'resonant depth' of acoustic space. This is its paradoxical nature as Georg Von Békésy once noted: the two-dimensional surface of the mosaic is 'a multidimensional world of interstructural resonance' (*GG*: 43). This multidimensional mosaic returns the reader of lineal texts to an earlier 'primitive' or 'audile-tactile' sensibility.

Benjamin is by far a more nuanced thinker than McLuhan, whose prose is often heavily rhetorical and satirical. Without doubt, Benjamin is also the more philosophically profound of the two. Yet McLuhan's work with its focus on surfaces and grammars, on forms and interfaces, and most especially on links between new and old technologies is not only provocative and stimulating but required reading for anyone trying to understand electric and digital convergences.

Writing the Galaxy

The Gutenberg Galaxy is a very scholarly presentation of ideas within an historical framework. Like Innis's *Empire and Communication*, it is dense and exciting in its gathering together of a huge, almost encyclopedic, array of studies, which in the humanist tradition draws on a vast number of disciplines: theology, history of science, art history, anthropology, psychology, literary studies, philosophy, sociology. One of the early reviews by Alfred Alvarez described the book as a 'lively, ingenious but infinitely perverse summa by some medieval logician, who has given up theology in favor of sociology and knows all about the techniques of modern advertising' (Marchand: 155). The description was apt. McLuhan's starting point is the comparative studies of the oral and written poetry in Homeric studies carried out first by Milman Parry and later by Albert Lord. Such studies had revealed differences in patterns and functions of oral and written poetry. McLuhan asks, if there have been comparative studies of the contrasts between 'the forms of oral and written poetry', why have historians not extended these insights into studies of the divergent 'forms of thought and the organization of experience in society and politics' that stems from literacy? McLuhan is clear to emphasize 'form' in his opening statement, foregrounding the central shift in his thinking throughout the 1950s, again in accordance with the experiment inspired by both Innis and Giedion, away from content towards an examination of forms of discourse. There is a profound reflexivity in *The Gutenberg Galaxy*, similar to that which we find in Innis's work, concerning the nature of the frameworks employed in the creation of knowledge. We have only recently become aware of formal differences in the epistemological frameworks of different historical periods, McLuhan speculates, because we are now living through a fundamental transformation in our perceptual modalities. If the artistic strategies that came into being during the Elizabethan period were the result of the experience of living in a divided world (Cruttwell, 1955), McLuhan speculates that the contemporary situation of electronic culture, of living 'at such a moment of the interplay of contrasted cultures' has made it possible to analyze their differences and their effects (*GG*: 1). In other words, we are once again living through a period where the conflicting forms of oral and written cultures are co-present, through the meeting of the new electronic with literary cultures. However, McLuhan suggests that while earlier shifts were more gradual and difficult to discern, the post-war period of the twentieth century is experiencing an astonishing introduction of new technologies into every facet of ordinary life, enabling us to observe ourselves and other cultures as never before. From this standpoint then, we can discern a transition that is currently underway. This transition brought about by electric media is one back to oral culture and acoustic space. For obvious reasons the character of daily interactions and global interdependence in non-literate and post-literate societies is different. The global village is not a tribal village as McLuhan would explore in greater detail in his chapter on 'hybrid' space in *Understanding Media*.

The notion of historical return is one that McLuhan was developing throughout the 1950s. Electronic media have created a different environment. They have created a new acoustic space enabling, by addressing our audile-tactile senses, a new post-literate post-visual experience that returns us to the interplay of all of our senses, back to a rich sensory 'garden' of 'haptic harmony' of the Middle Ages (*GG*: 17). The electronic media are organic and biological and certainly like de Chardin's Noosphere, there is something utopian in this electric blanket:

> The invention of the alphabet, like the invention of the wheel, was the translation or reduction of a complex, organic interplay of spaces into a single space. The phonetic alphabet reduced the use of all the senses at once, which is oral speech, to a merely visual code. Today, such translation can be effected back and forth through a variety of spatial forms which we call the 'media of communication'. But each of these spaces has unique properties and impinges upon our other senses or spaces in unique ways. (*GG*: 45)

The new awareness created through the electronic media was discovered through the experiments in perception carried out in the arts – in Cézanne and the work of the symbolists which culminated in Joyce's experiments, and in the modern physics of Max Planck which 'since Cézanne' have abandoned the specialized visual space of Descartes and Newton. For McLuhan, the arts and the sciences have come to the same conclusions, made the same kinds of innovations in the creation of 'integrated' frameworks. McLuhan underlines Whitehead's famous assertion that the great discovery of the nineteenth century is the discovery of the method of discovery (*GG*: 45). Whitehead turns our attention to the process rather than to the products of discovery and it is from this insight that he will develop a new methodology.

While *The Gutenberg Galaxy* uses the mosaic method first explored in The *Mechanical Bride*, its methodology is reconceptualized. Although McLuhan has been criticized for using books to condemn book culture (Williams, 1967), he has clearly worked to redraft the linear structure of the book – essentially to make the book into a work of art. This is why the advent of the artists' book in the 1960s can be read in relation to the influence of McLuhan's ideas on artists (Cavell, 2002). McLuhan might maintain that such a phenomenon was more proof of the book's obsolescence – as literacy's environment is made visible through electric culture, the book itself becomes a work of art. Like *The Mechanical Bride, The Gutenberg Galaxy* is non-linear, divided into sections united by short 'glosses' which serve to highlight specific ideas. It is a text that takes as its shape the medieval manuscript, the transitional medium *par excellence*, as the interface of orality and literacy. It resembles in its form not only the audile-tactile and mosaic qualities of the medieval manuscript, but it would be perfectly adaptable to new electronic forms of hyper-text with multi-levelled constructions, quotes within quotes, net-worked integrated knowledge, and a plurality of interactive trajectories.

Unlike *The Mechanical Bride*, *The Gutenberg Galaxy* does not follow Poe's methodology outlined in 'philosophy of composi-tion' which is to begin at the end with the solution to the problem or desired effect and to work backwards. This retracing is the method of modern science and Freud's *The Interpretation of Dreams*. *The Mechanical Bride* examined commodity culture in precisely this way as an effect of Western modernity. The methodology required for understanding the origin and action of such forms as the wheel or the alphabet is, however, 'beyond this method of invention'. It is not 'the backtracking from *product* to starting point, but the following of *process* in isolation from the product. To follow the contours of process as in psychoanalysis provides the only means of avoiding the product of process, namely, the neurosis or psychosis' (*GG*: 45). As with *The Mechanical Bride*, psychoanalysis provides a very general way of making conscious the forces 'we have made ourselves'. McLuhan moves from retracing towards following the contours of a process, he shifts his attention away from a lineal conception of space towards an acoustic understanding. As he argues toward the end of *The Gutenberg Galaxy*, the metaphors of space used by Darwin, Freud (influenced by Darwin), and Kant would be incon-ceivable without literacy. McLuhan is interested in the end of Euclidean space – continuous, uniform and infinite space – and the rebirth of sound based paradigm (ibid.: 251).

The Gutenberg Galaxy seeks to establish a theory of cultural change by tracing the ways in which 'forms of experience and of mental outlook and expression have been modified, first by the phonetic alphabet and then by printing' (ibid.: 1). Thus, McLuhan is looking to understand how specific technologies of language (ways of encoding reality) affect societal structures, cultural forms and most fundamentally forms of pedagogy, which is how ideas and technologies are internalized to become society's ways of organizing time and space. Fundamental, for McLuhan, is the corporeal experience of how reality is mediated, and thus experienced, through these technologies and, crucially, how these new mediations have reconfigured our sensory ratios by emphasizing one sense (the eye) over all the others.

McLuhan's second book represents an attempt to account for the rise of visual culture in the West, with a specific emphasis on Western Europe and North America. McLuhan argues that writing and movable type created a quite unexpected new environment – 'it created the PUBLIC' (*GG*: i). In a manner that recalls what Benedict Anderson has called the 'imagined community' of nations, McLuhan describes an imaginary sense of belonging to a whole created through the daily newspapers. We know that this argument is derived in part from Innis's research, yet we also know that, starting from his doctoral thesis on Thomas Nashe, McLuhan's interest in the popular press was a central one, namely his understanding that the vernacular created a particular form of identification with place. Thus, Gutenberg technology consolidated a sense of the public and the nation: 'What we have called "nations" in recent centuries did not, and could not, precede the advent of Gutenberg technology any more than they can survive the advent of electric circuitry' (*GG*: i). Here we find a fundamental difference between McLuhan and Innis. For Innis, the nation-state is formed through writing – any kind of writing, while for McLuhan, it is the phonetic alphabet and moveable type. Essentially, it is the press that enabled the rise of a particular kind of rationality that reduces and abstracts the world to a code. For Innis, it is writing and not the phonetic alphabet that is the major historical technological development which had led to a space bias or, as McLuhan would assert, visual bias in Western culture. For McLuhan, it is the linear and abstract structure of the phonetic alphabet, its 'one thing at a timeness' that provided the essential linear abstract structure of Western modernity and its rational enterprises.

With the exception of oral culture, historical phases are presented in chronological order in McLuhan's account. The first is oral, the second is the emergence of the phonetic alphabet and scribal tradition, the third is the Guttenberg revolution, the invention of print and moveable type. The final stage in his account is the electronic age, which represents a return to the orality of earlier non-literate cultures, and enables us to view the characteristic and visual bias of literacy. If Innis privileges Greek civilization in his account of the history of communications, McLuhan clearly privileges the Middle Ages as a utopian moment of unity and diversity, orality and literacy. It is perhaps this concentration that makes McLuhan's work so useful for thinking about the character of modernity. His analysis is continuous with his early work in that his interpretation of shifts in technologies of communications is measured in pedagogical terms precisely because this is how such technologies are internalized to become intrinsic parts of the culture. Walter Ong's work regarding educational reforms brought about by print is an important and acknowledged influence on McLuhan, but also because the rise of scribal culture or the book was finally pedagogical and epistemological. Let us look at this in more detail.

Like Innis, McLuhan follows an historical chronology of civilization that corresponds to a history of communication – taking the shift from orality to literacy as a fundamental benchmark of the rise of Western modernity. *The Gutenberg Galaxy* differs from Innis's account in one important respect. While for Innis oral culture is Greek culture, McLuhan begins his study of communications by looking at contemporary non-literate cultures in Africa and in some of the First Nations communities in Canada. Oral culture is non-literate rather than pre-literate; that is, it is very much a part of our present day with both aboriginal and electronic cultures coming to the fore. It is the acoustic character of the media that have made apparent the cultural edifice created by literacy. *The Gutenberg Galaxy* claims then to examine literacy from the standpoint of non-literate cultures. It is expressly by taking multiple points of view (multi-cultural, multi-disciplinary) that a better understanding of the modern era is possible. McLuhan's starting point is the comparative studies of the oral and written poetry in Homeric studies carried out first by Milman Parry and later by Albert Lord, which had revealed differences in patterns and functions of oral and written poetry. Parry's study had examined the poetic process under oral conditions and contrasted it with the conditions of auditory suppression produced by literacy. McLuhan argues that missing from the examination is the 'effect on the organism when the visual function of language was given extraordinary extension and power by literacy' (*GG*: 3).

McLuhan turns to the work of biologist J.Z. Young as well as to the University of Toronto anthropologist Edward Hall to set up a dialectical structure for his study. Young speculates that the 'effect of stimulations' either internal or external is to create 'disturbances' which break up the unity of the brain's patterns. The brain responds by seeking to re-establish equilibrium or completion. While this is admittedly highly speculative, it could, Young surmises, help us to understand 'how we tend to fit ourselves to the world and the world to ourselves' (*GG*: 4). Using this biological model, McLuhan will see literacy and printing as 'disturbances', which by either suppressing or extending human sense have created new 'cultural completions', a new cultural landscape. Thus, McLuhan seeks to understand their action in terms of interactivity; these technologies are not simply foreign objects imposed on bodies, but 'stimulations', which produce a particular response, which in turn produce other connections and action patterns that 'in turn will determine future sequences' (ibid.: 4). Hall's notion that technologies are extensions of the human sensorium provides further insight into a model of *techne* that is complex rather than simply reductive. All technologies, according to Hall, can be read as originating in the body: 'The evolution of weapons begins with teeth and the fist and ends with the atom bomb'. The same can be said of clothes, houses, furniture which extend our biological thermostat, money stores labour, transportation replaces feet. Indeed, language and speech are forms of 'outering' which allow for the accumulation of experience and knowledge that makes for easy transmission.

It is the manner in which knowledge is imparted, pedagogy, that is central to McLuhan's account of the book: both how technology has aestheticized ideas and how it (new media) can be used to reveal this process and create new forms of knowledge. McLuhan argues that all of these extensions of sense, whether the wheel, the alphabet, or the radio, constitute central closed systems as opposed to our private senses, which 'are endlessly translated into each other in that experience we call con-sciousness'. Our extended senses, tools, and technologies have been incapable of interplay or collective awareness. But now in the electric age the very 'instantaneous nature of co-existence' among our technological instruments has created a crisis quite new in human history: now that 'sight, sound and movement are simultaneous and global in extent', we can no longer isolate technological events, now just as our private senses have always enjoyed 'a ratio of interplay' so too must our extended senses (technologies, tools) engage in a ratio of interplay. McLuhan is not simply saying that communications media are imitating the processes of consciousness but rather these are extensions of consciousness.

Just like the new physics, history itself must be written in terms of fields and dynamic interactions. Classical physics provided a static and rigid framework that was independent of 'dynamic processes' (*GG*: 5). McLuhan will argue that Cartesian and Newtonian procedures were constituted by the phonetic alphabet, by a system of abstraction that organized the material world into particular patterns, and consequently perceptions, into a single point of view. The upheaval that quantum physics wrought on classical physics is connected to the new perceptual modalities fostered by the electric environment. We must take care not simply to make of electricity some essential environment. McLuhan sees J.Z. Young's explanation of electricity not as 'flow' but rather as a 'condition of observation'. Thus, physicists no longer use terms to name things in the physical world the way one would the pieces of a machine. Instead, such terminology is used 'as part of a description of the observation of physicists'. For McLuhan, this insight is crucial as Young understands that changes in speaking and acting are 'bound up with the adoption of new instruments'. Thus, *The Gutenberg Galaxy* is 'a prolonged meditation on this theme' which is enabled by quantum physics (ibid.: 6). It is a theme that for McLuhan is fundamental to the writing of history, one that great historians like Alexis de Tocqueville are able to accommodate by creating an interplay between different modes of perception (oral and written), and in this way reacting to his world not in sections but 'as to a whole *field*' (ibid.: 7).

The event that finally spurred on McLuhan to put the quotes that he had been collecting over a 20-year period for *The Gutenberg Galaxy* was the publication of J.C. Carothers' article, 'Culture, psychiatry and the written word', which set up a comparison between literate and non-literate African communities (Marchand, 1989: 153). The central theme of Carothers' article is an examination of the sensory effects of literacy. He argued that the difference between literate and non-literate culture was an emphasis on either eye or ear, that literacy forced a separation of the sense of sight from the rest of the senses. Carothers' essay contains many of the ideas that McLuhan had been developing over a 20-year period. McLuhan recasts Carothers insights to set up his own argument which can be read as a critique of modernity embodied in one central opposition: the disharmony between eye and ear. This represents a profound fragmentation of the senses, for the ear in McLuhan's and Carothers' understanding is very much tied to a synthesis of all the senses. McLuhan refers to it as 'audile-tactile'.

'The ear is connected to touch which is the interplay of all the senses' (*GG*: 65). The opening scene of David Lynch's film *Blue Velvet* (1986), enacts the McLuhanesque dichotomy between eye and ear: a young man in a small suburban town finds an ear in a field near a gas station. It is a strange body part to find lying in a field. One could read the film, a non-linear surreal detective story, through this ear which stands in opposition to the long unending spaces and well-tended identical lawns of suburban America. This reading is especially apt if the ear is read to belong to McLuhan's galaxy. For it is a culture of the ear, of non-linear acoustic space, that has risen up to join the older more permanent forms of orality in non-Western cultures that represents the end of Western civilization. Given McLuhan's love of oral and medieval culture, it is clear that he holds much hope for new forms of electric culture as a means to counter the reductive and dominating epistemological forms of visual culture in the West. In Lynch's universe, the utopian aspiration of an acoustic space is castrated into an image of hell *à la Hieronymus Bosch*. *Blue Velvet* is perhaps the negative impulse inherent in *The Gutenberg Galaxy*.

The path to redemption for McLuhan is in the 'common sense'. McLuhan draws his ideas from the medieval theory of sensory perception. The Thomistic theory maintains that all the senses play a part in experience, the senses are unified in a gestalt through the sense of touch (Aquinas gets this from Aristotle). A balance of all the senses at once, a common sense, according to Thomistic theory is necessary for proper perception. Like Innis's belief in the need for a balance between time and space in the technologies governing institutions and social organizations, McLuhan interprets the cultures produced by specific forms of communication through the senses called upon within the communicative exchange. The Thomist paradigm informs his prescriptive stance, and his hopeful view that the electric media hold within their form the capacity to enable a balance between all sense perception.

Thus we find at every level of McLuhan's description of communications technology an inclination for sensory openness, disciplinary openness, openness to cultural difference and to a plurality of experiences that is utopian. This openness is expressed through a concept of participation, most importantly participatory action in the process of communication. This has a particular inflection in the cultural context of post-war America, and later in the counter-cultural youth movements of the 1960s to which McLuhan was deeply sympathetic. He saw the hippie movement as an expression of the new consciousness produced through the technological environment.

For McLuhan, participation defines art's capacity to stimulate and unite the psyche–soma. It is both physically involving and intellectually creative, and it invites performativity rather than passive readership. W.B. Yeats referred to active sensorial participation in an artwork as walking through a garden, as the 'the interplay of all the senses in haptic harmony' (*GG*: 17), of which music was the highest manifestation. The music theme is important for McLuhan and will run through many of his writings. As we saw in the previous chapter, Innis preferred the permanence of sculpture to the ephemerality of music. This would also account for their different interpretation of orality, which for Innis is in the past and for McLuhan is very much a thing lived and of the present (ibid.).

Carothers explains cultures of the ear and eye in terms of space conception. The non-literate rural populations of Africa live in a world of sound, while the Western Europeans inhabit a world of vision. In the acoustic world, sounds are 'indicators of dynamic things – of movements, events, activities, for which man, when largely unprotected from the hazards of life in the bush or the veldt, must be ever on the alert'. While in the industrialized cities of the West which are highly visual and sequential, Europeans must develop an ability to filter them out, to 'disregard them' (*GG*: 19). Words in these worlds take on different roles. In the oral cultures of Africa that Carothers studied, words have their own force, they affect the world, they are dramatic, emotional and magical. In oral culture, the ear is a receiving organ while the eye is much more an instrument of the will (i.e., 'evil eye'). In Western cultures, words are separated from action and from corporeal subjectivities through writing and most especially through printing. When words are written they become static objects, and lose the temporal materiality of the auditory world and the spoken word. Here subjectivity itself is affected: while the spoken word is inflected with human emotion and directed at someone, the written word is directed at no one in particular (save a general readership).

The spoken word is impossible to avoid, while the written word can be put down according to the reader's whim. The spoken word takes place in time and the oral discussion inherently involves personal contact and a consideration for the feelings of others. Recall Innis's assertion that oral culture is time-based and spiritual: 'the oral tradition implies the spirit but writing and printing are inherently materialistic'. Thus, when the word becomes visible it becomes indifferent to the viewer in a 'world from which the magic "power" of the word has been abstracted' (1951: 130). The result of this separation of word from action leads Carothers to speculate upon the way that this verbal thought becomes neutral, something internalized and contained in minds. This will produce serious socio-cultural and psychic differences in the area of 'free ideation' between the two worlds, which for McLuhan is crucial to understanding the history of writing: 'In a highly literate society, then, visual and behavioural conformity frees the individual for inner deviation' (*GG*: 20). Thus oral cultures like those of Russia view guilt as extending to thought, which is not understood to exist privately. It is precisely a sense of individuality and privacy that emerges through the visual language according to Carothers. Oral communities are tribal, members consider themselves to be part of a larger group or clan, and interdependence and interpenetration are what hold people together, whereas literate cultures, through the internalization of thought, produce highly individualized and private selves.

For McLuhan, cultures will be divided according to sense ratios. Ear and eye, sacral and profane, simultaneous and static, tribal and individuated. McLuhan will try to comprehend cultural differences in terms of communication traditions, and specifically in terms of the phonetic alphabet. Africa, India, Russia, China and Japan, for example are seen as being still largely 'audile-tactile' cultures, while North America and Western Europe are cultures of the eye, standardized, and repetitive. Although the Chinese invented printing in the seventh and eighth century, their culture has remained largely one of the ear. This is precisely because it was not part of a capitalist system, the purpose was 'not the creation of uniform repeatable products for a market and a price system' but was 'an alternative to prayer-wheels' (*GG*: 34). Moreover, printing ideograms is entirely different from typography based on the phonetic alphabet. Unlike the phonetic alphabet, which separates sight and sound and meaning in a purely abstract form of notation, the ideograph, like the hieroglyph, is a complex *gestalt* which involves all the senses at once. In addition, ideograms require scholarly interpretation to be read. These are the reasons that Eisenstein, for example, was able to apply some of these principles of hieroglyphic and ideogrammatic writing to cinematic montage. The sensuous and intellectual participation that these forms of writing invited provided an important model for theorizing the workings of cinematic montage.

McLuhan views the phonetic alphabet above all others as having created a new sensory environment in the Western world, one which was based on abstraction, and designed to maximize production. This is important. McLuhan does not describe a simple causality whereby phonetic alphabet equals abstract rationality and reductive forms of logic. Rather, his description is far more dialectical. Just as the Chinese did not use printing for the market and for industry, it is a new social formation that enabled and was hospitable to new forms of writing and new technologies of representation, which in turn produced a certain 'cultural ecology'. Within this new ecology technologies are mediated by institutional (religious, educational and commercial) applications. The technologies themselves, in their very materiality, like language are part of the common culture.

Fundamentally, what McLuhan will object to in the humanist tradition that rises up around the use of books in the Renaissance is a lack of historical consciousness, that is, a lack of a sense of time. It is no accident that McLuhan's book ends with Minerva's owl, a creature that was so important to Innis's 'plea for time' and, according to McLuhan, was the first essay of Innis's that he read. McLuhan's suggestion is that any extension of the sensorium by technological means has the effect of setting up new ratios among the senses. Languages that are a technology constituted by the outering of all our senses at once are themselves immediately subject to the impact of any mechanically extended sense. That is, 'writing effects speech directly, not only its accidence and syntax but also its enunciation and social uses' (*GG*: 35). It is Innis who hit upon the '*process* of change as implicit in the *forms* of media technology' (ibid.: 50).

The Gutenberg Galaxy is concerned with the history of this impact and the results for learning and society. It is the focus on learning and ways of knowing that will guide McLuhan's writing of this history of 'a continuous drive ... toward the separation of the senses, of functions, of operations, of states emotional and political'. This fragmentation leads to the abstraction found in three-dimensional pictorial space and chronological forms of narrative which appear to us in West, as 'normal'. McLuhan wants to highlight, with the help of Gombrich and William Ivins and others, the history of a particular representational regime. When he moves to examine the fact that non-literate cultures do not read three-dimensional images in the same way as literate audiences, his point is that cultures of the ear are used to a higher degree of participation in everyday life. Individuals from societies where oral cultures continue to thrive are far less passive because the oral cultures constitute a more dynamic and intimate relation between word and world. Not unlike the description of the Middle Ages, McLuhan's sympathetic descriptions of cultures esconsed in the aural traditions highlight the holistic and dialogical aspects of experience. The descriptions of a community in Africa watching a film and actively engaging with the narrative are essentializing to be sure. They resemble Leavis's nostalgia for a past Elizabethan culture where everything in the society was integrated through a common culture (*GG*: 37).

There is no doubt that Africanists would find McLuhan's descriptions crude and inadequate. His views of 'tribal society' are Orientalist and reflect the colonial mentality that Spivak, among others, would later criticize when she calls McLuhan a 'mad scientist' (1999). Andrew Ross's objection that McLuhan's work, with its celebration of 'tribal' consciousness, served to reinforce cultural imperialist ideology in the early sixties is another important criticism (1989: 125). Still, it should be noted that when McLuhan writes that the printed word plays a role in 'staying' what Joseph Conrad referred to as the 'Africa within' Western experience, he is not making an argument in favour of the printed word but rather in support of a new global multicultural connectivity that is both geographic and temporal. To be sure there is a great deal of political naïveté and a Catholic utopianism at work, yet there is also a highly developed 'project' that takes multiculturalism to be its core. This multicultural and anthropological inflection is what distinguishes the history of Canadian cultural theory (Stamps, 1995). McLuhan's interpretation of aboriginal cultures came from radical anthropology which sought to challenge conceptions of what constitutes normative perceptions and time and space. For example, he quotes Carpenter's study of the Aivilik Inuit:

> I know of no example of an Aivilik describing space primarily in visual terms. They don't regard space as static, and therefore measurable; hence they have no formal units of spatial measurement, just as they have no uniform divisions of time. The carver is indifferent to the demands of the optical eye, he lets each piece fill its own space, create its own world, without reference to background or anything external to it ... In the oral tradition, the myth-teller speaks as many-to-many, not as person-to-person. Speech and song are addressed to all ... The work of art can be seen or heard equally well from any direction. (Carpenter quoted in *GG*: 66)

This last quote emphasizes the multidirectional space orientation of oral cultures that McLuhan wishes to study. McLuhan, like Carpenter, is critical of simple appropriations of these cultures by contemporary art: 'primitivism has become the vulgar cliché of much modern art and speculation' (*GG*: 67). He is also critical of the romanticization and commodification of oral cultures, which becomes a refuge for print-saturated citizens. He warns against those uniformly processed individuals of commercial society who think they can simply 'return' to marginal spots that remain untouched by print as tourists and consumers, whether geographical or artistic. The 'transcendental imagination' and art are packaged as 'compensation for a top-sided life', a life that is divorced from the somatic experiences of the life-world (ibid.: 212). Thus, while we do need to be wary of his conflation of discourses of the Other as oral culture, there is in McLuhan's analysis an awareness of the pitfalls inherent in using the terminology and cultural indices of the Other. Certainly, his friendship and his collaborations with Carpenter, his links to Dorothy Lee and his readings of other anthropologists from Gregory Bateson to Margaret Mead, provide him with an awareness that is grounded in a respect for differences.

8

Sacred Technologies, Historical Imagination

In tracing the history of literacy, McLuhan was also investigating the history of the human spirit. He was interested in the 'desacralized cosmos' as a 'recent discovery' that he correlated with literacy and with the splitting apart of word and action. While there are different modalities in which to experience the sacred, whether in the religious experience of time, ritual, human consecration, or in the vitality of physiological acts, the desacralized world is a product of modern consciousness. In *The Sacred and the Profane* (1961), Mircea Eliade analyzes this difference in terms of space. He argues that for religious cultures, space is not homogenous. Sacred spaces are not Euclidean, they are pluralistic, unique, and filled with qualitative differentiation, orientations and time. While McLuhan is interested in many of the same issues that Eliade explores, he takes issue with *The Sacred and the Profane* because it sets up an opposition between religious cultures and rationality.

McLuhan believes that Eliade is a victim of literacy for 'supposing that the "rational" is the explicitly lineal, sequential, visual'. In his desire to counter visual culture, Eliade plays with an opposition, which makes of the sacred something wholly irrational. The irrational itself could all too easily be encompassed and regimented by the manifestos of Marinetti and Maholy-Nagy who misunderstood the origins and differences between the sacred and profane experience. If Blake were alive today, he would be 'anti-Blake' because 'the Blake reaction against the abstract visual is now the dominant *cliché*' (*GG*: 71). Rationality for McLuhan has a particular meaning which is not simply a product of literacy – rather ratio-nality refers to ratios of the senses. Literacy changes those ratios to emphasize the visual sense at the expense of the others. Literacy, then, and this is a central argument, should not be conflated with rationality. All forms of communication require rationality because they involve corporeal exchange and sensory experience.

McLuhan is too much of a Thomist to ever accept that ratio-nality is a product of literacy. He cites Aquinas's medieval sense doctrine: 'the senses delight in things duly proportioned as in something akin to them; for, the sense, too, is a kid of reason as is every cognitive power' (ibid.: 107). At the heart of McLuhan's critique of the rise of literacy is a sense that 'Typographic Man' has lost a feeling for the sacred in the experience of the world. The printed phonetic alphabet produces a visual culture that disconnects and dislocates the human sensorium from experience; this disconnection from place as from people erodes the sacred. It is this loss of the sacred that informs McLuhan's phenomenology of literacy.

McLuhan's framework is very compatible with Bergson's critique of Western science. They are both indebted to Augustine. Science based on a visuality produces tools which translate the world into the language of one sense only – which is Blake's point in wanting to be free of 'single vision and Newton's sleep'. McLuhan sees his own critical task as disrupting the hypnotic sleep produced by the magnification of this visual perception: 'The sleeper awakes when challenged in any other sense' (ibid.: 73). Sacred and profane states never exist in their pure forms. The profane existence, Eliade underlines, always contains traces of religious value. Each age exists in the process of translation, metamorphosis and mutation. This is why as noted earlier, periods of translation occasion creative ferment, i.e., Classical Greece, the Renaissance and the present time which all saw the translation of one mode of communication into another. The concept of the interface, a concept McLuhan gets from modern physics, helps us to understand the way that the meeting of two cultures can be like 'astrological galaxies' that cross through each other, creating a metamorphosis of both structures, a change in configuration. In this liminal state, models and their sensory bias become visible as a form of consciousness:

> Just as we now live on the frontier between five centuries of mechanism and the new electronics, between homogeneity and simultaneity, the sixteenth century Renaissance was an age on the frontier between thousand years of alphabetic and manuscript culture, on the one hand, and the mechanism of repeatability and quantification on the other. (*GG*: 141)

It is new forms of awareness that McLuhan wishes to stimulate through his historical display of epistemological frameworks. Thus, the techniques he developed throughout the 1950s culminate in a method which he sees as intrinsic to the twentieth century: 'The method of the twentieth century is to use not single but multiple models for experimental exploration – the technique of the suspended judgement' (ibid.: 71). This technique is borrowed from Giedion, like the idea of 'anonymous history'.

McLuhan's dramatic sketch will draw on dozens of massive studies: the landmark work by Febvre and Martin, *L'Apparition du livre*, Curt Bhuler's *The Fifteenth Century Book*, Walter Ong's *Ramus: Method and the Decay of Dialogue* and the 'indispensable' book by E.P. Goldschmidt, *Medieval Texts and Their First Appearance in Print*. Following these four studies among others, McLuhan focuses very specifically on the difference between the manuscript and the printed book.

The Scribe and the Press

McLuhan examines the progressive disappearance of the body in the mechanical reproduction of writing. The mechanical printed page may have seemed like a continuation of the manuscript to both producers and consumers but they were radically different. In the same way that there is nothing in common between the 'mosaic image of television and the pictorial space of the photograph', the printed book produced a new form that would change the culture. From the fifth century BC to the fifteenth century AD, the book itself was a product of scribal practice. Only one-third of the history of the book is typographic. This is an important fact since McLuhan wants to highlight the relatively short history and hegemony of the book in learning.

McLuhan sees the alphabet as a 'translation' and a 'reduction' of embodied interplay of the senses, of synesthesia and tactility which were still a very important aspect of the manuscript culture. He wishes to foreground the oral aspect of manuscript culture, and examines the history of writing as integrally tied to a history of reading, to a performance which links auditory and kinesthetic actions to the visual apprehension of the text. Reading throughout ancient and medieval times referred to reading aloud (*GG*: 84). To start with, there was far more hearing than reading during this period and literature was produced for public recitation. Texts were governed by rules of rhetoric and were written to be read aloud. Thus, reading itself was, even when silent, an action that involved the movement of lips or at least the movement of vocal chords to be understood. Reading was connected to a whole system of corporeal mnemonics in sacred rituals, meditation, and study. Meditation consisted of the act of memorizing, combining 'muscular memory of the words pronounced and an aural memory of the words heard' (Leclercq, cited in *GG*: 89). It is this act that inscribes sacred texts onto bodies. Like the *vers libre* of modern poets like Gertrude Stein, E.E. Cummings, Pound and Eliot, medieval texts were intended for oral presentation, experienced, masticated and ingested. It is this oral and musical (for the monks the reading carrel was a 'singing booth') aspect of manuscript culture that differentiates it so profoundly from typographic culture (ibid.: 92).

Writing at the medieval university was never separate from the writing body. Writing was important because it was a sign of good *pronuntiatio* of oral Latin and proper *grammatica* ensured oral fidelity. Clashes in medieval teaching procedures were between the old forms of dictation and new forms of oral disputation. Before printing, teachers would dictate the manuscript book (which cost a great deal to purchase) to students who might sell it or use it for their future careers. Degrees awarded could depend on the candidate's library. Thus, students made their own books based upon their teacher's dictation from other books. But teachers often added something to the dictation, or summarized and personalized concepts, which gave rise to a new literature. Writing itself was not simply a matter of copying but was a physical practice, part of a practice involving the pleasure of writing and the acquisition of the texts (ibid.: 98).

By analyzing the oral aspects of manuscript culture, McLuhan is trying to move away from the literary bias that he finds in other studies of literacy. What stands out in his description of medieval culture is an experience and relation to space itself. As Giedion would maintain in *Mechanization Takes Command*, medieval culture, though full of daily physical hardships, also produced spaces that brought to everyday life a sense of 'comfort', and 'dignity' (*GG*: 147). It is an experience of integrated space, the difference between place and location, which is commonly used to depict medieval culture – sometimes in highly romantic ways. Nevertheless, an experience of space is generally what differentiates medieval culture from Renaissance culture. For the sake of brevity, let me clarify this difference beyond what McLuhan presents in *The Gutenberg Galaxy*.

We can understand the distinction between place and location by grasping the difference between medieval space and the *Quattrocento* perspective of Renaissance painting. Maurice Merleau-Ponty has explained this shift:

> In spontaneous vision ... at every moment I was swimming in the world of things and overrun by a horizon of things to see that which could not possibly be seen simultaneously with what I was seeing but by this very fact were simultaneous with it ... my glance, running freely over depth, height, and width, was not subordinated to any point of view because it adopted and rejected each one in turn ... I had the experience of a world of teeming, exclusive things which could be embraced only by means of a temporal cycle in which each gain is simultaneously a loss. [The] world crystallizes into an ordered perspective within which backgrounds resign themselves to being merely backgrounds, inaccessible and vague as required, where objects in the foreground lose something of their aggressiveness, order their interior lines according to the common law of the spectacle ... The

whole scene is in the past, in the mode of completion and eternity. Everything adopts an air of propriety and discretion. (1973: 52–3)

In medieval times there was a feeling of belonging to a world, of having a place or of being localized within the world and connected to it – of 'swimming'. Things and our experience of things took place simultaneously, 'my gaze' was not subjected to any one point of view but could experience all points of view. Hence there existed in this experience, and in its representation as 'temporal cycle', both a gain and a loss that comes with simultaneity. As Arthur Koestler has remarked, the medieval world was finite, complete and interconnected like 'a babe in the womb' (1961: 19). This is the acoustic space of 'all-at-onceness' that electric media will hearken back to. This is the sacred space that Eliade refers to in his study. But when the universe was opened up by infinity, place or home gave way to mere location, one view among an infinity of views relative to an infinite scheme. It is within the infinite world that the cosmos is desacralized.

The discovery of electro-magnetic waves in the late eighteenth century instigated a return to and search for new forms of sacred communion. Pierre Teilhard de Chardin's 'noosphere' is based on this discovery that he sees as 'biological' and organic in opposition to mechanism. This noosphere creates a space in which 'each individual finds himself henceforth (actively and passively) simultaneously present, over land and sea, in every corner of the earth'. McLuhan calls the noosphere a 'cosmic membrane' or a 'technological brain for the world' that wraps the earth through the 'electric dilation' of the senses (*GG*: 32). Unlike de Chardin, McLuhan does not subscribe wholeheartedly to the new cosmic consciousness. Instead he wishes to investigate the 'process' by which these modalities of being in the world became desacralized so that 'we can at least make a conscious and responsible choice whether we elect once more the tribal' connectivity of acoustic space. McLuhan cautions that just as our senses are 'outered', Big Brother gets inside our heads: 'So, unless aware of the dynamic, we shall at once move into a phase of panic terrors, exactly befitting a small world of tribal drums, total interdependence, and superimposed co-existence' (*GG*: 32). Consciousness of the effects of technologies is McLuhan's sole objective: 'The theme of this book is not that there is anything good or bad about print but that unconsciousness of the effect of any force is a disaster, especially a force that we have made ourselves' (ibid.: 248).

Despite the fact that McLuhan says he does not privilege literacy or electric culture, the notion that acoustic space is a return to tribal and oral forms of connectivity is highly utopian. Acoustic space is a medieval space of the feminine, a space of the womb, of nature and of home. McLuhan adds to his list of medievalists and art historians, among them Smalley's *Study of the Bible in the Middle Ages*, Erwin Panofsky's influential study of Gothic architecture, Otto von Simson's work on Gothic cathedrals and numerous other writers cited by these authors in a sometimes delirious conversation. He considers how this experience of space is intrinsic to an epistemology of 'light through' rather 'light on' objects: 'Probably any medieval person would be puzzled at our idea of looking through something. He would assume that the reality looked through at us, and that by contemplation we bathed in the divine light, rather than looked at it' (*GG*: 106). Such a relationship is tied to a *sensus communis* which is a central principle in Aquinas's sense doctrine, linking transparency in architecture with tactility. Tactility itself is a way of remembering, and indeed the medieval manuscript is tied to oral culture through the gloss, which served its users as oral lecture notes. As we noted earlier, *The Gutenberg Galaxy* is constructed through such glosses, referencing in its mode of organization the manuscript culture that McLuhan seems to value above the printed book.

McLuhan compares the scholastic technique of aphorism to the Ciceronian method, which simply explicates a problem with the aim to persuade rather than engage analysis. Francis Bacon would write and McLuhan would quote him approvingly: 'Aphorisms, representing a knowledge broken, do invite men to inquire farther; whereas Methods, carrying the show of a total, do secure men, as if they were at farthest' (*GG*: 102–03). Bacon (the 'Senecan who was in many respects a Schoolman') as well as Abelard's aphoristic writing provide McLuhan with models of a methodology that was steeped in the oral culture of dialogue (ibid.). It is a model that McLuhan will utilize to describe the contemporary environment of media cultures. It is also a method that he returns to in his posthumously published study *Laws of Media*.

The Art of Memory

Sacred Scripture was not only read but memorized, and recited. This enabled the reader through recitation to recreate the thoughts, which before transcribed were oral, to better penetrate the ideas. McLuhan notes the steady development of a new visual bias in the later medieval study of the Bible. *Memoria* was the fourth branch of rhetoric and was increasingly supplemented by architectural and imagistic means which functioned as *aide-mémoire* (*Letters*: 339). A significant aspect of the issue of memory and writing is the influence of typography on the art of authorship. Goldschmidt points out that manuscript culture was producer-oriented, and the consumer who was also a producer looked for the relevant use rather than sources. The invention of printing seems to have done away with anonymity or made it visible, while the Renaissance produced new ideas on fame and 'intellectual property'. The writer of the manuscript had no reading public beyond a few colleagues with whom to share knowledge, bearing in mind that 'the manuscript book is slow to read and to move' (*GG*: 132). Thus, when an author died, for example, his papers were easily the source of confusion – handwritten, these could either be his own composition or a copy made by him of someone else's manuscript. This confusion between scribe and author complicated procedures for library cataloguing with volumes of numerous smaller pieces. This ambiguity and anonymity concerning authorship characterized a great many of the medieval texts. Dialects made reading and writing difficult, not to mention a lack of paper that led to the practice of reducing spaces between words that increased the difficulties in reading.

The significant shift in thinking that takes place from scribal to typographic printing is the assumption that mechanical writing is 'uncontaminated by human agency'. This new sense of objectivity was profound and would lead gradually to all those forms of production and social organization from which the Western world has come to define itself. *The Gutenberg Galaxy* does not aim 'to do more than to explain the configuration or galaxy of events and actions associated with Gutenberg technology' (ibid.: 139). For McLuhan, such actions and events are not simply a 'bad thing', rather, we should use the opportunity of living in a period of transition to 'retain the achieved values' of literacy. For the electric age, according to de Chardin, is not mechanical but organic, and has little understanding of the values produced by typography. *Gutenberg Galaxy*'s aim is to historicize those values and to situate the typographic revolution as an historical rather than natural occurrence in the West. The modern era for McLuhan, defined both culturally and scientifically in terms of the rise of literacy and print culture, is resolutely ocularcentric. Like Innis, McLuhan recognizes the period beginning with the Renaissance as intrinsic to unraveling modernity. While the printing press, according to Febvre and Martin, did nothing to 'hasten the adoption of new theories of knowledge', they did introduce into everyday life a standard, a '*homogénéité de la page*' that would act as the formulas not only for the new science and art of the Renaissance but for trade and politics as well. (*GG*: 143)

Following John Dewey, McLuhan wants to explore alternative modes of inscribing reality, different methods of learning and teaching, and to celebrate new and old modes of writing. McLuhan is concerned with 'packaged' forms of knowledge, which exclude the reader's participation in the making of understanding. The printed book was not just a teaching tool. Like the manuscript, it was a portable 'teaching machine' enabling independent and private study. Peter Ramus' educational programme, as Walter Ong has shown, was aligned with the press and geared towards processing students through a curriculum that was in Ong's words, 'the doorway to reality, and indeed the only doorway' (*GG*: 146). Educational reformers missed the nature and effects of this new tool in the shaping of knowledge – a trend that continues to this day.[1] Ramus introduces a new educational system for the self-educated mercantile class, one that promoted practical qualities and applied knowledge, that was more related to numbers than to letters.

The most substantial accounts of the Gutenberg transformation of society come from literature: Rabelais's *Gargantua*, Cervantes' *Don Quixote*, the *Dunciad* by Pope, and *Finnegans Wake*. These literary works each in their own way recount the manner that print came to transform and mediate experience. Rabelais likens the printing press to the wine press from which it originates, seeing it as a technology which intoxicates as it flattens differences between things and people. Like Shakespeare, Rabelais stands at the frontier between two cultures, he is a 'collective rout of oral schoolmen and glossators suddenly debouched into a visual world newly set up on individualist and nationalist lines' (*GG*: 149). Rabelais's medievalism is apparent in the promiscuous tactility of his writing, which consciously splashes against the 'tidy new visual wall of print culture'. Rabelais's audile-tactile writing reminds McLuhan of Joyce who maintained that the world 'is comprised of a single book'.

If Rabelais could write of the modern world, it is because he was so well aware of the nature of print culture. Joyce comes from the other side, from the 'Charge of the Light Brigade', the world of television. Both use audile-tactile forms of writing to challenge the effects of typographic cultures. Tactility itself was lost to printing until writers like Hopkins (one of McLuhan's favourites) and the French Symbolists brought it back in the nineteenth century (*GG*: 151). Part of the separation of touch from print was evident in the 'great divorce' between numbers as the language of science and letters as the language of civilization. The mechanization of scribal action spread along with innovations in industrial modes of production fostered by the change from 'mill to mallet', from continuous circular movement to alternative sequence.

A passion for exact measurement and quantification came to dominate the Renaissance. Space and time from the mid-sixteenth century in Europe were subjected to new forms of precise measurement, translated into a new visuality and new procedures of control. This is the age of the telescope and the portable camera obscura – devices that confined the infinite celeste to the dark chambers of one internal perspective. Both Leonardo da Vinci and, two centuries earlier, Roger Bacon had described a technology which, by means of mirrors, could enable someone 'inside' to witness 'outside' occurrences normally not accessible to ordinary vision. As McLuhan points out, this is the phenomenon that led Giovanni Battista della Porta in his *Magia Naturalis, sive de Miraculis Rerum Naturalium* (1589) to warn readers that what he was revealing about the camera should probably be kept secret. Kept secret precisely because of the secrets this new form of surveillance might reveal and the trickery it might enlist:

> Nothing can be more pleasant for great men and Scholars, and ingenious persons to behold; that in a dark Chamber by white sheets objected, one may see as clearly and perspicuously, as if they were before his eyes, Huntings, Banquets, Armies of Enemies, Plays and all things else that one desireth. Let there be over against that Chamber, where you desire to represent these things, some spacious Plain, where the sun can freely shine, upon that you shall see trees in Order, also Woods, Mountains, Rivers and Animals that are really so or made by Art, of Wood, or some other matter ... those that are in the Chamber shall see ... so plainly, that they cannot tell whether they be true or delusions: Swords drawn will glisten in at the hole. (*GG*: 128)

The camera obscura provides a new way to translate the fundamental sensorial plurality of the world into one vision. A new kind of packaging: 'the natural magic of the camera obscura anticipated Hollywood in turning the spectacle of the external world into a consumer commodity' (ibid.). The conception of self and the universe transforms the sense of *place* (always a central one) into *locatedness* (in relation to an infinite number of locations). McLuhan remarks:

> point of view originates in the discovery of a fixed position as creating perspective, or vanishing point. It was this discovery in the fifteenth century that we associate with the end of medieval art. It was the same discovery taken up by map-makers and by navigators that made the world voyages possible. For prior to the discovery of space as homogeneous and lineally continuous, it was not known that one could simply proceed on and on in a straight line on a single plane. ('New media and the new education' in *RPUM*: iii)

The codification of space into a linear visual sequence had been underway in perspective painting since Brunelleschi's famous experiment applied the mathematics of perspective to painting in 1425 (ibid.: 17). The fact that the printing press is only invented in 1450 is of some significance and could prove embarrassing in terms of McLuhan's argument. Yet such criticisms miss the point of McLuhan's book, which is precisely not to attribute an effect (modernity) to a single cause (the press) at a single moment in time (1450). McLuhan works against a single linear theory of causality. In fact, towards the end of *The Gutenberg Galaxy*, he turns to Edmund Whittaker's explanation of a new spatial, certainly acoustic, configuration in *Space and Spirit* (1948), which challenges the linear causality of the Newtonian Cosmos. I quote the passage from Whittaker's book because for McLuhan it serves to explain both the title and procedure of *Gutenberg Galaxy*:

> In the argument as usually presented the language used is appropriate to the case when each effect has only one cause, and each cause has only one effect, so that all chains of causation are simple linear sequences. If we now take into account the fact that an effect may be produced by the joint action of several distinct causes, and also that a cause may give rise to more than one effect, the chains of causation may be branched, and also may have junctions with one another; but since the rule still holds, that the cause always precedes the effect in time, it is evident that the proof is not essentially affected. Moreover, the argument does not require that all chains of causation, when traced backward, should terminate on the *same* ultimate point: in other words, it does not lead necessarily to the conclusion that the universe acquired its entire stock-in-trade in a single consignment at the Creation, and that it has received nothing since ... the recent trend of physical thought (as will be evident from what has been said about the principle of causality) is in favor of the view that in the physical domain, there is a continual succession of intrusions or new creations. The universe is very far from being a mere mathematical consequence of the disposition of the particles at the Creation, and is a much more interesting and eventful place than any determinist imagines. (*GG*: 252)

While McLuhan may tell us in the Preface that he is seeking to understand causal operations in history, he is really looking to create a collage where multiple causal relations and effects can be juxtaposed in a way that is intrinsically decentred.

To attribute the printing press to Gutenberg is as nonsensical as attributing the automobile to Ford. The printing press is a locus of inventions and innovations – 'Gutenberg invented nothing'.

Indeed, the movable type required the introduction of linen paper making, an innovation that entered Europe from China, specific oil-based inks, wood engraving, as well as casting. While McLuhan comments on the multiple innovations needed to support one invention, his interest is in the responses to the invention – in the new uses and cultural environments that will be created out of it. That is, he is concerned with the transformations brought about with the printing press: the rise of a new book trade, printing and publishing houses, book sellers, the emergence of calligraphy as an art or a hobby. On a larger scale, the Gutenberg galaxy encompasses a cultural transformation: a new kind of individuality and nationalism, rationalism and scientific quantification. McLuhan points out that this history is opaque. Yet it is a history that must be written, not in terms of technology but in terms of actions and social practices precisely because machines are what humans make. It is the social organization not only of that making but of what the making produces that needs to be highlighted. McLuhan's technique for writing history draws on new theories of reality in physics but also a methodology that he borrows from the Italian scholar Vico whose work I shall discuss shortly.

The Gutenberg Galaxy is a configuration of inter-actions. Such actions centred on the translation of non-visual events in motion to static visual modes for purposes of quantification – this in fact became the very principle of applied knowledge (*GG*: 155). Typography, in its uniformity and repeatability, in its standardized grammar and forms of presentation, enabled language to become transparent, the meanings behind words to be reduced to a singularity, to become entirely self-evident so that Descartes could instruct his public to read without stopping. Typography makes language into a 'portable commodity' rather than a tool for perception and exploration (ibid.: 161). 'Printed books themselves are the first uniform, repeatable, mass produced items in the world', and as such furnish the culture into which they spread with 'endless paradigms of commodity culture' (ibid.: 163). Printed books are staples and as Innis was able to show, these created a system of production, distribution and indeed, a price system and wealth (ibid.: 165). Printed books separated voice from word, destroying oral culture. They also produced a new sense of the self, an insight that McLuhan gets from both Ong and Carothers as discussed earlier. With the silent reading of the book the voice turns inward, with literacy comes an internal monologue and the stream of consciousness writing that Joyce invented. This internal life creates a sense of privacy in the process of thinking. Literacy also produces a new sense of individuality and exclusiveness; the Artist as outsider emerges with literacy.

McLuhan points out, 'the painters explained perspective or fixed point of view to the public when print was scarcely known. Aretino became the "scourge of princes" when print was young, ... Petrarch developed the sonnet as a mode of self-expression and self-analysis'. This is because artists until the present time, were always as Wyndham Lewis understood 'engaged in writing a detailed history of the future because [they were] aware of the unused possibilities of the present' ('New media' in *RPUM*: i). McLuhan believes that artists have throughout history always been ahead of technicians. This romantic conception of the artist as alienated outsider is created through the typographic logic, which comes to define consumer society. An intrinsic member of this group of outsiders is the Romantic 'figure of woman', which McLuhan points out is made to stand for the whole: Her 'haptic bias, her intuition, her wholeness entitle her to marginal status'. While women could not be entirely homogenized, made into a uniform, specialized and repeatable commodity through print, it was movie and photo advertising which subjected her to visual uniformity and repeatability (*GG*: 212) This was the insight that he drew upon in his analysis of ads in *The Mechanical Bride*.

Historical Imagination

Historians typically equate the birth of the 'historical imagination' along with nationalism with the Renaissance. Myron Gilmore maintains that, whereas in the Middle Ages human experience throughout time was seen as unified and continuous, in the sixteenth century differences between distinct periods became a source of investigation. History emerges as an object of study, as an academic discipline rather than a sacred telos. The study of law, Gilmore points out, underwent an important transformation at the end of the sixteenth century. No longer understood as universal and absolute, laws were seen to reflect an historical contingency (1979: 97). Merleau-Ponty indicates that the conception of the past in terms of history coincides with the *Quattrocento* and with the advent of print culture; thus the medieval world of simultaneity disappears into a world frozen in and distanced by time, a world where things 'no longer call upon me and I am not compromised by them' (1973: 53). A universe in which the body is fixed and separated from a space which extends far beyond its realm. Innis concurs with this notion that history 'in the modern sense' is about four centuries old. Innis comments on changing concepts of time and importantly on the powers that came with the ability to control time:

> The linear concept of time was made effective as a result of humanistic studies in the Renaissance. When Gregory XIII imposed the Julian calendar on the Catholic world in 1582 Joseph Justus Scalinger following his edition of Manilius (1579) published the '*De emendatione temporum*' and later his '*Thesaurus temporum*' (1606) ... With his work he developed an appreciation of the ancient world as a whole and introduced a conception of the unity of history at variance with the attitude of the church. While Scalinger assisted in wresting control over time from the church he contributed to the historical tradition of philosophy until Descartes with his emphasis on mathematics and his unhistorical temper succeeded in liberating philosophy from history. (*Bias*: 62–63)

McLuhan would extend Innis's concern with history to consider the effects of a divided psyche–soma on subjectivity. What happens to sense perception during this period in which subjectivity is suddenly seen as an impediment to knowledge, in which head and heart, body and mind, art and science, letters and numbers, poetry and music are separated? Descartes' distrust of sense experience reflected the impact of the new visual culture and separation of the senses. Sense perception comes to define subjectivity insofar as it is misleading; consciousness is no longer capable of mirroring nature but is set apart in the interior realm of thought: 'Thought is a word which covers everything that exists *in us* in such a way that we are immediately conscious of it. Thus all operations of will, intellect, imagination, and the senses are thoughts' (Descartes: 52). The constitution of subjectivity as deep interiority – the 'interior landscape' as McLuhan called it – characterizes the transition from a medieval to a modern Western conception of the world in the sixteenth and seventeenth centuries. Descartes' separation of thought into clear and distinct ideas is the internalization of word into thought.

Vico and the Romantics

It is Giambattista Vico, the Italian renegade scholar who challenges Descartes' mathematization and abstraction of the world by proposing a methodology that is rhetorical, historical and grounded always in the present moment. McLuhan is introduced to Vico through Joyce, and Vico will provide an important source of inspiration for McLuhan from the 1950s onward. The structure of Joyce's *Ulysses* was drawn from Vico's *New Science* where he proposed a methodology for writing history that was uniquely radical and intertextual. For Vico history can only be written to take account of objects made and traces left: literature, law, myths, institutional regulations – all forms of discourse that constitute human society and experience. We can only know the past through its artifacts. Vico is the first to recognize the entire contents of human consciousness and unconsciousness as 'memory theatres' and to conceive of history as writing bound up with the imagination. Memory theatres were non-literary, they were premised on 'topics or places' that were given an architectural form for the convenience of the rhetorician or orator. With the printed word, the 'whole fabric of these theatres collapsed' and the relation between memory and place was lost (Letters: 339). Vico will use this lost art form as a metaphor for his historical methodology that takes language itself as the object of historical research.

> Vico, like Heidegger, is a philologist among philosophers. His time theory of 'ricorsi' has been interpreted by lineal minds to imply 'recurrence'. ... Vico conceives the time-structure of history as 'not

linear, but contrapuntal. It must be traced along a number of lines of development'. For Vico, all history is contemporary or simultaneous, a fact given, Joyce would add, by virtue of language itself, the simultaneous storehouse of all experience. And in Vico, the concept of recurrence cannot 'be admitted at the level of the course of the nations throught time': 'The establishment of providence establishes universal history, the total presence of the human spirit to itself in idea' (*GG*: 249–250).

The new tribal cultures produced by electric media are not to be interpreted as a return to older forms but as a new cultural manifestation that we can interpret through older non-Western cultural formations.

If Vico provides a methodology for challenging the single vision of Renaissance perspective, it is in the end with the Romantics and ultimately with Joyce (all of whom were influenced by Vico) that McLuhan will conclude his exploration. The Enlightenment context of the mechanization of writing and the social scientific is satirized in Pope's *The Dunciad* as a cultural apocalypse: 'Art after Art goes out, and all is Night' and in Blake's 'single vision and Newton's sleep'. McLuhan shares this modernist project to rekindle the imaginative contours of experience extinguished by the *techne* of literacy. Imagination is that ratio among the perceptions and faculties which exists when 'they are not embedded or outered in material technologies'. This outering produces closed systems and puts an end to the interplay among the senses. John Ruskin will seek to rekindle the historical imagination when he defines *the* aesthetic programme for the English Romantics. In the 'grotesque imagination' of Gothic architecture and in pre-Raphaelite mythologies, Ruskin does not locate a history of the Middle Ages but the performance of imagination and the excessive flesh and density of the symbol. Ruskin decries the mechanization of truth as a simple matching of object with abstract visual standard, by situating imagination in the making of truth, in the 'ratio between the mind and things' (*GG*: 265).

McLuhan recognizes that these new conventions emanated from changes in 'the structure of feeling' for, as Raymond Williams underlined, the rise of a new market society created a new context for art. While Blake, Ruskin and the Romantics sought to counter the effects of industrial culture by focussing on 'the common property of imaginative truth' (Williams, quoted in *GG*: 273), J.S. Mill and Matthew Arnold devoted themselves to fighting for the individual liberty and for culture in the face of mass culture. But neither of these sides 'has meaning alone', nor can we simply blame mass culture or capitalism for the situation. For McLuhan, Joyce's *Finnegans Wake* provides a middle ground between these two positions. It is a history of writing which suggests a way out of the 'Night' described by Pope, 'the Night from which Joyce invites the Finnegans to wake' (*GG*: 263).

The Gutenberg Galaxy offers Pope's Mannipean Satire, the Romantic's 'esemplastic imagination' and Joyce's stream-of-consciousness writing as means to awake from modernity and the instrumentalization of all aspects of experience into a new awareness. Such a 'liberation', Joyce believed might come from Marconi technology which materializes and manifests 'the mythic or collective dimension of human experience' (ibid.: 269). It is electric technology which enables a new awareness of human interpenetration and interdependence, it gave Joyce 'access to language on a new basis' (*Letters*: 341).

Transitions

The conclusion of *The Gutenberg Galaxy* promises a book called *Understanding Media* that will examine the co-existence of two technological worlds and the sense of trauma brought about by their dramatic interface: the 'new electric galaxy of events has already moved deeply into the Gutenberg Galaxy' (*GG*: 278). The notion of 'co-existence' counteracts the idea of a simple transition. Rather, literacy and electricity inter-act, electricity produces mutations in the older structures which created electricity. That is, it is no accident that mechanical culture gave rise to its opposite, creating new hybrid forms of sensibility and cultural objects. This is what is often misunderstood about new media: their connection to the older media forms is one of mutation and this relationship will be further developed in *Understanding Media* as McLuhan describes electric media in terms of organic culture. If we were to think about the relation between books and computers at the present time, for example, Internet 'chat-rooms' which are forms of talking, but consist of writing, a number of interesting questions arise with regard to this new mutation in writing messages. Writing itself in these instances is still writing. But it is a new kind of writing, an abbreviated, iconic form of written conversation that produces new configurations of sense and perception, new experiences of identity and discarnality. People are writing as never before and the inexperienced refer to it as 'talking'.

McLuhan's work calls attention to new forms of culture and their relation to a history of communication. So writing, whether it is on paper or on screens, with a pencil or a keyboard, is still the translation of thought into a system of visual codes. But there has certainly been a change in the very character and indeed experience of writing. Writing on the Internet in its ephemerality is inflected by speech in diametrically opposed ways to the function of writing as sediment of living memory. I use this simple example to illustrate the way that McLuhan's presentation of the history of literacy and the shift to electric cultures invites a whole new set of explorations into changes in the nature of communication. McLuhan's analysis of communication technologies is always comparative (different national practices, different technologies) and historical.

In *The Gutenberg Galaxy* electric culture emerges from the literate world as a mutation transforming everyday attitudes and institutions into those grotesque gargoyles described by Ruskin (*GG*: 226). Gargoyles represent the grotesque imagination, which is capable of illuminating the present and accessing the unconscious of a culture. Hence, all the 'talk', Internet chatting, cell phones, email communication, is precisely this 'outering' of inner thoughts. Indeed, 'illumination' and 'anxiety' are the key effects of this new age. Because all that is hidden is shared, illumination begets 'Anxiety'. The gargoyles are the metaphors for a dialectical transformation underway, a new consciousness growing out of and totally penetrating the old.

This metamorphosis can be seen in the transformation of the child-like adolescent into the self-sufficient 'tribal' teenager. McLuhan's concern with teenagers is a theme that will increasingly highlight some of his most deterministic and exciting ideas. We might point out that the emergence of a shared youth culture is directly tied to the 'teenager' as a new demographic for the popular mass media. Yet, McLuhan would argue that it is a direct result of the internalization of technology which has produced that being known and feared, the 'TV child'.

The last passages of *The Gutenberg Galaxy* are pure science fiction. They have that grammatico-rhetorical sensibility that was very much a part of the style and satire of *The Mechanical Bride* and his best essays published throughout the 1950s. McLuhan begins to assemble a roster of romantic and gothic metaphors that will serve to define the new spaces of the present techno-logical moment. His metaphors evoke the new environment as if it were a shimmering galactic fog, an outer veil transparent and sensorial, enveloping and bewildering, a new space for which we will need to prepare, to change our thinking. As he would say in a 1959 CBC television discussion with graphic artist Harley Parker and American scholar Robert Shafer: 'But look at what is about to happen – automation, tapes, synchronized information coming from numerous directions all at once, very much like our global village in which the single line or structure seems to yield to a non-lineal complex' (*RPUM*: Appendix i: 1).

This New World, McLuhan tells us, is already here: 'we are living in a period richer and more terrible than the "Shakespearean moment"' (*GG*: 278). As opposed to point of view, the techniques of 'suspended judgement', and the collage techniques of 'anony-mous history' are part of the new perception discovered by the art and physics of the twentieth century, it is the method for seeing through to the last galaxy. The electric galaxy is a metaphor for a new consciousness and expressive culture that is organic, simul-taneous, pattern- and process-oriented, driven by the interval, acoustic and tactile, defined by the breaking down of boundaries and categories of a previous era of impersonal assembly line linearity. Electrical media create new forms of interdependence, interpenetration, interdisciplinarity and interactivity. And it is as a guide to this New World that McLuhan will become a famous and famously failed prophet. Introducing us to menacing demons and electric angels in a world of growing media conglomerations (not unlike Rabelais's giants) on a path towards total implosion, a path that is seemingly beyond the control of any one person but a trajectory that we must learn about and learn to program. It will be McLuhan's task over the next two decades to show, adopting a more forceful and rhetorical garb than previously worn, what ('the hell') is *happening*.

Conclusion

The formalism of *The Gutenberg Galaxy* enabled McLuhan to understand literacy and electric communication historically. The electronic galaxy is the culmination of changes in the way thought is distributed across space and time. This is Innis's insight and it is basic. Changes in a society's communication technologies can be understood in terms of how these reorganize and are biased toward either the space or time structures of social and economic institutions (Innis, 1951). McLuhan builds on this. Changes in a society's organizational structures have a profound effect on both our social and cultural experiences of space and time (knowledge systems, forms of culture, etc.) and also, in the first instance on our physical relations to the world. That is, McLuhan looks for homologies across different levels of society and sensory experience, both macro processes (multi-national mergers, the rise of tribal nationalisms) and micro experiences (discarnate perceptions, televisual relations). This gets translated especially in his writings of the 1960s and on, in positivistic analyses. He is interested, for example, in studying the differences between children who grew up with no television and those children reared on television.

The Gutenberg Galaxy needs to be read closely, and most of the criticisms regarding McLuhan's technological determinism stem from the later photo-collage and concrete essays. To read *The Gutenberg Galaxy* requires time but, as McLuhan said of Innis, it is worth the effort. As I have tried to show, each paragraph is a library that provides us with juxtapositions of writing which offer up profound insights into historical transitions and the modern age. What is driving change? Who is implementing and developing the technologies, choreographing the new electric events? *The Gutenberg Galaxy* never answers the question of origins because its framework is designed not so much to trace causalities as it is to show a network of forces at play. It is intended to present a community of thinkers in action, to trace the living contours of effects. The objective of the book is not to present a theory of these effects of technological change but to show a mosaic of writing about writing. Change itself is not presented as determined by any one force, technological development as we saw with his description, for example, of Gutenberg's 'invention' is complex and layered, a combination of efforts and countries, economies and technologies so that to trace things back to one causality is senseless. Hence the metaphor of the 'galaxy' refers us to a framework of fragments that encompasses a multiplicity of material forces.

Lists

Throughout *The Gutenberg Galaxy*, McLuhan formulates dialectical oppositions that are useful for describing cultural modalities and media grammars within an historical framework. While he was critical of dialectical thought for making the world into a tidy synthesized picture, he uses oppositions that emanate from the cultures and discourses he describes. His oppositions are themselves the product of literacy.

Eye	Ear
visuality	tactility
literacy	orality
neutral	magical
private	communal
nation	tribe
individuality	collectivity
private identity	corporeal identity
uniform	plural
repeatability	multiplicity
profane	sacral

real	mythic
exclusive	inclusive
mallet	mill
linear	point
sequential	simultaneous
continuous	discontinuous
disunity	unity
visual space	acoustic space
mechanical	organic/electric
internal thought	action
unconscious	conscious
point of view	field
novel	theatre
being	becoming
matching	making
diachronic	synchronic

Note

1 McLuhan often cites a favourite example, the failure of Wilbur Schramm to understand that print is his only 'criterion of reality' which is why he simply correlates children's television watching with socio-economic status (*UM*: 19).

PART III
Global Theatre

9

The Project for Understanding Media

McLuhan's project, as I have been describing it, provides a method for studying the effects of the forms of communication on cognitive functions and culture, on social relations and knowledge systems, and finally on global interactions. There is no doubt that McLuhan's work from the early 1960s onwards appears increasingly non-dialectical and often ahistorical. He begins numerous collaborations with artists and designers and his books (many of them photo-collages) are far more aphoristic and rhetorical than works of rigorous scholarship. His media studies become more performative, and his research is increasingly concerned with curriculum for the new discipline of Communication Studies, as well as for popular consumption.

While *The Gutenberg Galaxy* tells us that the term 'environment' could serve just as well as 'galaxy' to describe the worlds created by technology (*GG*: i), it is not a term that seems entirely appropriate to the book with its 'textura' of quotations, discourses and ideas. It is not until *Understanding Media* that McLuhan shifts his metaphors to focus on space as immediate environment, stressing surround and disorientation – environ – rather than distant spheres of symbolically mediated spaces and hence, temporalities. Indeed, the prose of *Understanding Media* seems decidedly more steeped in satire but less bound to a collage aesthetic of quotation and exegesis. I would argue that it is important to understand this in relation to a new intellectual format, an intellectual 'put on' that he would connect to his texts. Phillip Marchand has described the notion:

> By 'putting on' audiences and trying to outmaneuver opponents in debate, McLuhan projected a protean face of an actor, capable of assuming different expressions without being committed to any one of them. Aside from tucking in his chin before speaking, he avoided any kind of pose or set of mannerisms that would leave an audience with a well-defined impression of him. (1989: 181)

McLuhan's public performance as a media celebrity should not be read as separate from his writings. Instead, we can see those writings, like all of his works, as serving a cognitive function, connected to a pedagogical project to promote discovery, wonder, and analysis through experience. Famously, McLuhan graded his students' papers not on the basis of accurate facts or even coherent arguments but on the number of new ideas proposed. His project was to stimulate those ideas. For some, including other professors at the University of Toronto, this approach was deeply problematic, lacking in the rigorous standards that define the university as a place of higher learning committed to excellence (Marchand: 224–225). As we saw in the previous chapters, McLuhan was deeply suspicious and indeed uninterested in maintaining the 'standards of excellence' defined by an institution that he felt was deeply out of touch with the contemporary world. His famous Monday evening seminars at the Centre for Culture and Technology were set up to develop interpretations of the contemporary world in a dialogical and communal context, and to extend the interdisciplinary explorations of media analysis initiated in the 1940s at St Louis University and in the 1950s in the Communication and Culture Seminar to a living educational project at the Coach House.

Arguably McLuhan's writings and lectures through the next two decades were provocations: open-ended, experimental, sometimes maddening and other times funny, yet always aiming to produce a response. Humour, the 'gag' or punning, were central tools in these challenges. McLuhan was interested in precisely all those things that draw attention to language as play and as common culture. Eco, for whom *Finnegans Wake* also constitutes a pivotal work on the history of writing, underlines the pun's creative capacity to generate new meanings:

> The pun constitutes a forced contiguity between two or more words: sang plus sans plus glorians plus riant makes 'Sanglorians'. It is a contiguity made of reciprocal elisions, whose result is an ambiguous deformation; but even in the form of fragments, there are words that nonetheless are related to one another. This forced contiguity frees a series of possible readings – hence interpretations – which lead to an acceptance of the terms as a metaphoric vehicle of different tenors … ('Role': 73–4)

We need to read McLuhan's puns as creative engagements with the life world. This is how they were always intended. The companion book to *The Gutenberg Galaxy* was never written although there are two books that go under the title of *Understanding Media*, the second of which made him famous. Let us begin with the first incarnation, which is in many ways the more substantive of the two.

Report on Project in Understanding New Media

In 1959, McLuhan would begin work on a media literacy guide for high-school students called *Report on Project in Understanding New Media* (*RPUM*) (1960). The book was commissioned by the National Association of Educational Broadcasters (NAEB) under an Education Act (Title VII), which was overseen by the Pentagon. McLuhan was asked to develop a syllabus that would introduce Grade 11 students to contradictory effects of the media. This would eventually form the basis of *Understanding Media*; a second edition published in 1964 made McLuhan a 'household name'. The difference between the two books is striking. One is clearly a media guide in the rhetorical style of *The Mechanical Bride* minus the visuals. The report reads as a record of research questions and is a thoughtful media literacy book – it is tentative, filled with questions, exercises, histories of media technologies (typewriter, telegraph, press, film, television, photography, and so on), graphs (which are almost indecipherable) and study guides designed to create an awareness of a new environment in relation to an old environment, of technologies and art history in a national context. These are useful teaching tools. Here are some samples:

> Projects and Questions – Film (Movie)
> In view of the various cultural backgrounds of England, France, America, Russia, India and Japan, what qualities would you expect to appear most in the movies made in these countries?
> In his *Film as Art*, Rudolph Arnheim for example says that the American film-maker excels in the single shot; the Russian in montage. Why should this be?
> Why should the European, the Russian and the Japanese have regarded the film as an art from the first? Why should the English-speaking world have such difficulty in seeing popular forms of entertainment as art forms whether the movie, the comic strip, or the common advertisement? (*RPUM*: 116)

Four decades of developing theoretical frameworks and close textual analyses would probably rephrase the questions in a more nuanced and less essentialist manner but the general form of the interrogation says something to us about McLuhan's views of the media: that the same technology is not uniform but will have different effects and different kinds of interaction within different national and cultural environments. That is, the history of the cinema, like the history of media, reflects the plurality of the world. In another question he asks how the Americans sold the 'American way of life' around the globe: 'Consider the role of uniformity and repeatability as indispensable to competition and rivalry. How could competition thrive where unique expression and achievement are stressed?'

These questions are open-ended and discussion-oriented. But certainly we can anticipate how McLuhan would explicate national differences in terms of their historical relation to oral and typographic cultures, as he does in the second edition of *Understanding Media*. In his chapter on the movies, he explains his admiration of Eisenstein's work in cinema which signalled a new direction in film form (if he had seen Vertov's visual acoustics in *Man with a Movie Camera* (1929) he would have said the same thing of him). Eisenstein, as we saw in Chapter 2, initiated experiments in montage that crossed the boundaries of art and science to create new forms of cognition that retraced perceptual experience. His experiments worked against the traditional linear forms of narrative cinema that had grown out of the more print-dominated cultures of the USA where the cinema was produced according to linear models of mass production. This mode of production enabled Hollywood to sell the American way of life around the world:

> The Hollywood tycoons were not wrong in acting on the assumption that movies gave the American immigrant a means of self-fulfillment without any delay. This strategy, however deplorable in the light of the 'absolute ideal good', was perfectly in accord with film form. It meant that in the 1920s the American way of life was exported to the entire world in cans. The world eagerly lined up to buy canned dreams. The film not only accompanied the first great consumer age, but was also incentive, advertisement, and, in itself, a major commodity. Now, in terms of media study it is clear that the power of film to store information in accessible form is unrivalled. (*UM*: 291)

Russia's oral culture traditions, not to mention its mass illiteracy meant an entirely different usage of film and, indeed, the view of film as language. A relation such as we saw in *The Gutenberg Galaxy* would draw in a consideration of the development of commercial culture and the commodification of art. While the diminution of cultural production to either oral or printed culture can lead to an over-simplification and reductionist view of material processes, it is certainly a useful way to consider the relation between, for example, narrative cinema and the novel or the development of national cinematic traditions. One of the criticisms that I will take up at the end of this chapter concerns the linearity of McLuhan's overall framework, moving from orality to literacy to electricity.

In his report, McLuhan builds on the earlier ideas he developed with *Explorations* and in essays like 'Notes on the media as art forms' and the 'Classroom without walls'. He proposes new educational methods that call upon an experimental pedagogy to combine the techniques of art, encourage experimental uses of electronic media and, above all, dialogue and interaction in the classroom. In a manner that recalls Innis, he opposes the 'Gutenberg teaching machines' which he takes to be the one-way flow of information, the discouragement of discussion, the reduction of learning to books and information, what Innis called the 'useless knowledge of useful facts' ('Adult education' in *Bias*: 205). Innis, however, did not make complete generalizations about book culture as McLuhan tends to do in all his writings. The danger for Innis lies not with books *tout court* but with textbooks and the commodification of learning. As such, Innis (and this is no doubt what McLuhan admired in his thinking) warns against the loss of a humanistic education within the capitalist enterprise:

> The breaking down of ideas and the emphasis on factual information have been evident in the narrowing of professional education and of arts courses. Textbooks of systematized knowledge have been altogether too much in evidence. Courses have been carefully calculated with a view to the inclusion of all the relevant information during the three or fours years of undergraduate work. The results have been a systematic closing of students' minds. Initiative and independence have been weakened. Factual material, information, classification reflect the narrowing tendencies of the mechanization of knowledge in the minds of staffs and students. Professions become narrow and sterile. The teaching profession suffers perhaps most of all. A broad interest in the complex problems of society becomes almost impossible. (ibid.: 208)

For Innis, the links between commercial interests and universities would have disastrous consequences for intellectual freedom and for the future of the university.

McLuhan is more cautiously optimistic, believing that links between industry and university were inevitable and could in fact present important opportunities for collaboration. This is an idea he would develop more fully in *Understanding Media* and in his lectures. In the twenty-first century we would be moving into a complete transformation of education and industry, the linking of education and information. Therefore universities, like large corporations, would have to adapt to the changing environment brought about by the new media. Collaboration between artists, corporations and universities would be necessary for survival and would be inevitable. The role of media literacy, beginning in high school and developing into liberal arts programs in universities, would be to teach students how to think and question assumptions in order to both understand and indeed counter what was already out there but also to contribute to and use the media in intelligent ways.

But, like Innis, McLuhan is wary of the consumer curriculum, which works to separate teaching and learning functions. This issue is central to the 'explorations' method and to McLuhan's claim that he was first and foremost a student of media rather than a teacher. McLuhan argues that dialogue and questioning should take precedence over the learning of 'facts' and examinations based upon knowledge of facts. In the information environment facts are readily available, however, insights into the meaning of these facts are not. This is the function of the new education. Its aims are informed by Heinrich Wofflin's *Principles of Art History* (1915) which revolutionized 'the study of many matters besides art'. Wofflin was Gideon's teacher and his view that it is the effect and not the 'sensuous facts' that should be of concern were at the heart of his and McLuhan's structuralist approach. McLuhan proposes to study the physiological effects of different media. Two dimensional images 'are in effect very tactile, resonant and auditory' while three dimensional representations are primarily 'visual, pictorial, retinal – abstract and exclusive of the non-retinal'. It is precisely this first regime that Georg Von Bekesy called upon for his *Experiments in Hearing* and it is this 'field' approach that will form the basis of the new education geared at a comparative analysis of the effects of media forms (*RPUM*: 1–2)

McLuhan recommends that electronic media be utilized so that students learn to use and analyze the technologies that make up their everyday realities. He suggests that the new education should be guided by the artists of the past ten decades who anticipated the electronic environment and its effects on patterns of apprehending space and time. The English Romantics gave imagination a role in the apprehension of the natural world through the creation metaphors, which functioned as forms of knowledge. Thus, Nature was invented as it was transformed into a landscape in the 'ceaseless quest for the inclusive and integral image'. Since Poe and Cézanne, artists have been creating cognitive forms that involve all the senses in a 'dance' of forms, involving audiences in the production of meanings. These artists do not speak to their readers but through them.

Of course these ideas on pedagogy and media frustrated those consumer-oriented audiences, but it also challenged them to reconsider the role and function of art as cognition. Art, as it came to be defined as avant-garde resistance, stood in relation to everyday life but also apart from it and sought a new function that writers such as Baudelaire and Flaubert would define as sociological. McLuhan argues that education in the future, if it is to be relevant, must utilize the same cognitive models developed by such artists. We should do away with guided tours through books and replace these with tours through the city. Exploration, participation, and dialogue should take place 'in a total field of unified awareness', which is an aesthetic engagement with pedagogy and culture. In short, 'the medium is the message'.

This neologism, perhaps McLuhan's most famous and indeed controversial one after 'global village', was adapted from an Ashley Montagu lecture called 'The method is the message' (Carpenter, 2001: 244). Régis Debray has related it to Cochin's less famous idea that 'method engenders doctrine' (1996: 101). But it is an idea that was part of McLuhan's thinking from the start: from the work of Richards, from the modernist artists and writers he so admired (ranging from Cézanne to Eisenstein) and from the history of mentalities carried out by scholars like Giedion and Innis. The 'medium is the message' is the foundation for the experimental pedagogy he was proposing: 'I have insisted that any new structure for codifying experience and of moving information, be it the alphabet or photography, has the power of imposing its structural character and assumptions upon all levels of our private and social lives, even without benefit of concepts or of conscious acceptance' (*RPUM*: x). Thus, the new curriculum is fundamentally a media literacy – one that seeks to make students conscious of the invisible structures shaping their perceptions, engaging students in their perceptions to produce ideas about the world, locating homologies at various levels of experience – cognitive, cultural, political. This would become the first chapter of the second edition of *Understanding Media* and has become a short-hand for McLuhan's technological determinism.

Indeed, McLuhan's language of imposition comes close to sounding like a simple technological determinism only if we read it in isolation from the kinds of contextualizing questions around national identity and multiculturalism (an awareness produced both through museum culture and the media) that he proposes in the rest of the syllabus. The changes being brought about by these new media are the themes developed throughout *The Gutenberg Galaxy*. McLuhan uses the metaphor of war that American governments may more readily understand, such as: '[W]e are living through intense nuclear bombardment from within our own cultures, we have achieved almost total clairvoyance of our own condition and of our debts to earlier ages'. Change itself is the matrix of this new world replete with an 'all-at-onceness' experience that demands a new syllabus: gone are individual subjects, these are replaced with multidisciplinary explorations driven by the 'sensitivity of the greatest artists'. All boundaries are broken down: not only the lines between subjects, but those physical structures that distinguished teaching and learning, producer and consumer, art and nature, and finally he slips in 'culture and commerce' (*RPUM*: xi).

This last dissolution between 'culture and commerce' would seem to contradict his call for a non-commodifiable curriculum as well as his use of modernist artists from the Romantics on, as models of exploration. These artists did not simply 'explore' but had as a project (as McLuhan well knew) a resistance to instrumental (i.e., commodifiable) culture. It is no doubt this area of the political economy of culture that will come to present many of his critics, on both the left and right, with the most difficulties. We will see this lack of political commitment in McLuhan's simultaneous involvement with artists and business executives as evidence of his belief in a higher unity of the different spheres of cultural experience in the electric cosmology of integrated experience.

For the young who have been brought up on television, these distinctions no longer existed according to McLuhan. There is no point in trying to adjust to these changes slowly: 'We simply have to know, and understand, exactly what is happening'. In order to do this we need a new curriculum based on the insights of art and geared toward media studies. McLuhan ends his address by telling the broadcasters who had commissioned his study that 'we must all become creative artists in order to cope with even the banalities of daily life' (*RPUM*: xiv). The artists that McLuhan will come to collaborate with throughout the rest of his career are the multi-disciplinary artists and graphic designers like Harley Parker and Quentin Fiore. In fact, he could be said to have recognized that designers (being artists who merge culture and commerce) would be the central artistic players of the twenty-first century as Hal Foster's *Design and Crime* (2002) well testifies. McLuhan did realize that someone would have to design the new information environments that were coming into existence. As he would write in his later collage collaboration, *Culture is Our Business*, artists create the 'anti-environments' to make visible the invisible environment and as a means of 'adjustment and perception' (1970: 3).

The curriculum that McLuhan's *Report* was proposing is aesthetic and creative, driven by an imaginative or cognitive (the same thing for him) engagement with the real world outside the classroom. While McLuhan distinguishes between the world inside and outside the classroom (hence his call for a classroom without walls), he does not distinguish between real and imaginary, since he argues that the whole world became art the instant Sputnik produced an image of the globe. This notion of the collapse of nature into art would have an impact on thinkers like Baudrillard and Virilio who develop notions of simulation for describing an experience of dislocation in the mediatized world (Genosko, 2001). Of course, all of these insights come to McLuhan from different sources: the Romantic philosophers from Nietzsche to Heidegger, writers like Flaubert and Baudelaire, Lewis, Pound and Joyce, and of course Eisenstein. Thus, while McLuhan's neologisms may have seemed to some offhand and superficial, a great deal of work had gone into his curricula.

Report on Project in Understanding New Media suggests a pedagogical project that would be more appropriate to university undergraduates rather than high school students. Its experimental approach to media studies presented sophisticated and open-ended approaches to analysis of the media as an environment. The syllabus was read and ridiculed on the Floor of the House of Representatives and printed in the Congressional Record (Carpenter, 2001: 253). In other words, the whole project was shelved.

Like *The Mechanical Bride*, this project was the culmination of many years of teaching. In the Leavisian tradition McLuhan's courses were concerned with the 'analysis of the present scene' (*Letters*: 157). One of the criticisms of his report by James Russel of the National Educational Association's Educational Policies Committee complained that McLuhan had failed to include a serious consideration of the effects of computers in the classroom, which the distinction of print and non-print communications does not cover. To this McLuhan would respond:

> Post-digital computation returns to the pre-digital just as post-literate education returns to the dialogue. However, what the computer means in education is this. As information movement speeds up, information levels rise in all areas of mind and society, and the result is that any subject of knowledge becomes substitutable for any other subject. That is to say, any and all curricula are obsolete with regard to subject matter. All that remains to study are the media themselves, as forms, as modes ever creating new assumptions and hence new objectives. (in Stearn, 1967: 159)

One can see why the NAEB did not take kindly to McLuhan's report since he was essentially arguing for a radically revised programme that would not describe the impact of new media on education but insist that the new media are the subject matter to be taught.

McLuhan's media literacy report was eventually significantly revised and published almost twenty years later in a book co-authored with his son Eric McLuhan and Kathryn Hutcheon called *The City as Classroom: Understanding Language and Media* (1977), a title that references the earlier essay co-written with Carpenter, 'Classroom without walls'. *The City as Classroom* was rewritten in a prose that was far more accessible than the *Report*, while continuing to emphasize what is stressed so emphatically in *The Mechanical Bride*: the need to give students the analytic tools to understand the culture that is everywhere around them. The Introduction to *The City as Classroom* asks, 'What's in a school?' This is not a rhetorical question but in McLuhanesque fashion asks students to consider the school 'as a place of work', to analyze the meaning of work and of its placement, its layout and interior design within the architecture of the school (1977 : 84). They go on to ask:

> Does the community want you to be separated from the work force? Ask local leaders in business and education. Could you join the work force before you reach school leaving age? Contact your local labor

union leaders and ask for their opinion of the school-leaving age in your area. Can you discover the reasons behind the legislation? Ask your vice-principal to explain the relation between school funding and school attendance.

Do you and your (classmates) … regard the classroom as a kind of prison? … Do the days of your school life seem like 'doing time' until you are eligible for the labor market? (*CC*: 60)

The City as Classroom investigates the relation between the room where classes are held and the experience of learning. It asks students to hold a class in the teacher's lounge, to consider the design of desks and chairs, the idea and function of rows.

This book, like all of McLuhan's work published in the 1970s, received very little critical response. I would argue that such a book is still, if not more, relevant today. If as Hal Foster maintains, the meeting of art and commerce has resulted in a perversion of the avant-garde reconciliation of art and life under the banner of design, then, arguably, there is more need than ever before for a critical media-based pedagogy:

> Beware of what you wish, runs one moral of modernism as seen from the present, because it may come true – in perverse form. Thus, to take only the chief example, the old project to reconnect Art and Life, endorsed in different ways by Art Nouveau, the Bauhaus, and many other movements, was eventually accomplished, but according to the spectacular dictates of the culture industry, not the liberatory ambitions of the avant-garde. And a primary form of this perverse reconciliation in our time is design. (Foster, 2002: 19)

Apart from its generalizations, and its negation of local specificity, Foster's argument is difficult to resist and one needs to situate McLuhan's programme historically – that is, before the rise of 'designer everything'. Although Foster includes McLuhan in his indictment of designer culture (ibid.: 24), one could contend that a text like *The City as Classroom* may well provide one form of critical consciousness in the present environment. This is doubly so since its pedagogical programme is directed towards the ideology of designed things in such a way as to engender an historical awareness of form in the Innisean sense of open humanistic inquiry.

10

The Electronic
Call Girl

The second edition of *Understanding Media*: The Extensions of
Man (1964) is far less a work of experimental collage and rhetorical juxtaposition, far less encyclopedic in its approach than *The
Gutenberg Galaxy*. This was a direct consequence of McLuhan's
editors at McGraw-Hill who refused the use of quotations for
anything more than argumentative exposition. As we saw with
The Gutenberg Galaxy and *The Mechanical Bride*, the use of
quotation was a strategy to create interfaces with existing
research and ideas. Block quotation rather than paraphrasing
ideas served to foreground historical frameworks and philosophical sources in a way that preserved their discourse and thus
served to create a more heterogeneous and encyclopedic textu-
ality. This absence is what makes the second edition of
Understanding Media seem far less historical in its approach.
While the second edition does not have the scholarly depth and
breadth of *The Gutenberg Galaxy*, it is a far more readerly text.
Having sold over 100,000 copies when it was first published and
now in its tenth printing, it is without doubt McLuhan's most
influential book.

Understanding Media was edited to be more fluid, accessible,
and popular. This accessibility was something that McLuhan
wanted and he jokingly referred to the book as 'The Electronic
Call Girl', an expression he used to describe television (Marchand,

1989: 169). Unlike *The Mechanical Bride*, the book engaged with living culture, with a culture that was fleeting and ephemeral, but as with *The Mechanical Bride* it was produced by the same patriarchal capitalist culture. *The Mechanical Bride*'s engagement with advertising was an easy task, McLuhan maintained, since the mechanical landscape was readily visible in the context of the electric environment. Understanding the 'Extensions of Man', the sub-title of *Understanding Media*, was a far more difficult task that required the tools and insights of art, as he had noted in his *Report*. These were tools McLuhan had been using since the late 1940s yet they would become increasingly more apparent in his artistic collaborations and concrete essays – the first of which were the playful graphics of *The Medium is the Massage: An Inventory of Effects* (1967) with Quentin Fiore.

McLuhan's writings need to be situated in terms of their aesthetic and pedagogical aims. Rather than providing an answer to, or a grand theory of, the media, his work provides a set of tools for making media grammars visible, especially their spatio-temporal assumptions. While *The Gutenberg Galaxy* was a work of exploration in this regard, *Understanding Media*, as McLuhan himself has said, needs to be read just as it was first conceived – as a proposal, an exercise book, and a practical guide. Both books are influenced by television – process-oriented, open-ended, continuous and fragmented. Yet while McLuhan insisted that his work does no more than provide a framework for examining the media, he presented various neologisms for discerning their different properties, which are by now familiar to most students: media hot and cool, media reversal, narcosis and hallucination, hybridity and media as translators, implosion. These ideas are presented in the first part of *Understanding Media* which culminates in 'The nemesis of creativity' where McLuhan makes the case that art will provide some 'immunity' against the technological environment that has overtaken the world.

Flows

McLuhan's historical periodization of communication is informed by the shift from orality to literacy, and the present-day environment is interpreted as a return to oral culture but with all the attendant characteristics of electricity: decentralization, implosion, outering, instantaneous connection. As he indicated at the beginning of *The Gutenberg Galaxy* and reiterates in *Understanding Media*, we cannot understand the new electric environment in terms of 'flow'. Electricity does not produce a materiality that runs like water:

> Most scientists are quite aware that since we have acquired some knowledge of electricity it is not possible to speak of atoms as pieces of matter. Again, as more is known about electrical 'discharges' and energy, there is less and less tendency to speak of electricity as a thing that 'flows' like water through a wire, or is 'contained' in a battery. Rather, the tendency is to speak of electricity as painters speak of space; namely, that it is a variable condition that involves the special positions of two or more bodies.
>
> There is no longer any tendency to speak of electricity as 'contained' in anything. Painters have long known that objects are not contained in space, but that they generate their own spaces. It was the dawning awareness of this in the mathematical world a century ago that enabled Lewis Carroll, the Oxford mathematician, to contrive *Alice in Wonderland*, in which times and spaces are neither uniform nor continuous, as they had seemed to be since the arrival of Renaissance perspective. As for the speed of light, that is merely the speed of total causality. (*UM*: 347–348)

The metaphor of flow is not a productive one for McLuhan because it suffers from the kind of functionalism he detected in Wiener's cybernetic theories. It gives the impression that communication is linear and that receivers are passive receptacles of content. Raymond Williams, for example, has used this notion to discuss the experience of television as an incessant one-way flow of messages that dissolve into one another (1974: 86–96).

Williams is responding to the way the medium was developed as a capitalist media along the lines of radio. Theorists of globalization or deterritorialization like Arjun Appadurai, Manuel Castells or Gilles Deleuze and Félix Guattari have used this term to describe the movements of people and information from different parts of the world. It is perhaps ironic that the man who made the global village a globally understood metaphor was afraid that the metaphor would hearken back to a rationalist conception of linear space, a conception and metaphor which, as physics has shown, is an inaccurate understanding of electricity as a container and one-way movement. Thus, McLuhan prefers the painterly connotations of spatial terms like 'field' or Lewis Carroll's construction (mathematically correct) of warped spaces. These impressed McLuhan precisely because they are discontinuous, not uniform, reflecting the heterogeneity of the cultures of the world.

In this sense Deleuze and Guattari's notion of 'rhizomatic' spaces and nomadic thought offers the metaphor that comes closest to the properties of McLuhan's acoustic space. Rhizomes express multiplicity without unity, discontinuity and the interval between two singularities. It is the resonant interval that allows McLuhan to claim that one could study Shakespeare to understand modern technology and get a fairly complete picture. Who but McLuhan and the advertising industry would juxtapose Shakespeare (or Plato) and television? It is precisely such juxtapositions that often infuriated McLuhan's critics and which also make his writings uniquely insightful and historically grounded. McLuhan does not produce a detailed history of technology, as, say, Elizabeth Einstein does in her brilliant study of the printing press. However, he forces us to relate all new innovations to older technologies; that is, he insists that obsolescence and novelty are intricately tied together. As he explored in *The Gutenberg Galaxy*, Shakespeare was writing on the cusp of a transition to print and therefore was able to comment upon its formal effects. For example, in *Romeo and Juliet*:

> But soft! What light through yonder window breaks?
> It speaks and yet says nothing. (9)

There are many more such examples that McLuhan playfully scatters throughout *Understanding Media* to foreground this early awareness of the limits and new epistemologies introduced by printing. Similarly, we are living through a transition created by electronic media, and because of this, forms of communication are once more visible. Thus, McLuhan's preference for fields over flows is prefaced on the importance of history in any analysis of technology.

'Technology is Explicitness'

The insight that 'the medium is the message' is of course not McLuhan's, but the neologism encapsulates and packages the approach of so many thinkers into a slogan that challenged established hermeneutical practices. McLuhan sees this approach across numerous disciplines from art history and philosophy to physics and experimental medicine. For example, Hans Selye's stress theory of disease deals with 'the total environmental situation' and proposes this method to study the media: 'not only the "content" but the medium and the cultural matrix within which the particular medium operates' (*UM*: 11). What McLuhan offers is fundamental to any critical understanding of the media. It is to see the media not only in the context of communication, but as environments that have an effect regardless of the message they carry.

The first example that McLuhan uses is that of electric light, and this is the example that Umberto Eco (1967) has criticized. McLuhan's choice is unfortunate for Eco because electric light is not a medium like the telegraph or television. It is 'a medium without a message'. It is the electric light example that leads McLuhan to write:

> This fact, characteristic of all media, means that the 'content' of any medium is always just another medium. The content of writing is speech, just as the written word is the content of print, and print is the content of the telegraph. If it is asked, 'What is the content of speech?', it is necessary to say, 'It is an actual process of thought, which is in itself non-verbal'. (*UM*: 8)

Most media analysts are focused upon content and use, which like 'the juicy piece of meat that the burglar carries to distract the watchdog of the mind' distracts from the formal environment and its effects on our bodies (ibid.: 18). McLuhan's choice to study electricity is strategic, for electric light, as several recent studies of night-time economies have shown, lends an awareness of how a medium of communication creates actions and forms of association, whether this is 'brain surgery or night baseball' (ibid.: 8). He wishes us to see the technological media as staples like cotton or wood. In so doing, we become aware of how such staples are both tied to global economies and to the way we experience culture – the study of communication is the study of the 'total situation'.

Eco criticizes McLuhan for not distinguishing between the channel, the code, and the message. Yet the semiologists forget to include the medium and the situation in their analysis of the code (Debray, 1976: 70). McLuhan is concerned with effects while Eco is interested in meaning. If McLuhan does not distinguish between 'cornflakes or Cadillacs', it is because he is concerned with how the technological mode of production reorganized human relations, association and patterns of experience. That is: 'What we are considering here, however, are the psychic and social consequences of the designs or patterns as they amplify or accelerate existing processes. For the "message" of any medium or technology is the change of scale or pace or pattern that it introduces into human affairs' (*UM*: 8). In the early 1960s, the General Electric Company had not yet discovered that it was in the same business as AT&T and McLuhan rightly predicted that it would. Ultimately the example of electric light is pedagogical because it provides an invaluable instance of how people fail to study media at all' (ibid.: 9).

There is also a mystical aspect to McLuhan's choice of light, which underlies his utopian view of the electric galaxy as a return to orality and a mystical unity. He cautions, in a manner not unlike Bergson, in a letter to Jacques Maritain written in 1969: 'Electric information environments being utterly ethereal foster the illusions of the world as spiritual substance. It is now a reasonable facsimile of the mystical body, a blatant manifestation of the Anti-Christ. After all, the Prince of this World is a very great electric engineer'. On the other hand, he writes 'we are doing these things to ourselves' and should therefore not simply submit to them 'unconsciously or irrationally'. Moreover, McLuhan believes that the instantaneousness of information and the very high speeds at which things occur may enable new forms of pattern recognition for the first time in human history (*Letters*: 370–1).

One of McLuhan's contributions to communication studies is a consciousness of space as produced, of time as living culture, of culture as living time. He drew attention to the architectural space of the school in the city, but also to the city as an educational space not simply filled with rhetoric that is a new form of education, but constructed by it. Theorists of space from Henri Lefebvre to Edward Soja share this insight. McLuhan has focused attention on the background and the spaces that both shape and are shaped by everyday experiences. While he recognized that the different uses of technologies will produce different kinds of representations, different spatial and temporal configurations, he is ultimately not interested in how technologies are used but in the uses that technologies create. As he would explain to one of his staunchest critics, the neurologist Jonathan Miller:

> What I am saying is what Wordsworth said in his phrase: 'the child is the father of the man'. This seemed like a wild statement at the time. All he meant was that youthful environments shape adult attitudes. All I am saying is that any product or innovation creates both service and disservice environments which reshape human attitudes. These service and disservice environments are always invisible until they have been superseded by new environments.
>
> When we last met, you seemed to concur as a neurologist with the fact that inputs are never what we experience, since any input is always modified by the entire sensorium as well as by the cultural bias of the individual. (*Letters*: 404)

Unfortunately, Miller did not see the nuance in this argument and wrote a very critical book on McLuhan's ideas, which he saw as flimsy and chaotic. While Miller misreads important aspects of McLuhan's thinking (not least television is a hot medium), he nevertheless raises one important question when he locates a central weakness in McLuhan's research programme. McLuhan, he claims, does not reference the crucial debate between Noam Chomsky and Benjamin Lee Whorf with regards to the biological or cultural basis of language (1971: 110). McLuhan was certainly influenced by Whorf's writings as well as Dorothy Lee's observations on the influence of language on experience. He was also interested in the machinations of the brain and in neurophilosophy before it was a field of study. As his comments above make clear, he would not see Chomsky and Whorf in opposition but rather as thinkers working on the different environments, 'the entire sensorium as well as the cultural bias' that make up the human landscape. Thus, guns and automobiles provide examples of technologies that have imposed themselves on space, transforming cities into highways, boundaries into prisons. Embedded in technologies are forms of power that are never simply neutral but are imbued with the ideological contexts they grew out of (*UM*: 11). Fundamentally, language is architectural – it is both a product of physical bodies and an environment in which we live.

Cool

The difference between low and high definition media was one that McLuhan had introduced in his *Report on a Project in Understanding New Media*. In the second edition of the guide he popularizes and extends the concept of hot and cool media. It is expressly because McLuhan sees all media as environmental that he develops a taxonomy of 'hot' and 'cool' media to describe their meteorological effects on our bodies. These are categories that he gets from Eastern modes of thought and from vernacular characterizations of jazz (the brassy big bands of the 1920s were said to be 'hot baby' while the small improvisational groups of the 1950s are 'cool man'). A hot medium like radio is distinguished from a cool one like the telephone because of the way 'it extends one single sense in "high definition"'. This *gestalt* theory of the media enables McLuhan to set up categories according to which each media either provides a great deal of 'high definition' information requiring very little participation on the part of the audience in terms of filling in the missing information, or 'low definition' requiring the audience to complete the message. McLuhan is able to set up a series of oppositions that are discursive probes rather than empirical categories: the photograph (high/hot) and the cartoon (low/cool), the lecture (high/hot) and the seminar (low/cool), the Waltz ('a hot, fast mechanical dance suited to the industrial time in its moods of pomp and circumstance') and the Twist ('a cool involved and chatty form of improvised gesture'), movie (high/hot) and television (low/cool), and so on (*UM*: 27).

These characteristics would enter into a common lexicon in McLuhan's media grammars to popularize his writings, as the anthology *McLuhan: Hot and Cool* (1967), edited by Gerald

Stearn, would illustrate. But as concepts they remain among his least developed and confusing. They are set up to describe the electric age – 'we of the TV age are cool' – and intended to provide evidence of a general movement toward greater immersion, involvement and coolness in the electric galaxy. Yet if this were true, the question arises (one that first time readers inevitably pose) as to how colour or high definition television could be read as cool? Or why radio, which uses only one sense, is more involving than television? The same goes for home entertainment units with surround sound or new environmental forms of entertainment like 3D or Imax cinema that are high definition but part of the electric galaxy. Often McLuhan's use of these categories is crude and can lead to the kind of functionalism he sought to challenge in his earlier critique of terms like 'mass communication'. Moreover, he takes the concept of media environment to embarrassing extremes with passages like:

> We are certainly coming within conceivable range of a world automatically controlled to the point where we could say, 'Six hours less radio in Indonesia next week or there will be a great falling off in literary attention'. Or, 'We can program twenty more hours of TV in South Africa next week to cool down the tribal temperature raised by radio last week'. Whole cultures could now be programmed to keep their emotional climate stable in the same way that we have begun to know something about maintaining equilibrium in the commercial economies of the world. (*UM*: 28)

It is difficult to simply attribute these kinds of comments to McLuhan's rhetorical approach because they reflect a growing positivism in his writings of the 1960s and the 1970s. Such statements provide an important warning to the medium theorists who forget about content and about the specificities of place, global power and local resistances.

The consequences of ignoring the content of the media in analysis are just as serious as ignoring the technological basis of the media. For those involved in analyzing media imperialism and for those of us who are raising children (I would argue girls, in particular), the changes in modes of media delivery cannot be divorced from the content of the images. McLuhan's 'blind spot' (Kroker, 1984) is not only political economy but also the actual content of images, as Eco posits, which do in fact carry effects around such things as identity formation and notions of history and truth. Michael Moore's intelligent film, *Bowling for Columbine* (2002), mounts a provocative and convincing analysis of the effects of the American media on violent crimes, arguing that the news media and the government help to create a society of fearful citizens.

McLuhan's reactionary assertions contradict many of the other ideas he presents in the book: the conviction that national boundaries are breaking down, that electric media are producing interdependence and new forms of sympathetic intercommunication that are 'tribal' and local rather than national. McLuhan's insight that the new context in which the unconscious is becoming conscious and in which 'people declare their beings totally' is antithetical to a language of imposition and control that we find in the passage above.

Interface/Intermedia

Understanding Media continues to be unique and highly original because of its explorations of the relations between different media technologies. Following Innis, McLuhan locates homologies between modes of transportation and the communications media that grew out of them, as structural social organizations of space in political and economic life. For example, McLuhan sees the railway as a reflection of a typographic mentality and as a national container. Thus, Québec separatism arises out of the electric age. A new audile-tactile experience of the electric grid 'would permit Québec to leave the Canadian union in a way quite inconceivable under the regime of the railways. The railways require a uniform political and economic space. On the other hand, airplane and radio permit the utmost discontinuity and diversity in spatial organization' (*UM*: 36). McLuhan's homologies are always stimulating. We could analyze the new local movements that, as Castells has put it, transform the previous slogan 'act locally, think globally' into 'act globally, think locally' in terms of the Internet's capacity to create new political grassroots within a global configuration (2001). McLuhan also discerns an important development in identity formation. While nation-states cannot withstand the pressures of electric media, he maintains that tribal identities will multiply. The new 'global embrace' enabled by electric media will lead to an experience of both homogeneity and of difference. We should always bear in mind, however, that McLuhan's homologies reveal important relationalities enabled by technologies, yet social processes cannot be reduced to media technologies, which must remain indeterminate and fundamental, as he argued convincingly in *Gutenberg Galaxy*.

When McLuhan moves into the public sphere in the mid-1960s, he will often use homologies to make proclamations that are reductive and undialectical: 'the telegraph created the civil war' which is perhaps where his 'charlatanesque' reputation originated (Interview in *Understanding McLuhan*, CD-ROM). It is important to recall that his methodology is dedicated to a phenomenology of the media. Just as with the natural environment, he sees the media in terms of movements that create stress and, when they are pushed to their limit, produce breaks and reversals. He attributes the idea of reversal to many sources, from the *I Ching* to Aquinas's principle of complementarity inherent in all created forms. McLuhan would cite Aquinas's *Summa*: 'And therefore in the preceding time, by which anything is moved towards a form, it is supported by the opposite form; and in the final instant of its time, which is the first instant' (*Letters*: 371). It is Joyce's *Finnegans Wake* that would congeal the notion of reversal around communications media most brilliantly for McLuhan.

Joyce would take up the idea of complementarity in Aquinas and in the writings of Italian Renaissance philosopher Giordanova Bruno, who maintained that opposites, when pushed to their extremes, will become indistinguishable and unified, so that hot and cold for example will come to be one in the same. Joyce gives the reader 'a set of multi-leveled puns on the reversal by which Western man enters his tribal, or Finn, cycle once more, following the track of the old Finn, but wide awake this time as we re-enter tribal night' (*UM*: 35). The last sentence in *Finnegans Wake* returns to complete the first sentence of the book so that the reader is invited to begin again. Here Joyce was playing with Vico's concept of 'ricorso' which is not simply a return but always a new return, a new retelling. Perhaps more than the heretic Bruno, it was Vico's philosophy of history that Joyce appropriated for his treatise on the history of writing, which he explores through the dreaming mind. The reader who has gone through the book will begin again but with a new experience that will determine the way she makes her way through the second reading. There is no sense of a return to an origin, nor of the circle but of the spiral of time where there is no beginning or end.

Vico's periodization is cyclical rather than linear, moving through three main stages in theocracy, aristocracy and democracy. At the end of the third stage after a period of destruction there is a 'ricorso' to the first in a never-ending cycle of change. *Finnegans Wake* postulates this return to a tribal consciousness but with all the consciousness of what has come before. This non-linear structure is typical of oral societies, in the Hebrew or Eastern mode of thought where problem and resolution are tackled as one and the same thing. 'The entire message is then traced and retraced, again and again, on the rounds of a concentric spiral with seeming redundancy. One can stop anywhere after the first few sentences and have the full message'. Frank Lloyd Wright's design for the Guggenheim is based on a spiral that is an expression of the electric age 'in which a concentric pattern is imposed by the instant quality, and overlay in depth, of electric speed'. It is the concentric as an infinite intersection of planes that is necessary for insight and absolutely essential to the study of the media since 'no medium has its meaning or existence alone but only in constant interplay with other media' (*UM*: 26).

In this way McLuhan does not separate different media but rather seeks to understand them in terms of whole networks of obsolescences, absorptions and hybrid energies. All media come in pairs with one acting as the content of the other. The usefulness of the electric light as an example is that because it has no content, students of media can observe the way it transforms the structures of time and space, work and society. They will come to understand the 'form of power that is in all media to reshape any lives they touch' (ibid.: 52). All other media are hybrid, they are the result of a meeting which produces 'a moment of freedom and release from the ordinary trance and numbness imposed by them on our senses' (ibid.: 55). The interface between two different media was pioneered by artists such as Dickens, Shaw, Eliot, Joyce, Eisenstein, the Marx Brothers, Chaplin, and many more, who were able to produce new forms of entertainment and art. It often takes a great artist to anticipate the hybrid created by the clash of cultures, which takes place often during wars and migrations. The new cultural mixes are produced more fundamentally by the electric fusion of Eastern and Western modes of awareness, the meeting of literate and oral cultures. The effect of literacy on oral cultures is far less complex than the meeting of oral cultures and literacy. McLuhan compares the difference to fission versus fusion (ibid.: 50).

McLuhan will use this idea to preface his account of the electronic implosion of the material universe. There is not an information explosion but rather an implosion whereby the material world is translated into information. Electric speed creates new forms of interconnectivity around the world and in all forms of learning. The transportation theory of communication (Shannon–Weaver model) is rejected by McLuhan in favour of a model of communication that interprets media messages in terms of translation and therefore transformation of experience: 'All media are active metaphors in their power to translate experience into new forms'. Words, as a primary 'technology of explicitness' (????: 57) to use Lyman Bryson's phrase, translate immediate sensory experience into our 'uttered or outered senses'. McLuhan sees a trend whereby every day more and more of ourselves is being translated into the form of information, moving 'toward a technological extension of consciousness' (ibid.: 60). While this extension does contain a utopian kernel, it also makes servo-mechanisms out of all those processed by it.

Media as Disease

Part I of *Understanding Media* outlines the overall framework and general ideas that will inform McLuhan's readings of the different technologies in the second half of the book. He relies on a medical paradigm, Selye's stress theory of disease, to theorize the impact of the media as a metamorphosis akin to a disease. The first symptom of this new electric environment, which is the result of the extension of the human nervous system is numbness and narcosis. Just as Werner Heisenberg is influenced by Chinese philosophy and medicine, so Selye is interested in a total and inclusive approach to the field of sickness. McLuhan interprets the effects of technologies by which we amplify our senses as a huge 'collective surgery' which has infected the whole social body:

> For in operating on society with a new technology, it is not the incised area that is most affected. The area of impact and incision is numb. It is the entire system that is changed. The effect of radio is visual, the effect of the photo is auditory. Each new impact shifts the ratios among all the senses. (*UM*: 64)

McLuhan sees the electric environment as a homeostatic system. According to Selye's theory, any physical extension is an attempt to maintain equilibrium. They regard any technological extension as an 'auto-amputation'. In the midst of the electric environment, we numb our central nervous system when it is extended 'or we will die'. The new media support an awareness of others and of social responsibility. They compel commitment and participation through their creation of Anxiety, for in 'the electric age we wear all mankind as our skin' (ibid.: 47). The Australian artist Stelarc has produced a performance based on this idea. He has created a programme that enables viewers in another country to touch parts of his body on a computer screen that activates muscle stimulations. He performs movements (over a period of hours) based on the touch of others around the world.

There is an underlying contradiction in McLuhan's account of the electric environment. On the one hand, we live in an age of anxiety, an age of boredom and apathy. We have passed through the different stages of alarm, resistance and exhaustion that accompany any disease or life stress. Yet this age is also characterized by a consciousness of the unconscious, by an outering and a need to have people 'declare their beings totally' (ibid.: 5). We are involved with each other as never before and what is needed is a 'deep faith that concerns the ultimate harmony of all being' (ibid.: 5–6). As he states to Maritain, we cannot be fooled into believing the electric media to be harmonizing and yet we have produced these technologies and we need to understand how they work on us. It is important to bear in mind that despite McLuhan's stated objectivity, there is a 'profound faith' driving his teleology. This profound faith rests not only with the technology but with the artist.

The Future of Art

McLuhan often cites Wyndham Lewis's famous dictum that the 'artist is always engaged in writing a detailed history of future because he is the only person aware of the nature of the present' (*UM*: 65). Artists are able to perceive the effects of technologies decades before they have transformed the environment. Art may prove to provide protection against shifts in sensory ratios, against numbness and narcosis, by foregrounding the structures and perceptual modalities that technologies produce. The electric media have, however, caught up with the artist and perform the same function of making structures visible, enabling integrated instant and total field awareness. With our central nervous system numbed, we have become aware for the first time of technology as an extension of our physical bodies. The electric media are self-reflexive and make the technological supports visible. This insight is more visible today than it was in the 1960s. If McLuhan were alive today, he would note (as many have) the way in which the media (television, the Internet, multimedia) have incorporated all those avant-garde techniques of the modern period (from the Romantics on). Lev Manovich has argued that the avant-garde techniques that came into being at the dawn of the computer are today's software. He has proposed, in a manner that builds productively on McLuhan's work, that the content of the new media are the old media, in particular the media innovations of the historical avant-garde of 1920s (the films of Dziga Vertov) have become the basis and metaphors for today's software (Manovich, 1999). Thus the new media are 'meta-media' or 'post-media'. McLuhan would argue that all media are meta-media, all media are created through interfaces, all media have for their content older media. Moreover, Eisenstein (McLuhan was not familiar with Vertov's films) and the Russian avant-garde who influenced McLuhan's thinking on the media were influenced by Joyce and by the Symbolists of the previous century. It would not be the 1920s that McLuhan would point to but the discovery of electromagnetic waves in the eighteenth century that would be a founding moment in the history of the new perceptions pivotal to electric media. McLuhan would agree with Manovich that the present context for new media is different. These are integrated and interconnected in a way previously unknown and do require a new kind of media theory (Manovich, 2001: 48).

This is not to say that because 'our technology is ahead of its time' that we do not need artists. Rather, McLuhan argues that the artist has moved from 'the ivory tower' to the 'control tower' and should be trusted to chart the course for society. Artists generate forms of knowledge that may help to guide society: 'The artist is the man in any field, scientific or humanistic, who grasps the implications of his actions and of new knowledge in his own time. He is the man of integral awareness' (*UM*: 65). Experimental art can give us the precise specifications of psychic violence to come from technologies; art can protect us by serving as a warning system and social conscience needed to navigate the electric environment.

McLuhan also speculates on the function of the intellectual who will move into 'the role of command and into the service of production' as everything is translated into information and higher education becomes a necessity for everyday life. He maintains that this liaison and mediating role between old and new forms of power has always been a function of the intelligentsia (ibid.: 37). These words were written before McLuhan's rise to fame. When he became Canada's 'intellectual comet', many viewed him as a 'sell out', lecturing to advertising executives and the corporate elite. We know that his role as a public intellectual and media guru did in fact have a far more 'radical' intent. McLuhan confessed to his closest friends that he was on a mission from God and that his 'spreading the word' was all part of a grand scheme, which, in the end did not treat his message very well (Carpenter, 2001: 256).

11
Murder by Television

Rebel without a Cause (1955) dramatizes the sudden visibility of middle-class teenagers and a concomitant concern over the media in 1950s' North America. The story-line synopsis by director Nicholas Ray was inspired by an actual case study from Robert Lindner's 1944 book of the same title. It was about a delinquent teenage psychopath in the post-war years. Ray's film is set in the suburbs of LA and features that icon of cool, James Dean. One pivotal scene that is particular to Ray's film features Jim's (Dean) ineffectual father asleep in front of a blank, flickering television. The image comes to stand for the moral vacuum and inevitable dissolution of the nuclear family. A modern sensibility crystallized in the escapism and speed of the automobile and, by extension, the empty consumerism of television is expressed in *Rebel*'s death drive as teens find entertainment by driving to the edge of a cliff and sometimes off it. The tragic irony that Dean would die that same year in an horrible car crash was not lost on J.G. Ballard nor on Andy Warhol whose writings and art works delved into this intersection of television, consumerism, and the car crash so endemic to that drive for perfection, that 'mechanical bride' through which men transcend the limits of corporeality for the sake of it.

Unlike Ballard or Warhol, McLuhan's interpretation of this context, and especially of the teenager, was not fuelled by fascination nor repulsion but, rather, by a need to situate a new consciousness intricately tied to the situation created by technology. It is a consciousness best understood through television, which is both its product and its origin. Using Edith Efron's taxonomy, McLuhan describes television as 'The Timid Giant' because it is unsuited to deal with hot issues. It has injected 'rigor mortis into the body politic'. Like the Rebel without a cause, television is essentially apolitical, it is a ritual container of emotion, of reactions rather than actions that invites participation in depth: 'TV is a medium that rejects the sharp personality and favors the presentation of processes rather than of products' (*UM*: 309). We might surmise that James Dean's stardom was a product of a television mentality that McLuhan spent several years on and off television trying to analyze. McLuhan's rise to stardom in the mid-1960s was no doubt connected to his claim to have some understanding of this medium and its effects. While Wilbur Schramm interpreted cartoons and television watching in terms of how immoral content was corrupting the youth, McLuhan felt that the new tribal identity of the teenager was an inevitable product of a new electric environment that was beyond our control: 'Before TV, there had been much concern about why Johnny couldn't read. Since TV, Johnny has acquired an entirely new set of perceptions. He is not at all the same' (*UM*: 312). McLuhan's writings on the media crossed the generation gap and were as attractive to parents looking to understand the TV child as they were to a new generation of media savvy teens just wanting hip discussion.

While McLuhan's book is committed to intermediality, he does privilege one medium above the rest. His reading of the electric environment as an extension of our nervous system into space is without doubt through television. Yet it is not television as a sign system but television as prosthetic that is his central concern. In his early *Explorations* essays, it was television, and live television in particular, that informed the interdisciplinary methodologies of the Communication and Culture Seminar. This methodology sought out contours and processes rather than static categories and products. While the electric telegraph connected to typography had created the multi-perspectival space of the modern press and supported nationalism, television was altogether different. As Joyce maintained, it was a medium that enabled viewers to share in each other's simultaneous realities. More importantly, it allowed viewers to share a simultaneous reality – a 'cybernation':

> The mode of the TV image has nothing in common with film or photo, except that it offers also a nonverbal gestalt or posture of forms. With TV, the viewer is the screen. He is bombarded with light impulses that James Joyce called the 'Charge of the Light Brigade' that imbues his 'soulskin with subconscious inklings'. The TV image is visually low in data. The TV image is not a still shot. It is not photo in any sense, but a ceaselessly forming contour of things limned by the scanning-finger. The resulting plastic contour appears by light *through*, not light *on*, and the image so formed has the quality of sculpture and icon, rather than of picture. (*UM*: 312–13)

McLuhan reads the television image in terms of its material properties, specifically in terms of the low resolution technology of the early 1960s. The question as to what happens with high definition television is tautological. For McLuhan, an improved television image would no longer be television (ibid.: 313). This response is unsatisfying to say the least. What is surprising, however, is the extent to which his description of early television continues to provide useful descriptive categories.

Television as Sculpture

At a meeting of the 2002 American Society of Cinematographers hosted by Kodak Inc., a group of film teachers was invited to a demonstration of the differences between digital rear projection and film frontal projection. The terms used to celebrate the superiority of film over digital video, although contradicting McLuhan's distinctions between film and television technology nevertheless relied on the idea of media specificity. In an attempt to stave off the onslaught on digital cinema, the physiological effects of the film versus video experience were highlighted by an industry desperate to keep film alive. While there was no scientific evidence presented, the notion that film 'involves' while video 'hypnotizes' was the central premise of the presentation.

Although we might be dubious of Kodak's motives, and despite media convergences, film and video are different technologies that produce different kinds of sensations.

Television is a cool medium because its multipoint screen or 'mosaic mesh', produces a 'convulsive participation', a filling in that is hallucinatory as opposed to the hypnotic effects produced by higher resolution media like cinema and radio. Television's 'broken line' emphasizes 'the sculptural contours' of things presented (*UM*: 158). Regardless of whether television is high or low definition, its 'light through' rather than 'light on' character produces the viewer as screen, and the world as sculptural. In effect, with the advent of digital cinema and high definition video, the differences between film and video are still important even though some would like the distinction to disappear. Many artists have been emphasizing the differences, the sculptural quality of digital video projected on a large screen to create new kinds of landscapes.

Inuit artist Zacharias Kanuk and his long-time collaborator Norman Cohn have preferred video to film in the creation of what they see as new hybrid forms to represent narratives about and based upon oral story-telling traditions and northern landscapes before discovery. Kanuk's film *Atanarjuat: The Fast Runner* (2002) is one of the most beautiful examples of video's sculptural and audile-tactile qualities which are, as with all Kanuk's and Cohn's videos, sculptural and inseparable from the sense of process, immediacy and non-linearity that stands in opposition to the historical tale that depends on centuries of oral story-telling. Here we can see the insights afforded by McLuhan's formalism: precisely that if the artists had shot on film instead of digital video, they would have produced a different work of art. The politics behind *Atanarjuat* are complex, involving exclusion from funding sources, institutionalized racism and the government's refusal to recognize and fund the project. For Kanuk and Cohn it was essential to maintain the specificity of video for political as well as aesthetic reasons – video is not simply a small medium but transferred to film, it becomes a new medium, full of sculptural quality with an important link to television – an important communicative and historical bond in the Inuit community of Igloolik.[1]

Sculpture, for McLuhan, lies at the frontiers of sound and vision, creating an *audile-tactile* experience (*UM*: 158). The content of television is cinema that is transformed into art as it passes through television. We may argue that the cinema was an art form long before television became a popular medium. Yet it is expressly when it was shown on television that it became distinguished from television as a serious art worthy of study. With the advent of television as an institutionalized cultural form, Film Studies emerges as a university discipline out of English departments to treat films as texts equal to literature. McLuhan, of course, would be quick to point out that the history of English Studies coincides with its absorption by the popular press, as we saw with Matthew Arnold's defence of poetry. We might argue that it was with the advent of computers and the Internet, television has more recently emerged out of Film Departments to become an object of aesthetic study – Television Studies. This formulation would seem far too linear and occludes important institutional histories and particularities; it omits fiery debates and cannot explain, for example, why radio has never been established as a proper area of research and theorization. Yet it is a useful way to think about how disciplines take root. McLuhan would argue that once a technology becomes obsolescent, it becomes not only a visible environment but also a work of art.

It is to McLuhan's credit to have recognized television's gestalt, which he famously compared to an abstract painting along the lines of Seurat or Rouault. One can just imagine the outrage that such comparisons incited. Yet it was precisely such comparisons that excited artists (Nam June Paik, Wolf Vostell, Woody Vasulka and others) and encouraged new kinds of experimental art forms (video art) that played not only with the technological boundaries of perception and the physical spaces of galleries but also with institutional boundaries of popular culture and high art. But more than an analogy for modern art, television accomplished the goals of modern art: 'TV is the Bauhaus program of design and living, or the Montessori educational strategy, given total technological extension and commercial sponsorship. The aggressive lunge of artistic strategy for the remaking of Western man has, via TV, become a vulgar sprawl and an overwhelming splurge in American life' (*UM*: 322). McLuhan is ambiguous about what has been accomplished and about the benefits of this 'vulgar sprawl'. Besides creating cultural interfaces between Europe and America, and diversifying consumer tastes in automobiles and clothes, the benefits are not always clear in *Understanding Media*.

Television as Touch

McLuhan was, however, most interested in television's potential as an educational technology. Working with a group of university students at Ryerson University in the mid-1950s, he and psychologist Carleton Williams were involved in some of the first research projects to investigate the differences in information retention using different media: the same material was communicated to students through television, radio, a printed text, and a lecture. They found that the greatest retention of information occurred with television. Yet during the second trial, each medium was intensified (the researchers pushed each medium to its formal limits) and radio surpassed television in its capacity to translate information ('The Ryerson media experiment', *RPUM*: 138–158).

According to McLuhan, this 'flip' occurred because television's low resolution and participatory structure do better with content that is not too defined – that is, cooler, and more improvisational. Television would do well with poetry or with rehearsals because it is process oriented and incomplete. One of the best CBC documentaries was organized around pianist Glenn Gould's rehearsing (*RPUM*: 139). In a way, McLuhan did not so much anticipate reality TV with its rough contours and unpolished edges as recognize the 'fit' and, as he noted in *The Mechanical Bride*, there was in public culture a growing appetite for reality.

My own interest in medical dramas was triggered by one of McLuhan's somewhat misdirected but nevertheless useful insights: since the very beginning of television in the late 1940s, there has been an alliance between television and medicine. In *Understanding Media*, written at the high point of shows like *Ben Casey* and *Dr. Kildare* (1960–66), McLuhan maintained that doctor shows were a natural by-product of television. Like the cool medium, the medico involves the viewer in depth by making the body the centre of the drama. In fact, writes McLuhan, 'in closed-circuit instruction in surgery, medical students from the first reported a strange effect – that they seemed not to be watching an operation, but performing it'. (*UM*: 328) As McLuhan's formalist theory goes: the convulsive participation produced by television enhances corporeal anxiety, the doctor show is seen to soothe this anxiety while playing upon the tension between seriality and closure, life and death, doctor and patient. With very few exceptions the portrayal of doctors and hospitals in the cinema focuses on the patient, illness and closure because the cinema as a hot medium encourages passive participation.

Indeed, as film historian Lewis Jacob has observed, negative portrayals of doctors in Hollywood is a pattern specific to the Depression in the 1930s, one that was fuelled by the simple fact that the market-driven interests of organized medicine in the USA during this time were painfully apparent (Turrow, 1989). But McLuhan is not so interested in this political economy. His explanation is bound to the specifics of the medium as having a determining influence. According to his theory, television encourages active participation and thus focuses not on the patient but on the doctor who becomes the centre in a narrative that is process-oriented, organized consistently on the never-ending business of healing illness. Thus, it is no accident for McLuhan that the medico as a genre is born through television, because medicine and television share the same goal. Both have the power to overcome fragmentation and heal the global body. Television, like the physician, is a tactile medium. But facility is not the 'contact of skin and object', it is the 'interplay of the senses' (*UM*: 314).

It is precisely the synesthetic aspects of the mosaic mesh, which like the fishnet stocking, invite touch for completion. Touch for McLuhan is the interval, it is the 'space of the gap, not the connection' (*Letters*: 368). Television as extension and prosthetic creates a sense at once of loss and plenitude – the more it keeps you *in touch*, alleges McLuhan, the less you feel. A sense of amputation and the numbness produced by amputation are the necessary costs of this experience of unity.

According to McLuhan, one of the most significant televisual events in the history of American television was John F. Kennedy's funeral. In a section he calls 'Murder by television', McLuhan discusses the experience of collectivity which is now mythological in the history, not only of American television, but of America. This was a moment when everything, except for television, came to a halt (including television advertising) and the nation mourned. Rather than the actual assassination, which was not captured by television, the funeral was perfectly suited to the medium, which, as noted above, is a technology of reaction and not action. The disembodied collectivity designated by the Kennedy assassination is, of course, profoundly Catholic: transcendence takes place through a sacrificial body, both Kennedy's and by extension our own, which is but a small price for omniscience and ever-lasting life. The Kennedy funeral demonstrated 'the power of TV to involve an entire population in a ritual process' (*UM*: 337).

Television as Reverse Shot

McLuhan argued that television 'claims the viewer as its vanishing point'.[2] He could only come up with this idea because he has created a comparative framework that is historically grounded. He maintains that we cannot describe television, as we could the cinema, in terms of an organization of space inherited from seventeenth-century rationalism; nor can we think of it in terms of a subject-system securing a centre of production. Not only did 1926 mark the coming of sound to the cinema, but also the first official television transmission by John Logie Baird in England. Just as sound was being employed *to bring the cinematic image to life*, a new technology – one of direct transmission – was being devised *to bring life to the viewer*. The Renaissance dream of omniscient seeing, of seeing life as it unfolds at a distance, was to become reality. Taken up in the modernist telos, breaking down epistemological barriers, exceeding the expanded present of Abel Gance's polyvision in his spectacular *Napoléon vu par Gance* (1926), and the simultaneity of Griffith's parallel montage, the television transmission transforms the viewing situation into a *reverse shot*. McLuhan considers the differences between the projected image and the image which is essentially projected onto the viewer (Kodak makes this a point of contention against digital cinema which may well 'hypnotize' its viewers). The difference is significant and he knows that while television may contain the cinema as content, it is a different medium, producing a different kind of viewing experience. The direct transmission while always mediated through the technology (as both apparatus and service environment) would come to define an immediacy that can never be apprehended, a constant flux which does not reduplicate but *is* the flux of the life it claims to deliver.

Walter Benjamin was right to detect in the emergence of mechanical reproduction a growing tendency to bring things closer, to equalize by making objects and people more intimate and less distinct:

> To satisfy the human interest of the masses may mean to have one's social function removed from the field of vision. Nothing guarantees that a portraitist of today, when painting a famous surgeon at the breakfast table in the midst of his family, depicts his social function more precisely than a painter of the 17th century who portrayed his medical doctors as representing this profession, like Rembrandt in his 'Anatomy Lesson'. (1969: 243)

Benjamin's insight into the 'human interest' portrait anticipates the advent of broadcast television, the 'close-up' medium. He chooses Rembrandt's 'Anatomy Lesson' to delineate an earlier moment, a culture of distance and distinction. Yet, one might locate just the reverse in the 'Anatomy Lesson'. Rembrandt's painting marks the opening up of the sacred privacy of the body, announcing the new publicity and so-called freedom of the Enlightenment. It does not demarcate social distinction so much as the construction of the average body and non-distinction. We can discern, then, a certain continuity between the 'human interest' answered by mechanical reproduction and the context of the Enlightenment. This continuity – found in the desire to 'bring things closer', to penetrate boundaries and equalize vision – can be seen to characterize the very movement of capital.

It is this very movement that aligns film and television as capitalist media. Using the analogy of a cutting objectivity central to Benjamin's 'Work of art' essay, we can surmise that television surpasses film's atomizing capabilities. More than the film camera, the television apparatus can be likened to a surgeon, penetrating the invisible private sphere, offering intimate views of the everyday under the guise of the 'human interest story'. At the same time, the television monitor – a domestic appliance designed to blend in with home and public surroundings, to be watched in the light – equalizes spaces, eroding the difference between public and private, inside and outside, action and reaction. Television is not simply background McLuhan argues, it engages you, you have 'to be with it'. Within two decades of its first transmission, television was steered away from the large screen theatre television which John Baird and others foresaw, to be consolidated into the expansive new model of integrated circuits and controls offered by network radio. In their essay 'Broadcasting politics: communications and consumption', Kevin Robins and Frank Webster show how television has subjugated leisure life and the privacy of the domestic sphere to suit the organization of a market economy. For them Taylorism marks the first genuine information revolution as a rationalization of work that would come to include consumption in the development of that modern process we call marketing (1990: 36). It is this earlier rationalization of work and political economy that McLuhan claims emerges from the Gutenberg galaxy and that enables capital to break down the division between production and consumption, to subsume both the public and the private sphere to a common wealth that, as Hannah Arendt once maintained, has nothing common about it except that it is 'strictly private' (1958: 69). McLuhan argues that the most obvious psychic consequence of any new technology is just the demand for it:

> Once we have surrendered our senses and nervous systems to the private manipulation of those who would try to benefit from taking a lease on our eyes and ears and nerves, we don't really have rights left. Leasing our eyes and ears and nerves to commercial interests is like handing over the common speech to a private corporation, or like giving the earth's atmosphere to a company as a monopoly. Something like this has already happened with outer space, for the same reasons that we have leased our central nervous systems to various corporations. (*UM*: 68)

What has potentially been lost in the information revolution is our common sense, which has in effect become privatized. The structure of the television apparatus, and the history of its development as a consumer technology, must be taken into consideration, McLuhan tells us, if we are to more fully understand the role it plays in fusing marketing and education.

Information Implosion

At the Third International Conference on Computer Communication held in Toronto in the late 1970s, Yoneji Masuda predicted that the impact of the communications revolution on post-industrial societies would result in the increase of public utilities, the severe restriction and finally annihilation of the private enterprise system – that is, the complete realization of participatory democracy. Industrial expansion would, he insisted, by the twenty-first century give way to a complete information implosion: television consumption would be transformed into a flourishing of useful (cognitive versus affective) information exchanged between individuals all over the world (Masuda, 1981: 49–68). The first signs of the new information society were already visible, according to Masuda, in the link between television and computers. The most important aspect of this communications revolution is 'the complete objectification of information'; that is, the separation of information from originary context and hence, from competing ideological frameworks. Machines would become the productive source of information for the common good in the establishment of a global information utility accessible to all. This is what McLuhan would describe as the cosmic consciousness of the electric galaxy.

These visions of the information society are perfectly commensurate with McLuhan's interactive utopia. The crucial difference between an industrial and an information society for McLuhan is that in the electronic age 'the assembly line with its human hands disappears, electronic automation brings about a withdrawal of the work force from industry' (*UM*: 279). The fact that human hands have disappeared from the assembly line,

McLuhan tells us, is as basic a component of automation as tactility is to the TV image. The transmission of power – light, information and knowledge – is quite separate from the work operation that uses the power. Thus, what is accomplished, as McLuhan describes it, is the complete objectification of power. Information as power can service many different operations, it is mobile and unfixed; it is a broadcasting which unifies all processes of production. Electronic implosion as a new enlightenment breaks down the difference between consumption and production. The point is, according to McLuhan, that electronic technologies eliminate this difference: 'Just as light is at once energy and information, so electric automation unites production, consumption, and learning in an inextricable process' (ibid.: 19).

It is no accident that the separation of power as knowledge from the historical circumstances of its production, coincides with the workings of ideology in the modern state. Foucault interprets the power/knowledge relation in the light of a technology conceived somewhat differently. Still the basic characteristics are the same: its diffuse and boundless elasticity, its ability to unify production and consumption and its positive economy. So that, indeed, as Foucault writes: 'We are subjected to the production of truth through power and we cannot exercise power except through the production of truth' (1980: 93).

The electronic age, McLuhan maintains, marks the end of Euclidean space and the ideologies of standardized consumption by breaking down the epistemic boundaries dictated by the previously visual culture. Free from the ubiquities of time and space – as information is severed from origin and 'electricity as information' illuminates all that it touches instantaneously and simultaneously – *you are the vanishing point, you are the screen*. The clash of views in printed journalism, the distance it affords, gives way to a new participation in the TV exposé, to a depth sculpted by vision and hearing in a 'convulsive-sensuous participation', in a wondrous gestalt of touching and being touched, of producing and consuming (*UM*: 314).

This tactility is as basic as the elimination of human hands from the industrial process. A total integration of the senses, that depends in the first instance on the body's absence from the processes of production, its distance from the originary transmission of power. It is this paradox of distance and proximity that McLuhan of course avoids by insisting on another analogy: *the machine as human extension*. That is, only by reinstating human subjectivity at the centre once again does McLuhan avoid the alienating effects of a power severed from its origins.

It is telling that McLuhan's analogy describes the modern technology of the panopticon theorized by Foucault. Like McLuhan, Foucault sees the modern subject as constituted in and through the vanishing point, balancing between 'the object of knowing and the subject that knows' (1971: 312). However, unlike McLuhan he doesn't see this as an essential break with the ideologies of monocular vision. In the same way that Sartre's paranoid gaze in *Being and Nothingness* needs no other to feel itself watched (1956: 254–300), Foucault's panopticon is a technology of anonymous and omniscient power: 'The panopticon is a machinery that assures dissymmetry, disequilibrium, difference. Consequently, it does not matter who exercises power. Any individual, taken almost at random can operate the machine' (1979: 202). The reason the panopticon is so effective, operating along the same principles as the sovereign gaze, is that you never see it. Like the tactile in depth participation McLuhan describes, you feel it – it is a part of you.

Against the Situationists, like Debord, for example, Foucault rejects the notion of the society of the spectacle in favour of the society of surveillance. His famous rebuttal in *Discipline and Punish* reads:

> Our society is one not of spectacle, but of surveillance; under the surface of images, one invests bodies in depth; behind the great abstraction of exchange, there continues the meticulous, concrete training of useful forces; the circuits of communication are the supports of an accumulation and a centralization of knowledge; the play of signs defines the anchorages of power; it is not that the beautiful totality of the individual is amputated, repressed, altered by our social order, it is rather that the individual is carefully fabricated in it, according to a whole technique of forces and bodies. (ibid.: 25)

Despite Foucault's dismissal, the society of the spectacle is perfectly compatible with the positive economy of surveillance. If Foucault would privilege scientific discourse, *episteme*, over political economy in this analysis, it is only because he sees the two as inextricably bound. Adam Smith's *Inquiry into the Nature and Causes of the Wealth of Nations* (1776), for example, would not have been possible without the mechanical models initiated by Newtonian science which for McLuhan are part of the Gutenberg Galaxy. The circulation of blood, planets and currency is subject to universal laws, through what Arendt has called an 'astrophysical view of things' (1958: 265). This is also the view that characterizes the society of the spectacle. It is through the internalization of this view that the post-Enlightenment subject is constituted. In this way we can no longer speak of passive or repressive interpolation for the very process of panopticism leads to the erosion of the difference between passive and active, between production and consumption.

So, though McLuhan would insist that the exercise of power produces a 'centre without margins', he would also acknowledge that the televisual vanishing point depends on the constitutive viewpoint, the subject/object division, of earlier visual technologies. Like the panoptic machine, the 'mosaic mesh' is discontinuous, skew, and non-linear; it produces difference; different tastes and different desires (*UM*: 321). Television is a social technology *par excellence*, it is synaesthetic, synergetic and for this reason is so well suited to education and marketing which have imploded.

Jean Baudrillard's contention that the information implosion created by new communications technologies signals the end of the panopticon and the limits of capitalist expansion is perhaps premature (1983: 36). Utilizing McLuhanist imperatives, the new communications media of video, cable, integrated cable and satellite television claim to offer a greater range of versatility, of freedom and of choice. What they also offer, as Kevin Wilson points out, is more space to advertisers, more specific and targeted advertising to particular groups, and most importantly a closer than ever surveillance and monitoring of audiences.

Wilson gives an early account of how interactive home systems created a truly cybernetic cycle of production and consumption, because every consumption activity generated information back to the industry pertinent to the modification of future production (1988: 35; cf. Roberts and Foelr, 2004). This in turn will help to overcome the spectatorial independence created by other technologies like the Internet. So like the panopticon, broadcast and interactive technologies function within a positive economy. The information implosion is but another feature of capital's expanding rule.

Unable to see a continuity between industrial capital and its more advanced configurations, McLuhan insists on the mythic separation of literacy and the second orality offered by broadcast technologies. His great insight, however, is to have detected the very mobility of capital in the growing conflation of production and consumption, in the forging of centres without margins. It is precisely these centres, the illusory viability of their pluralism, that inform the processes of spectatorship under global capital.

Performing Media Studies

With *Understanding Media*, we need to consider McLuhan's pedagogical project as taking a new turn. Rather than shedding light on the new media, this project becomes part of it. That is, McLuhan very consciously enters into the electric galaxy of events to become an event himself, defining a new role that was not academic but belonged to the new public intellectual of the electric age. McLuhan's career can be divided somewhat crudely but accurately into two spheres, which are demarcated by his meteoric ascent into the electric galaxy of stardom. His 1960s' persona as a media guru coincides with a shift in his life away from writing towards performance. It is the public persona that he developed, McLuhan as a self-made cliché, the prophet, the media guru, that most are familiar with and that may account in part, for the lack of credibility or respectability that I have found accompanies the mere mention of his name in certain academic circles.

McLuhan's sin was to have speculated recklessly and to have been wrong about a lot of things. Up until that 'meteoric' rise to fame (a rise carefully manipulated and planned by the California 'genius scouts' Gerald Feigen and Howard Gossage), he had been describing the world at some distance. From 1966 to 1971, McLuhan became a highly produced symptom or cliché of the world he was describing (cf. Willmott, 1996: 136–155). Like the

English Vorticists of the First World War period, he was able to appropriate popular discourses and then become one himself.

The Vorticists were particularly conscious of the relation between the mass media and popular journalism and the creation of avant-garde art movements, art stars, famous art works. Since the birth of the avant-garde, it is clear that the press was responsible for collaborating in the production of a militaristic and bohemian image of art, an image of art as shock or resistance. That is, an art and artist that in their uselessness (the definition of bourgeois bohemians) were given a function. Art movements could be reduced to the discourse of the headline and artists, especially in the early twentieth century, would capitalize on this publicity machine by producing 'ready-made' headlines in the shape of manifestos and personas that would both simplify rifts and produce dramas for public consumption. The Vorticists recognized this and immediately set themselves against the Futurists as well as the Surrealists. Indeed, Wyndham Lewis and Ezra Pound went one step further and produced *Blast*, a publication which inflated newspaper headlines to set themselves against most things and 'blessed' a few things. McLuhan reprinted several manifestos in *Explorations* 8. Here is one of the best:

> Beyond Action
> and
> Reaction
> We would establish ourselves
> We start from opposite statements of a chosen world.
> Set up violent structure of adolescent clearness
> between two extremes.
> We discharge ourselves on both sides.
> We fight first on one side, then on the other, but
> Always for the SAME cause, which is neither side or
> both sides and ours.
> Mercenaries were always the best troops.
> We are primitive Mercenaries in the Modern World.
> Our cause Is NO-MAN'S.
> We set Humor at Humor's throat.
> Stir up Civil War among peaceful apes.
> We only want Tragedy if it has fought like Tragedy.
> We only want Tragedy if it can clench its side-muscles
> like hands on its belly, and bring to the surface a
> *laugh like a bomb.*

The Vorticist project was doomed to end, precisely because it was designed to be absorbed as contestation (Wees, 1972: 40). McLuhan interestingly used a similar rhetorical strategy, especially from the publication of *Understanding Media* onward. We can see where he derived his rhetorical and graphic appropriations, his structured oppositions, his bawdy humour and his *façade*.

McLuhan considers the newly created mediatized environment as a body that has transformed humans into 'servo-mechanisms' because they demand certain patterns of behaviour. According to his biographer, this is the reason he would never drive a car (Marchand, 1989: 168). While many reviews alleged that McLuhan was celebrating new media, there is an underlying melancholy discernible in *Understanding Media*. It is the tone that was reserved more strictly for the forms of production that had destroyed oral culture. On the one hand, the commercialization of new media has meant that we have 'leased' our senses. On the other, computers may well provide us with a cosmic communication beyond everything, able to transcend language/cultural differences, to create the dream of a universal phenomenology or common culture. Artists will help us to navigate these contradictions.

Notes

1 Zacharias Kanuk and Norman Cohn, talk given in the Faculty of Fine Arts, York University, Toronto, January 2002.

2 'The McLuhan is the message', *Telescope Revisited*, 20 July, 1967. CBC Television. *Understanding McLuhan* CDROM.

12

Globalization and Time

McLuhan's methodology needs to be examined in terms of its relevance for present-day theorizations of globalization and the new cultural formations that have both enabled and been defined by it. In particular, the meanings of McLuhan's most famous neologism, the 'global village' have been revived in the popular press but also in cultural geography as a means to foreground the paradoxical nature of globality and place. McLuhan's approach is formalist, comparative and medium-based. As discussed in the previous chapters, his 'medium is the message' includes the institutional and economic context in which the medium emerges as a social technology. Juxtaposing, for example, the bicycle and the cinema, or the radio and the typist is not intended to prove his historical periodization (oral – literate – electric) but rather functions to create an interdisciplinary, dynamic and historical ground through which to discern the movements of contemporary cultures. Such field approaches created historically by artists and scientist alike occasion reflexive and often new forms of knowledge: 'The painter learns how to adjust relations among things to release new perceptions, and the chemist and physicist learn how other relations release other kinds of power' (*UM*: 168).

McLuhan seeks to understand media as both an effect of and an influence upon the western human sensorium. This awareness must take on the paradox that technologies function both as physical extensions of human bodies and as invisible environments. He attempts to think of media not as continuous and progressive developments but as contiguous and, importantly, as belonging to a living changing environment, to a space–time framework and inter-national context. Even if the medium is the message, McLuhan fights against a model of communication as linear transmission stressing instead, very much like Benjamin, *translation*. In his examination, it is less a medium's use then the service industries that grow up around the medium that are of concern. McLuhan is interested in the kinds of practices – social, physical, and psychological – that are oriented around or engaged by specific technologies. What kinds of epistemological grounds do specific technologies produce and grow out of? What kinds of physical space–times are created by technologies – either external, imploded or internal psychological? McLuhan objects to simple analyses of technology that locate usage at the level of content. Technologies are not neutral but are used for specific purposes which they help to create. For example, the telegraph is used to communicate across space and leads to a whole network of practices and transformations in news reporting, in scheduling and in controlling movement. If we were to simply concentrate on the messages sent by telegraph instead of its relations to other technologies, to time and space, we would miss the underlying transformations that McLuhan sees as giving birth to the newspaper and to national cultural formations.

McLuhan's litany of examples do not substantiate or illustrate a theory of the media, rather, these function as singularities that enable the researcher/student to 'probe' the media in terms of a larger field of patterns, relationalities and structural homologies. His pedagogical project seeks to explore different media in terms of their heterogeneous materialities, in terms of the spaces and temporalities these produce without reducing them to a single framework (*LM*: 54).

The media that McLuhan studies cannot be accessed through empirical observation because their effects, that he would later frame as 'figure/ground' relations, are subliminal. These construct ways of seeing and ground assumptions. In his study of communications in history, Innis had noted that the situation for understanding is conditioned by the very media that dominate an age. The question is how to see beyond them or through them.

McLuhan responds to this problem in the same way that neurobiologists are currently trying to analyze consciousness. That is, he introduces media studies to quantum physics. In fact, for McLuhan, consciousness in the technologized world cannot be separated from the media. He develops a variety of analytic 'probes' to investigate the invisible environment created by the media. As metaphors drawn from experimental medicine and space exploration, probes serve to study symptoms, sensory ratios and new environments. From *The Gutenberg Galaxy* onward, the general form that McLuhan devises to set these in space finds justification in von Békésy's mosaic approach. In *Experiments in Hearing* Georg von Békésy would posit:

> It is possible to distinguish two forms of approach to a problem. One, which may be called the theoretical approach, is to formulate the problem in relation to what is already known, to make additions or extensions on the basis of accepted principles, and then to proceed to test these hypotheses experimentally. Another, which may be called the mosaic approach, takes each problem for itself with little reference to the field in which it lies, and seeks to discover relations and principles that hold within the circumscribed area. (*LM*: 4)

It is this approach which is called for when existing frameworks are uncertain, and for McLuhan such an approach is the most appropriate for studying the simultaneous field (which is an auditory rather than a visual field) of relations of experience. As we have seen, especially obvious in McLuhan's best work *Gutenberg Galaxy*, the mosaic is an iconic and historically grounded form that is discontinuous, abrupt and multi-levelled (*LM*: 55). It must be seen as an heuristic device gathering a variety of surfaces together – the hypertext in its multidimensional form is a construction that neatly encapsulates the spatiality McLuhan was calling for and that von Békésy was describing.

Space–Time Compression

McLuhan's famous Introduction to *Understanding Media* states that:

> After three thousand years of explosion, by means of fragmentary and mechanical technologies, the Western world is imploding. During the mechanical ages we had extended our bodies in space. Today, after more than a century of electric technology, we have extended our central nervous system itself in a global embrace, abolishing both space and time as far as our planet is concerned. (*UM*: 3)

Here we find the analogy between the human nervous system and the 'wired' planet, that is fundamental to McLuhan's ecumenical belief that the media may form a new unity among all the people of the world. Does McLuhan really believe that time and space are simply 'abolished' or have ceased to exist in this global embrace? The answer to this question is a qualified no. To start with, we know that McLuhan the rhetorician wishes to draw attention to changes in experiences of time and space brought about through new media technology. This statement and many more like it over the years have created a great deal of animosity towards the 'global village' metaphor as a space of simultaneous and instantaneous happenings where 'time has ceased and space has vanished'. In fact, we should consider another quotation from the same text that clarifies and indeed, qualifies this notion which originates from McLuhan's reading of post-Einsteinian physics:

> The total field created by the instantaneous electric forms cannot be visualized any more than the velocities of electronic particles can be visualized. The instantaneous creates interplay among time and space and human occupations, for which the older forms of currency exchange become increasingly inadequate. A modern physicist who attempted to employ visual models of perception in organizing atomic data would not be able to get anywhere near the nature of his problems. Both time (as measured visually and segmentally) and space (as uniform, pictorial, and enclosed) disappear in the electronic age of instant information. In the age of instant information man ends his job of fragmented specializing and assumes the role of information gathering. (*UM*: 138)

It is not the ontological dimension of space–time but rather the technological character of time and space that McLuhan seeks to foreground: the medium is the message. Juxtaposing the works of Adorno, Benjamin, Innis and McLuhan, Judith Stamps finds that these philosophers of modernity are part of a larger Western project to rethink the visual dimension of space–time relations by employing frameworks which draw out the temporal qualities of sound (1995: 151). Richard Cavell has maintained that McLuhan's challenge to the hegemony of visual spatial thinking is not a nostalgic return to oral culture (one which plagues Innis's thought) but a new space–time paradigm, heavily informed by physics, which he locates in acoustic space. Acoustic space, according to Cavell, 'encapsulates time as a dynamic of constant flux' and is inherently dialogical (2002: 22). This quality of space–time marks a fundamental difference between McLuhan and Innis. McLuhan would point out in his 1964 Foreword to *Bias of Communication* that Innis does not differentiate between 'the modalities of the visual and the audible' in his analysis of communications media. In effect, McLuhan will argue that different technologies, depending on which senses are amplified, will organize our experience of space–time differently.

We can turn to a short film (*The Telescope of Time*, CBC, 1967) to demonstrate McLuhan's conceptualization of space–time compression and the difference between visual and auditory space. The clip concerns distance since that is precisely what the paradox of the global village rests upon, the distance between things (spatial, temporal, epistemological, social, linguistic, etc.) is transformed through technology. We see McLuhan in trenchcoat and hat looking like a detective (his favourite literary figure being Sherlock Holmes) from a 1940s' film noir, sitting on a crowded subway, newspaper in hand, he speaks directly to the camera:

> Personally, I hate travel. I find it a kind of suspended animation that is very exhausting and disturbing because one is constantly adjusting to new spaces, new faces, and this is, I find, a great drain on nervous energy. Travel is many forms and this kind of horizontal travel on rolling stock is much more conducive to social life and reading and chat, whereas when you go up in an airplane, you are suspended in a kind of time zone, you are really out of space and you begin to work away at forming a destination image or syndrome that imprisons you in a kind of a hope bubble or pattern.

Here is McLuhan, offering comments on everything around him as he would do throughout his life but most publicly in the late 1960s. This is a great image of improvisational thought and it testifies to his method which is to take note of particular technologies and the different kinds of spaces created by them: the subway, unlike the car, will enable social encounters with strangers, while airplane travel is a projection into the future. These are the examples he uses in the first pages of *Understanding Media* as well where he explains that the 'railway medium … accelerated and enlarged' human capacities, creating new kinds of cities and social formations. As we saw in the previous chapter, the medium of communication must be understood in terms of their effects on time and space rather than what they are carrying: 'This [transformation] happened whether the railway functioned in a tropical or a northern environment, and is quite independent of the freight or content of the railway medium' (*UM*: 8).

Let us recall that the train carriage was an example that Einstein called upon to illustrate his theory of relativity and Bergson used to critique Einstein's theory as not grounded in real lived experience. Regardless of whether McLuhan was dealing with the real or the symbolic as Bergson distinguished, his train ride carries a diversity of temporalities which are both multiple and grounded in lived experience: the linear time of the subway train (the 'horizontal travel on rolling stock'), the time inside the train (the experience of simultaneously moving forward and being stationary), the time of reading (the multiple space–time relationships inside the mosaic of the newspaper), the different schedules accommodated by the different passengers (some are late, some have free time) – all this movement is through time and in time. In effect, there is a multiplicity of times contained in this single time of the train moving forward. The difference between train and airplane travel is perhaps key here as each produces different space–time experiences (linear and non-linear). And we could add to McLuhan's riff on time travel, our experience of the film (the film transferred to video) and the author of this book writing to you the reader about the images of the film. This kind of analysis foregrounds the complex relationships between media technology, between images and reality, and finally it seeks to foreground the hybrid archetypal character of all media. McLuhan believes that we 'live in a world much vaster than any which a scientist today has instruments to measure, or concepts to describe'. He quotes Yeats: 'The visible world is no longer a reality and the unseen world is no longer a dream'. (*UM*: 35) Walter Benjamin made similar remark about the way mechanical reproduction had enabled new realities previously invisible to be opened up.

McLuhan believes that informatic technologies are transforming reality and therefore our experience of time as experienced through space. Thus, it is not time and temporality but time as measure that will be transformed by the new technologies of instantaneous transmission. For the measure of time itself has a history as Wyndham Lewis's work has traced. Indeed, it is precisely an awareness of the history of time, of linear time, of 'city-time' that abstracts temporality from the physical world of bodies and agriculture that leads McLuhan to some of his most audacious statements. All this has become apparent in the changes brought about to time through the industrial revolution whose greatest invention, according to Mumford, was the clock. For McLuhan, it is not the clock but the phonetic alphabet that is 'the technology that had made possible the visual and uniform fragmentation of time' that we know clocks to bring (*UM*: 147). It is precisely this mastering of time that has meant in the industrial city a scheduling of human activity that is divorced from the physical environment. So that, as Mumford observed, we eat when it is time rather than when we are hungry. Or as the writings of Sebastian de Grazia's *Of Time, Work and Leisure* which McLuhan cites, '"free time" is not leisure since leisure is not part of the division of labour that creates the opposite of free time that is "work", nor the division of time that constitute "full time" and "free time"' (quoted in *UM*: 153). This is the political economy in which time itself is a container to be filled or something that runs out, time can be given or has to be protected like a precious commodity. Moreover, by the late 1950s McLuhan is engaged with Bergson's *Creative Evolution* and sees his concerns regarding the spatializatoin of time in terms of quantum theory, and he discerns following De Broglie 'a rapprochement' between wave mechanics and Bergson's philosophy of time (*LM*: 55). It is also the new physics of Max Planck, Werner Heisenberg and Louis de Broglie who introduced components of acoustic space into physics with quanta, indeterminacy, resonance and wave mechanics (*LM*: 44).

Thus, it is a more complex picture of physical space and time, of multiple, simultaneous, and discontinuous temporalities that McLuhan had been attempting to introduce into media studies since the early work with the *Explorations* group and especially since his encounter with radical anthropologists like Dorothy Lee and Carpenter. In the train sequence, his point would favour Bergson rather than Einstein with regards to time. Isabelle Stengers has framed their famous debate in 1922 in a manner that makes clear where McLuhan would be situated:

> Henri Bergson tried to defend, against Einstein, the multiplicity of lived times co-existing in the unity of real time, to argue for the intuitive evidence that makes us think that these multiple durations participate in the same world. Look at Einstein's response: he totally rejects, as incompetent, the 'time of philosophers', convinced that no lived experience can save what science denies. (Stengers, 2000: 40)

While McLuhan and others have noted the close relationship between Einstein and Bergson, Stengers points to their fundamental disagreement, which involves phenomenal reality and the irreversibility of time's arrow. Certainly, McLuhan's zealous pronouncements about space and time being abolished in the electric galaxy are over-emphasized in order to stress that the experience of time is centrally transformed by the technologization of space. That is, space and time are both different and bound together in space–time. This is why, as noted above, he is so critical of the notion of 'flow' with regards to the electric culture which he sees as a remnant of typographic culture, as if electricity (or people or information) could simply run like water or 'like the firing of guns' (*UM*: 148).

As a concept or metaphor, flow reduces time to a singular and linear space. McLuhan wishes to maintain the multiplicity of times within space without reducing time to space. In the electric age, fields or interfaces are more appropriate analogies for, while they are unified and inclusive, they are also heterogeneous: 'Now in the electric age of decentralized power and information we begin to chafe under the uniformity of clock-time. In this age of space–time we seek multiplicity, rather than repeatability, of rhythms. This is the difference between marching soldiers and ballet' (*UM*: 149). The juxtaposition of instrumental march (as in the march of time) with aesthetic non-linear motion of ballet is telling and indeed quite characteristic of McLuhan's ideogrammatic formulations. His point is clear enough. The new media offer a freedom of movements, of creative thought and aesthetic perceptions that the previous visual regime did not, these portend an opening rather than a closing of different forms of engagement, interactive and multi-planed rather than simply reactive and single file. Those that will benefit the most from the freedom enabled by the electric media will be 'the child, the cripple, the woman, and the colored person who appear in a world of visual and typographic technology as victims of injustice'. These oppressed people cannot live 'in a man's world' which is the product of homogenous and uniform industrial culture. But in the electric galaxy, 'in a culture that assigns roles instead of jobs' people will 'create their own spaces'. The same goes for education. The electronic media will create a new pedagogical situation in which difference will be accommodated instead of erased (*UM*: 17). Recent work in the area of cultural geography has developed ideas on locality, place and difference as a politic of the interval. Iain Chambers, for example, makes a good case to give place to 'immediate, discontinuous and irregular experiences', which are altogether less susceptible to a teleological harmony:

> It has been under the impact of feminism, race and ethnicity, that the abrupt edges of an earlier hegemony ... [have] been most sharply exposed. To reintroduce the uneven and fragmented experiences of the once obscured hidden and defeated means to reject a homogeneous and unitary sense of culture and politics, of history. Such considerations invariably result in a critical cutting edge in the more usual discussion of the 'political', where cultural details and differences are usually related to an instrumental footnote in the discourse. For those other voices are also part of the polis ... People speak 'out of place' and through this politics now confronts an excess of sense. It is not so much a question of reversing hegemonies but of displacing, simultaneously investing distinct realities and histories while maintaining their differences, provides us with the possibility of a shared set of interfaces and involvement, and a political sense of the commonplace. (1990: 79)

Chambers suggests a political engagement defined by the interface between diasporic cultures, along 'borderlines', in the common space between places.

Although McLuhan was enthusiastic about the possibilities for new kinds of political interface, there is also a deep regret about the kinds of experiences being lost in the electric galaxy. In his discussion of photography, for example, he considers the way that images (photographs and films) have reversed 'the travail' of engaging with different cultures by packaging them into images:

> Travel differs very little from going to a movie or turning the pages of a magazine. The 'Go Now, Pay Later' formula of the travel agencies might as well read: 'Go now, arrive later,' for it could be argued that such [people] never really leave their beaten paths of impercipience, nor do they ever arrive at any new place. They can have Shanghai or Berlin or Venice in a package tour that they need never open. In 1961, TWA began to provide new movies for its trans-Atlantic flights so that you could visit Portugal, California, or anywhere else, while en route to Holland, for example. Thus the world itself becomes a sort of museum of objects that have been encountered before in some other medium. (*UM*: 198)

Lost then is the interaction, conversation and reflection that comes from encounters with others in the world. Of course he is aware that it is citizens from Western capitalist countries that are doing the packaging and the travelling, a remnant from the time of Descartes and from imperial travels of conquest. His point is that the image has replaced the actual experience of movement. Technology as extension leads to a fierce amputation, a discarnate separation from the world. The simultaneous motion and stillness that we find with McLuhan on the train or in the plane produce distance from the world by abolishing it. The Situationist Guy Debord has remarked in a manner not unlike McLuhan, that the 'society which eliminates geographical distance reproduces distance internally as spectacular separation'. The spectator as tourist or the tourist as spectator implicitly denies access to geographical space: 'The same modernization that removed time from the voyage also removed from it the reality of space' (Debord, 1983: 167). Both McLuhan and Debord are clear about the fact that human circulation mirrors commodity circulation. What is accomplished is what Debord calls 'spectacular separation', or McLuhan calls 'amputation', the guarantee of equivalence through representation and, hence 'the banalization of the world'.

The deep disconnection that is created through electric media has also created a silence, a loss of communication between people and the world which is in the imploded world merely a museum of the already experienced. McLuhan recognizes the contours of time in terms of speed. Thus, he stresses over-mediation and dematerialization as a loss and effect of modernity. This is why both McLuhan and Innis value oral culture above all other forms of communication because while mediated through language, the oral tradition preserves continuity between past and present. Arguably, oral culture for Innis is less related to a public sphere as it is for McLuhan, than it is to an historical consciousness. Obviously there is the danger that the face-to-face interaction of oral culture is romanticized for its immediacy and authenticity. All forms of interaction are mediated and certainly one could criticize McLuhan's periodization for the opposition it sets up between orality and literacy. Writing exists outside literacy and most oral cultures have some form of writing. Yet such differentiations between face-to-face communication, telephonic, televisual encounters, and so on are useful categories for analyzing cultural formations. For McLuhan, human interaction in its present incarnation through the media, has the spatial qualities of a public sphere as Habermas has defined it (1989). But whereas Habermas would see the media as channels or technological supports for communication among citizens, McLuhan would see these technologies as constitutive of both the idiom and the character of citizenship and debate. The media are the public sphere.

Globality

While the global village may be marked according to McLuhan's formulation by an acoustic and oral character, its simultaneous character is profoundly discontinuous in a way that the village is not. This is why the global village is not a utopian concept or ideal state for McLuhan. In other words, the global village attempts to describe rather than celebrate a new situation, a new way of being in the Western world which is discarnate and discontinuous. As we have seen, McLuhan will have a dialectical reading of this state as humans become 'servo-mechanisms', or the 'sex organs' of the machine. This notion itself may seem simplistic but we need to keep in mind that the machine is constituted by social and economic processes and practices. On the other hand, there is inherent in this new situation of interconnectedness, the Catholic humanist 'faith in' a universal communication, communion. This hope is generally what has become the lasting interpretative frame for McLuhan's global village.

The neologism was in fact, 'borrowed' from Wyndham Lewis. As Carpenter has pointed out, McLuhan preferred the term 'global theatre' to global village because he felt it was more descriptive of the light show that Torontonians were witnessing from the 'surrealist cornucopia' of American culture imported via television and radio in the 1950s. Yet global theatre never struck the kind of imaginative chord among journalists 'who considered themselves neutral reporters, not theatrical producers'. So if global village stuck, it stuck first and foremost because it appealed to the media rather than being anything descriptive of the media (Carpenter, 2001: 244). Coming from Lewis it was most probably a term that was coined by journalists in the first place. Thus, it is with some irony that McLuhan will write in the opening pages of *The Gutenberg Galaxy*: 'The new electronic interdependence recreates the world in the image of the global village'. (*GG*: 31) This is an important detail to recall, and one that I would take quite literally, the global village is an image. This concept then takes McLuhan to a point where virtual space and physical space are fused as mythic form. Jean Baudrillard will interpret this as a dystopian space. For McLuhan it is mostly dialectical.

But McLuhan's most utopian proclamations come in the opening to Part II of *Understanding Media*, 'The Spoken Word' as 'the flower of evil' which is his homage to Bergson. Here it is not the global village but a 'cosmic consciousness' capable of transcending language that constitutes the utopian horizon:

> Our new electric technology that extends our senses and nerves in a global embrace has large implications for the future of language. Electric technology does not need words any more than the digital computer needs numbers. Electricity points the way to an extension

of the process of consciousness itself, on a world scale, and without any verbalization whatever. Such a state of collective awareness may have been the preverbal condition of men. Language as the technology of human extension, whose powers of division and separation we know so well, may have been the 'Tower of Babel' by which men sought to scale the highest heavens. Today computers hold out the promise of a means of instant translation of any code or language into any other code or language. The computer, in short, promises by technology a Pentecostal condition of universal understanding and unity. The next logical step would seem to be, not to translate, but to by-pass languages in favor of a general cosmic consciousness which might be very like the collective unconscious dreamt of by Bergson. The condition of 'weightlessness', that biologists say promises a physical immortality, may be paralleled by the condition of speechlessness that could confer a perpetuity of collective harmony and peace. (*UM*: 80)

McLuhan's relation to Bergson could help us to better understand what is meant by 'cosmic consciousness'. This is an expression that he borrows from the Canadian writer Richard Maurice Bucke's book *Cosmic Consciousness* (1901) which in a very secular manner theorized the evolution of consciousness towards an omniscience that would dissolve physical and psychological borders and boundaries (Cavell: 13). McLuhan maintains this is synonymous with the 'collective unconscious'. If Freud's work illuminates the psychic structures produced by literacy and industrial modes of production, then Jung's theories of primordial archetypes which are mythological figures or processes that repeat themselves across cultures and history can help us to understand the present moment.

Jung wrote the Introduction to the English version *I Ching or Book of Changes*, the ancient Chinese text brought to the West through the translation of his old friend Richard Wilhelm in 1950. McLuhan points out that the *I Ching* is being used in the contemporary world not because it is an escape from modern life but because 'its structure is once again understandable' (*CA*: 23). The *I Ching* uses the same binary system as the computer and includes the observer in the process of programming. Let us go directly to Jung for a more in-depth explanation:

The ancient Chinese mind contemplates the cosmos in a way comparable to that of the modern physicist, who cannot deny that his model of the world is a decidedly psychophysical structure. The microphysical event includes the observer just as much as the reality underlying the I Ching comprises subjective, i.e., psychic conditions in the totality of the momentary situation. Just as causality describes the sequence of events, so synchronicity to the Chinese mind deals with coincidence of events. The causal point of view tells us a dramatic story about how D came into existence: it took its origin from C, which existed before D, and C in its turn had a father, B, etc. The synchronistic view on the other hand tries to produce an equally meaningful picture of coincidence. How does it happen that A', B', C', D', etc., appear all in the same moment and in the same place? It happens in the first place because the physical events A' and B' are of the same quality as the psychic events C' and D', and further because all are the exponents of one and the same momentary situation. The situation is assumed to represent a legible and understandable picture. (*The I Ching or Book of Changes*, 1977: xxiv–xxv)

The concept of synchronicity rather than causality frames McLuhan's field approach to the history of communication as to understanding the present moment. McLuhan will look to Jung's work especially in *From Cliché to Archetype* (1970) to clarify the structures of experience and discourses produced by electric modes of production. The electric age with its decentred spaces and memory archives enables users to see archetypal patterns more readily. The concept of a collective unconscious, of 'psychic residua' which are the 'roots of consciousness' is not scientific but simply refers to 'numberless experiences of the same type' (Jung).

McLuhan had in the early 1950s concurred with Wyndham Lewis's (and Innis's) distrust of Bergson's argument that reality is made up of Time flux and that a cinematographic method has spatialized time. Lewis's *Time and Western Man* was deeply critical of Bergson and early on McLuhan praised Lewis's project to 'arrest the flux of existence in order that the mind may be united with that which is permanent in existence' ('Wyndham Lewis: His theory, his art', *IL*: 67). Lewis and the Vorticists focused on space through fragmented discontinuous collages which juxtaposed objects in space. These collages were especially influential for *The Mechanical Bride*, and Lewis's work would draw upon the 'world of Space as opposed to the world of memory and history', precisely as a way out of 'the nightmare of history'. McLuhan derives his central methodological image from Lewis in the form of the vortex and Poe's maelstrom which is the way to arrest the moment and perceive lived patterns of everyday life. We may recall that Innis's critique of the time philosophers rested on the notion that an emphasis on flux led to an 'obsession with the immediate' and did not permit an historical continuity and a sense of permanence. Yet from the *Explorations* essays onward, McLuhan develops a method that is influenced by the new physics and by a dynamic methodology that does not freeze the moment but engages with living historical processes.

McLuhan's utopian projection is also a reference to an earlier mythos of language as Divine Logos, as containing the thing referenced and we can see this mythos at work in his interest in clichés and archetypes. As discussed in the last chapter, McLuhan sees electric media as a *ricorso* of sorts. Bergson's views of speech and McLuhan's understanding of the written form as having created alienated experience emanate from the same theological premise, that of the fundamental unity of the world and the 'Pentecostal condition of universal understanding' (*UM*: 80). For McLuhan the communicative connections enabled by electric technology make possible a return to this earlier unified consciousness.

We find in the passage quoted above on the future of language as cosmic consciousness, an attempt to theorize the sensual involvement fostered by virtual communication (Horrocks, 2000). While McLuhan does imagine a future when the computer 'by-passes' language altogether to create 'a general cosmic consciousness', the central focus of his work rests on those things in the present, on the universality of what is unique to each culture: 'Each mother tongue teaches its users a way of seeing and feeling the world, and of acting in the world, that is quite unique' (*UM*: 80). Speech is the most creative manifestation of communication, it is the greatest art of humans (*CA*: 19). Speech also bonds communities as well as space and time through a carnal process.

Medium theorists like McLuhan and Innis seek to situate communication within a materiality that is historically conscious. At the same time, it is this historical consciousness that with McLuhan also includes mythological consciousness (Jung) which is a characteristic of oral culture: 'For, until literacy deprives language of this multi-dimensional resonance, every word is a poetic world unto itself, a "momentary deity" or revelation, as it seemed to non-literate men'. For McLuhan, Ernst Cassirer's *Language and Myth* 'presents this aspect of non-literate human awareness, surveying the wide range of current study of language origins and development' (*GG*: 25). Thus, McLuhan will find in new media forms, especially television and computers, a communication that is both verbal and non-verbal that does not separate signifier and signified. Deleuze and Guattari have praised this aspect, 'a linguistics of flows', in McLuhan's analysis of the media:

> to have shown what a language of decoded flows is, as opposed to a signifier that strangles and overcodes the flows. In the first place, for non-signifying language anything will do: whether it be phonic, graphic, gestural, etc., no flow is privileged in this language, which remains indifferent to its substance or its support, inasmuch as the latter is an amorphous continuum. The electric flow can be considered as the realization of such a flow that is indeterminate as such. (1983: 241)

What gives a flow, or for McLuhan it would be a medium, substance is the encounter with another medium: 'This fact, characteristic of all media, means that the context of any medium is always another medium' (ibid). This produces figures not the figural, archetypes which are always 'living entities' according to Jung. Thus, when George Steiner writes that McLuhan's contribution might have been to make a space for art that dies (with reference to the work of Cage or the Fluxus group), he mistakes McLuhan's concept of death which is always everlasting life or becoming. In *From Cliché to Archetype* which delineates the process of 'intermedia action', he quotes Yeats on the original:

> Those masterful images because complete
> Grew in pure mind, but out of what began?
> A mound of refuse or the sweepings of a street,
> Old kettles, old bottles, and a broken can,
> Old iron, old bones, old rags, that raving slut
> Who keeps the till. Now that my ladder's gone,
> I must lie down where all the ladders start,
> In the foul rag-a-bone shop of the heart.

The age of information, says McLuhan, produces a great deal of garbage (*CA*: 184). It is precisely the mechanism of creative recycling, metamorphosis and hybridity that stands as the true miracle of perception.

Localities

The global village essentially fuses two contradictory terms to make one 'organic whole'. Borrowing from Mumford's *The City in History*, the village even as extension still retains an integral space. The qualifying term of globality does not oppose space and place, or the local and the global. The fact that 'the whole of the planet is being shrunk or more to the point, imploding to the experience of a village, where everyone knows everyone else's business' is an effect of speed. According to McLuhan, it is the speed of electricity that breaks down the boundaries between work and home, distance and proximity, private and public, transforming the linear and homogenous spaces of modernity, creating an image of the world that mimics the cohesiveness and experience of the village.

It is movement, the movement of globalization, the rationalization and commodification of the world as picture as Hedeigger put it, that describes the global village as image. In McLuhan's work it is the everyday experiences of these images that produce possibilities for new kinds of intervals and relations.

Some theorists of globalization (Doreen Massey (1994), Arjun Appadurai (1996), Michael Peter Smith (2001)) have argued that the everyday needs to be rehabilitated and valued as a path forward: the local, the immediate of experience, the neighbourhood are not the means to some new version of strategic essentialism, or a romanticization of authenticity. Rather, the local provides a hopeful method of focusing on the materiality of experiences in a world of increasing movement and virtuality. The realm of the everyday is no less ephemeral than the world of global hyperreality because it is part of it or, rather, hyperreality is part of our everyday world. But it is by way of the everyday that we can act upon and understand not only how globalization acts upon us but how we interact and effect global processes.

John Tomlinson has underlined that the globalization we are currently experiencing is distinct from earlier forms of imperialism. In the context of the spread of cultural modernity, a language which emphasizes cultural domination and imposition is no longer entirely appropriate. This is not to say that imperialism has disappeared but that the tension is important. Tomlinson maintains that globalization is far less coherent or culturally directed than imperialism:

> For all that is ambiguous between economic and political senses, the idea of imperialism contains, at least, the notion of a purposeful project: the intended spread of a social system from one centre of power across the globe. The idea of 'globalization' suggests interconnection and interdependency of all global areas which happens in a far less purposeful way ... and which functions to weaken all nation states – including the economically powerful ones – the imperialist powers of a previous era. (1991: 175)

Taking his lead from Raymond Williams, Tomlinson distinguishes between cultural and economic imperialism. While earlier forms of empire were directed by political and cultural interests that worked in tandem to define a social mission (i.e., colonization/civilization), the processes of globalization that distinguish global capitalism are driven by the interests of the market alone. This distinction enables us to think about cultural practices and new global cultures in ways that do not simply reduce them to ownership or capitalist ideology (cf. Berland and Hornstein, 2000). In this way, we move beyond the binary opposition of modernism and mass culture that informed Innis's distrust of instructional technologies and Adorno and Horkheimer's analysis of the culture industry. Instead of the notion that mass culture is simply a uniform product imposed on passive consumers, a space for contradictory forms of empowerment, production and consumption is considered as an area to be examined.

The Internet may well embody the contradictory status of global cultural modernity. The source of a transmission, technology or service is blurred across national, regional and institutional boundaries, across public and private spaces, within the decentred economy of the user. McLuhan's revival in the 1990s is directly connected to the rise of the Internet and the advent of new portable hand-held 'do it yourself' forms of electronic media in North America and Western Europe (Levinson, 1999). McLuhan's belief that electronic forms of global communication would both connect (to some degree homogenize and unify) but also differentiate cultures appears apt:

> Since electric energy is independent of the place or kind of work-operation, it creates patterns of decentralism and diversity in the work to be done. This is a logic that appears plainly enough in the difference between firelight and electric light, for example. Persons grouped around a fire or candle for warmth or light are less able to pursue independent thoughts, or even tasks, than people supplied with electric light. In the same way, the social and educational patterns latent in automation are those of self-employment and artistic autonomy. (*UM*: 359)

And

> We live in an economic world in which information itself has become the main commodity. Packages and consumer goods are now a relatively minor commodity compared to just information. [Where does this information output, the fact that information is so readily available, where does that put the traditional family situation, for instance?] It means for one thing, for example, that the computer could become the basis of a cottage economy again. Just as the kids have gone back to the Middle Ages in their costumes and social outlook, role-playing, so our economy could go back to the cottage economy of a much earlier time. You could run the world's biggest factory in a kitchen by computer. In other words, the nature of instant speeds – telephones, telex, computer – is to decentralize all forms of management and all forms of hardware. The computer, literally, could run the world from a cottage.[1]

McLuhan's 'centre-without-margins' is a cultural rather than an economic model. It has proven useful for describing new and highly creative forms of community, something like the open source movement and locally based forms of protest and cultural production as well as more flexible administrative structures in urban civil society. McLuhan maintained that computers would support the expression of difference, breaking down national borders while fostering community identities as well as interfaces between cultures. The new electronic world would see a diversity of cultural scapes and flows from a global diaspora.

Since McLuhan privileges the cultural in his thinking, the 'centre-without-margins' model can tell us nothing about the economic structures which support the new technologies, cultures and knowledges he describes. His concept of the 'global village' collapses the global into the local, making it impossible to discern relations of power of any kind. This is why his media theories have always been more attractive to corporations like AT&T rather than to political activists. This is why also the analogy between the village and the mass mediated world was for Raymond Williams who grew up in a small Welsh village a senseless juxtaposition:

Much of the content of modern communications is this kind of substitute for directly discoverable and transitive relations to the world ... It is a form of shared consciousness rather than merely a set of techniques. And as a form of consciousness it is not to be understood by rhetorical analogies like the 'global village'. Nothing could be less like the experience of any kind of village or settled active community. For in its main uses it is a form of unevenly shared consciousness of persistently external events. It is what appears to happen, in these powerfully transmitted and mediated ways in a world with which we have no perceptible connections but which we feel is at once central and marginal to our lives. (1973: 295–6)

Williams was one of McLuhan's staunchest critics and he objects mostly to the rhetorical flair of McLuhan's neologisms and perhaps also, their lack of connection to the actual experiences of globality. Williams turns McLuhan's 'centre-without-margin' model on its head to describe the way in which dominant media play a central role in people's lives whose existence is marginal and who are disempowered when it comes to having an effect on the dominant media. Williams's remarks are much closer to those of Innis who maintained the centre–margin structure as a means to understand the workings of Empire. Certainly, Saskia Sassen's (2002) study of the supposed decentralizing role of the digital media industries has found that the new media industries are still very much located in the large urban centres of the industrialized nations. The digital divide is alive and growing stronger. This reality has made it imperative not to lose sight of the political economic infrastructures of media technologies and certainly never to take McLuhan's metaphors too literally.

Nevertheless, as I have been arguing throughout this book, McLuhan does take account of political economy as an historical system which has both produced and been produced by global technologies. Certainly, the current function of the information technologies in supporting new kinds of cultural formations, social interactions, communications circuits should not be exaggerated but nor are they inconsequential to many who have been marginalized by dominant media (Castells, 2001). These need to be studied in all their complexity and the two models offered by McLuhan (centre-without-margins) and Innis (centre–margin) are complementary spatial models that give us different perspectives on the kinds of relations that make up specific media contexts.

Ultimately, we need to remember in reading McLuhan's writings, that he is offering a pedagogical framework through which to get a hold of and understand the properties of everchanging mediascapes, 'situations that are in process' (*LM*: 116). In his last book, *Laws of Media*, co-written with his son Eric McLuhan, a new tool is introduced for precisely this kind of hermeneutical experimentation. The 'tetrad' is 'exegesis on four levels' directed towards making visible some of the hidden grammars and etymologies underlying human artifacts. The four laws derive from McLuhan's insights regarding new media that he had been developing over his career. He simplifies these into a template made up four simultaneous appositional parts that address the phenomenology of artifacts. Every artefact, McLuhan claimed, 'enhances' a sensory ratio, process or aspect. It will also make something else obsolescent. These ideas are basic. The last two 'laws' are more innovative. In *From Cliché to Archetype* McLuhan had claimed that archetypes stem from the recycling of past clichés. Thus, he argues, every artefact retrieves some obsolete process or object from the past. The last law was one that he had developed in his *Explorations* days and presented more fully in *Understanding Media* in the chapter 'Reversal of an overheated medium'. Any major artefact, when pushed to its maximum capacity or boundary, will break and 'flip' into opposite form. The most obvious example of this is found in the shift from mechanical to electric modes, from explosion to implosion. McLuhan finds examples of reversals throughout history and looks to Toynbee's *Study of History* and his chapter on the 'Reversal of roles' to substantiate his ideas: 'Today the road beyond its break boundary turns cities into highways, and the highway proper takes on continuous urban character' (*UM*: 38). The fact that processes of change and development may be fuelled by capitalist development is beside the point for McLuhan. Rather, he is interested not in causes but how forms become manifest, and how these manifestations are deeply interdependent:

| Enhances | Reverses into |
| Retrieves | Obsolesces |

The tetrad is a creative tool for thinking about objects historically and phenemologically. If one reads through the tetrads on offer in the *Laws of Media*, these are 'tentative' because the tool is still being 'tuned' (*LM*: 128–9). The tetrad is not a scientific instrument that will reveal hard facts but it is an experimental technique that may open up uncharted relations. Its dynamic structure seeks to translate the histories embedded in objects into a creative metaphor.

Most importantly, the tetrad incorporates reciprocity into its four parts and this is its most original aspect. While inspired by a roster of thinkers from Vico to Popper, the authors of *Laws of Media* cite *After Babel* by the humanist scholar and 'grammarian' George Steiner as a major inspiration. Steiner, like McLuhan, reacts against Hegel's 'sterile triadic model' and offers instead 'a four fold hermeneutic motion' to define the act of translating which is the process of interpretation. Steiner tells us that the hermeneutic motion is 'dangerously incomplete, that is dangerous because it is incomplete, if it lacks its fourth stage, the piston-stroke, as it were, which complete the cycles … The enactment of reciprocity in order to restore balance is the crux of the metier and morals of translation' (Steiner, cited in *LM*: 127). Thus, we return to the function of criticism as translation, and as 'an enactment of reciprocity'. We can see the tetrad as belonging to a long line of creative intellectual probes, all part of a critical apparatus to understand *what the hell is happening*. And so the last paragraph of McLuhan's last book carries in proper prophetic style, one of his familiar warnings:

> Another traditional understanding of the figures of speech holds that each is a unique posture of the mind and the imagination. Each is a vortex of energy and experience and a pattern of sensibility. The goal of science and the arts and of education for the next generation must be to decipher not the genetic but the perceptual code. In a global information environment, the old pattern of education in answer-finding is of no avail: one is surrounded by answers, millions of them, moving and mutating at electric speed. Survival and control will depend on the ability to probe and to question in the proper way and place. As the information that constitutes the environment is perpetually in flux, so the need is not for fixed concepts but rather for the ancient skill of reading that book, for navigating through an ever uncharted and unchartable milieu. Else we will have no more control of this technology and environment than we have of the wind and the tides. (*LM*: 239)

McLuhan's final point is an important one. If the humanities are to live up to their full potential as interdisciplinary endeavours, they need to engage with central questions related to pedagogy (i.e., ethics, knowledge formations and perceptual modalities) within situations recognized as simultaneous, multiple, relational, historical and ultimately unified.

Note

1 Interview with Ed Fitzgerald, *The New Majority*, 25 August 1970, CBC Television in *Understanding McLuhan* CDROM.

Afterword

Evidence of Things Not Seen

> Faith is the substance of things hoped for,
> The evidence of things not seen. (St Paul)

McLuhan combines a history of mentalities with a discussion of technologies, aesthetics and phenomenology. He sees human communication in terms of the miracle of perception and of language. As I have attempted to highlight throughout this study, McLuhan's approach to the media is premised on a faith in a common human bond. He was concerned with 'the evidence of things not seen' and he was occupied by 'the transparent meanings of miracles', that is, their symbolism (Carpenter, 2001: 247). Let me conclude this study with a film by Toronto artist Barbara Sternberg that centres on small gestures, a phenomenology of everyday life and symbolic exchanges that crystallize many of the themes touched upon in McLuhan's project. *Like a Dream that Vanishes* (1999) juxtaposes three interrelated puzzles: a philosophical discussion of miracles, cinematic ontology, and human communication. The film opens with scratched emulsion, a house at night, a woman swimming, flickering colors, a baby on a beach, roads – images marked by a beautiful materiality. We cut to John Davis, Professor of Philosophy at Queen's University in Kingston, Ontario, who lays out the film's central problematic with the eloquence and passion that comes from a lifetime of contemplating paradoxes: Do you believe in miracles? Divided into seven short parts, reference no doubt to the myth of

Creation, this question is defracted across the film. As John Davis takes this question apart, explicating David Hume's sceptical denouncement of miracles, Sternberg presents us with a montage of movements, reframing the argument in a rhetorical flash of light: a white lamb, optically printed lightening bolts, sun reflecting off of water, light streaks across emulsion. Sternberg cuts back to philosopher John Davis throughout the film; his presence and words inflect our reading of the images. An old man at the end of his life, Davis looks shyly towards the camera, speaking to the film-maker directly as if in conversation. Each time we return to him, the argument and the debates that ensued from Hume's famous challenge to religious belief are clarified in greater detail: possibly the definition of miracles was not accurate enough, perhaps we don't know enough about the laws of nature leaving the very character of a miracle inconsonant. Yet as the film unfolds, the argument against miracles appears increasingly incomplete, unresolved. Is it simply a word-game or can it tell us something about the world we inhabit?

In the juxtaposition of those small everyday gestures so familiar in Sternberg's films – film scratches, emulsion flares, Niagara Falls, children playing, teenagers drinking beer and smoking hash, a lake seen from a boat, two women in loving conversation, more children, the sky, the wind in the trees, light on water, old men debating in a town square, a woman blowing out a birthday candle, more children's parties, a man running on a dirt road, a young woman leaning over a bridge, a woman swimming – there is something present. In these images, silent for the most part, cut rhythmically to create a collage intensified by the contemplative music of Rainer Wiens, Hume's argument is displaced by the film-maker's sense of wonder.

Located in and through the connectedness of things, people and nature, the film sculpts an acoustic space that reconfigures the linearity of the argument. It lays the argument to rest on the brink of uncertainty, of excess – a mosaic of details reveals irreducible patterns of singularity. The birthday candle about to be blown out reoccurs throughout the film and is one of its central picturings: children blowing out candles, opening gifts, a woman leaning over, eyes closed, breathing a wish out into the darkness.

Such images speak to human yearnings, parochial faith: hoping, wishing, innocent belief in the future.

Experience

John Davis died shortly after Sternberg filmed the interview with him in 1998. This brings an added dimension to his reflections and presence in the film. Towards the end of the interview, he tells us that every culture has built into its very structure, the need to understand 'what it's all for', a need to make sense of the universe. Yet no one has solved the riddle, and the world is filled with contradictions and inconsistencies. Philosophy, he feels, has come full circle, is moving back to its origins of 'beginning in wonder'. He continues, 'the world is not a very tidy place, in fact, it's pretty messy'. Davis leans back in his chair and gives Sternberg a beautiful mischievous smile. This is the last time we will see him.

The fact that the world is a 'messy place' was the reason that McLuhan was attracted early on to the neo-realism of Zavattini. He was not as interested in theory as he was in developing methodologies for exploring situations in all their complexity.

Like a Dream that Vanishes does not resurrect anyone from the dead, nor does it promise a miracle, what it conveys, however, are the limits of the knowable, of the sacred contained in the very materiality of the life-world, in social rituals and languages, in the communication between people. The two lengthy sync-sound sequences in the film concern social interaction: two East Asian women sitting across from one another at a table, discussing a map, laughing, gesturing, engrossed in each other's directions. Teenagers hang out on a front porch in a Toronto neighbourhood, drinking and smoking pot to pass the evening hours. The camera does not intervene or pass judgement in either case, it simply captures at some distance the communication and the sharing that exists between people.

These social exchanges are grounded in gestures, words, clothes, meaningful glances. That is, they are in the cultural fabric and rhetorical forms that bind communities. The final sequences of the film record communities in movement. Marches, parades, and celebrations of solidarity are sites of communal identities and communication in Toronto: Chinatown, Caribana, the Gay and Lesbian Pride Parade. The very last image in the film returns us to the black-and-white sequence of a woman blowing out a birthday candle. It brings us to the wish and crucially to the gift. It is fitting that Sternberg ends the film on this image for gift-giving is perhaps the oldest of social rituals, initiating and maintaining relationships. It is a gesture that is undoubtedly at the root of community as Mauss's work on the society of the gift has shown. The gift as the manifestation of relationality, of the space between things is held out not as actuality but as potentiality, tied to the wish that disappears into darkness. It is this darkness that the film insists upon, and like a dream that vanishes, we are left swimming in the uncertainty not of a future tense but of the present moment, which is always passing. Inherent in this moment of communication, of wishing and of gift, there are always the social structures of ritual and emotion, of hierarchies and of power that generate changes and revolution. It is this space that McLuhan always reserved for the power of art as expression of human cognition and enchantment. To the accusation that he lacked 'the full understanding of the drama of human relations', he would respond:

> I have been *amazed* at the range of current drama and perhaps have been mesmerized rather than *illuminated*. There is a phrase of Aristotle's: *Causae ad invicem causae sunt*. This is the drama that I am involved in, and it is very difficult to find a beginning, middle, or end except in the most arbitrary way. What I have found is enormous enjoyment and thrill in experiencing the events that are on every hand. It seems to me that this steady enjoyment of these events is a sufficient value system insofar as it asserts the joy of mere existence. (quoted in Theall, 2001: 219)

Bibliography

Marshall McLuhan Cited Works

'The aesthetic moment in landscape poetry', in Alan Downe (ed.), *English Institute Essays*. New York: Columbia University Press, pp. 168–81 (1952).

'Aesthetic patterns in Keats' Odes', *University of Toronto Quarterly*, 12 (2): 167–79 (1943).

'An ancient quarrel in modern America', *Classical Journal*, 41 (4): 156–62 (1946).

'Canada: the borderline case', in David Staines (ed.), *The Canadian Imagination: Dimensions of a Literary Culture*. Cambridge, MA: Harvard University Press, pp. 226–48 (1977).

'Catholic humanism and modern letters', in *Christian Humanism in Letters: The McAuley Lectures, Series 2*. West Hartford, CT: Saint Joseph College, pp. 49–67 (1954).

'Coleridge as artist', in Clarence D. Thorpe, Carlos Baker and Bennett Weaver, *The Major English Romantic Poets: A Symposium in Reappraisal*. Carbondale, IL: Southern Illinois University Press, pp. 83–99 (1957).

Counterblast. New York: Harcourt, Brace and World (1969).

Culture is Our Business. New York: McGraw-Hill (1970).

'Culture without literacy', *Explorations*, 1: 117–27 (1953).

'Edgar Poe's tradition', *Sewanee Review*, 52 (1): 24–33 (1944).

'Excerpts from a paper given at the National Conference on Canadian Goals', *Financial Post*, 26 September, p. 57 (1964).

'Foreword' (1964) *Bias of Communication* by Harold Innis, Toronto: University of Toronto Press.

'Foreword' (1975) *Empire and Communications* by Harold Innis, Toronto: University of Toronto Press.

From Cliché to Archetype. New York: Viking (1970).

'G.K. Chesterton: a practical mystic', *Dalhousie Review*, 15: 455–64 (1936).

The Global Village: Transformations in World Life and Media in the 21st Century. New York: Oxford University Press (1992).

'Guaranteed income in the electric age', in Richard Kostelanetz (ed.), *Beyond Left and Right: Radical Thought for Our Times*. New York: William Morrow, pp. 72–83 (1968).

The Gutenberg Galaxy: The Making of Typographic Man. Toronto: University of Toronto Press (1961).

'Innis and Communication' *Explorations* 3 (August 1954): 96–126.

'James Joyce: trivial and quadrivial', *Thought* 28 (108): 75–98 (1953).

'Joyce, Aquinas, and the poetic process', in Thomas E. Connolly (ed.), *Joyce's Portrait*. New York: Appleton Century Crofts (1962).

'Joyce, Mallarmé, and the press', *Sewanee Review*, 62 (1): 38–55 (1954).

Letters of Marshall McLuhan, eds Matie Molinaro, Corinne McLuhan and William Toye. Toronto: Oxford University Press (1987).

'Living at the speed of light', *Maclean's*, 93: 32–3 (1980).

'Manifestos', *Explorations*, 8: n.p. (1957).

The Mechanical Bride: Folklore of Industrial Man. New York: Vanguard (1951).

'New media as political forms', *Explorations*, 3: 120–6 (1954).

'Notes on Burroughs', *Nation*, 195 (5): 7–19 (1964).

'Notes on the media as art forms', *Explorations*, 2: 6–13 (1954).

'People of the word', *Explorations*, 8: n.p. (1957).

'Poetic vs rhetorical exegesis: the case for Leavis against Richards and Empson', *Sewanee Review*, 52 (2): 266–76 (1944).

'Pound's critical prose', in Peter Russell, (ed.), *Ezra Pound: A Collection of Essays*. London: Peter Nevill, pp. 165–71 (1950).

'Radio and Tv vs. The Abced-Minded', *Explorations*, 5: 12–18 (1955).

Report on Project in Understanding New Media (1960) National Association of Educational Broadcasters: United States Department of Health, Education and Welfare.

'Space, time and poetry', *Explorations* 4: 56–62 (1955).

'Tennyson and picturesque poetry', *Essays in Criticism*, 1 (3): 262–82 (1951).

Understanding Media: The Extensions of Man. New York: McGraw-Hill (1964).

'Wyndham Lewis: his theory of art and communication', *Shenandoah*, 4 (2–3): 77–88 (1953).

With Edmund Carpenter, 'Classroom without walls', *Explorations*, 7: 22–6 (1957).

With Quentin Fiore and Jerome Agel, *The Medium is the Massage* (vinyl LP, produced by John Simon). Columbia Records of CBS, Inc. (1967).

With Quentin Fiore and Jerome Agel, *The Medium is the Massage: An Inventory of Effects*. New York: Bantam (1967).

With Quentin Fiore and Jerome Agel, *War and Peace in the Global Village*. New York: Bantam (1968).

With Kathryn Hutchon and Eric McLuhan, *The City as Classroom: Understanding Language and Media*. Agincourt, Ontario: Book Society of Canada (1977).

With Eric McLuhan, *Laws of Media: The New Science*. Toronto: University of Toronto Press (1988).

With H.J.B. Nevitt, *Take Today: The Executive as Drop-Out*. New York: Harcourt Brace Jovanovich (1972).

With Harley Parker, *Through the Vanishing Point: Space in Poetry and Painting*. New York: Harper and Row (1968).

Other Works Quoted

Abram, M.H. (1997) 'The transformation of English studies 1930–1995' Daeldalus (Winter): 105–131.

Adorno, T.W. (1977) 'Letters to Walter Benjamin', in *Aesthetics and Politics*, trans. and ed. R. Taylor. London: New Left Books.

Altschiell, J. Herbert (1990) *From Milton to McLuhan: Ideas and American Journalism*. London: Longman.

Appadurai, Arjun (1996) *Modernity at Large: Cultural Dimensions of Globalization*. Minneapolis: University of Minnesota Press.

Arendt, Hanna (1958) *The Human Condition*. Chicago: University of Chicago Press.

Arnold, Matthew (1993) *'Culture and Anarchy' and Other Writings*, ed. Stefan Collini. Cambridge: Cambridge University Press.

Barthes, Roland (1968) *Writing Degree Zero*, trans. Annette Lavers and Colin Smith. New York: Hill and Wang.

Barthes, Roland (1970) *Mythologies*, trans. Annette Lavers. London: Vintage.

Barthes, Roland (1977) *Roland Barthes*, trans. Richard Howard. New York: Hill and Wang.

Barthes, Roland (1978) *A Lover's Discourse: Fragments*, trans. Richard Howard. New York: Hill and Wang.

Barthes, Roland (1981) *Le Grain de la voix: Entretiens 1962–1980*. Paris: Editions du Seuil.

Bataille, Georges (1986) *Eroticism: Death and Sensuality*, trans. Mary Dalwood. San Francisco: City Lights Books.

Baudrillard, Jean (1983) *Simulations*, trans. Paul Foss, Paul Patton and Philip Beitchman. New York: Semiotext(e).

Baudrillard, Jean (1995) *Simulacra and Simulation*. trans. Sheila Glaser. Ann Arbor: University of Michigan Press.

Benedetti, Paul and DeHart, Nancy (eds) (1996) *Forward through the Rearview Mirror: Reflections on and by Marshall McLuhan*. Scarborough, ONT: Prentice Hall.

Benjamin, Walter (1969) 'The work of art in the age of mechanical reproduction', in *Illuminations*, ed. Hannah Arendt and trans. Harry Zohn. New York: Schocken Books.

Benjamin, Walter (1999) *The Arcades Project*, trans. Howard Eiland and Kevin McLaughlin and ed. Rolf Tiedemann. Cambridge, MA: Belknap Press.

Berland, Jody and Shelley Hornstein (2000) *Capital Culture: A Reader on Modernist Legacies, State Institutions and the Values of Art*. Montréal: McGill-Queen's University Press.

Black, David J. (2002) *Politics of Enchantment: Romanticism Media and Cultural Studies*. Waterloo: Wilfrid Laurier University Press.

Bordwell, David (1974–5) 'Eisenstein's epistemological shift', *Screen*, 15 (4): 37–54.

Bowler, Peter (1989) *The Invention of Progress: The Victorians and the Past*. Oxford: Blackwell.

Buck-Morss, Susan (1999) *The Dialectics of Seeing: Walter Benjamin and the Arcades Project*. Cambridge, MA: MIT Press.

Burch, Noel (1990) *Life to those Shadows*, trans. Ben Brewster. Berkeley, CA: University of California Press.

Burger, Peter (1984) *Theory of the Avant-Garde*, trans. Michael Shaw. Minneapolis: University of Minnesota Press.

Carey, James (1983) The origins of the radical discourse on Cultural Studies in the United States, *Journal of Communication (Summer)*: 311–313.

Cameron, Evan W. (1989) 'McLuhan's method (or: The Mad Hatter at tea with Austin and Wittgenstein)', unpublished lecture notes for address to the Conference of the Film Studies Association of Canada, University of Regina, Saskatchewan, 20 May.

Carey, James W. (1968) 'Harold Adams Innis and Marshall McLuhan', in *McLuhan: Pro and Con*, ed. Raymond Rosenthal. Baltimore, MD: Penguin, pp. 270–308.

Carey, James W. (1981) 'McLuhan and Mumford: the roots of modern media analysis', *Journal of Communication*, 31 (3): 162–78.

Carey, James W. (1986) 'Walter Benjamin, Marshall McLuhan and the emergence of visual Society', *Prospects*, 11: 29–38.

Carey, James W. and Quile, John J. (1970) 'The mythos of the electronic revolution', *American Scholar*, 39 (2)(3): 219–41 (395–429).

Carpenter, Edmund (2001) 'That not-so-silent sea', in Donald Theall, *The Virtual Marshall McLuhan*. Toronto: University of Toronto Press, pp. 236–61.

Carpenter, Edmund and McLuhan, Marshall (eds) (1966) *Explorations in Communication: An Anthology*. Boston: Beacon Press.

Castells, Manuel (2001) *The Internet Galaxy: Reflections on the Internet, Business and Society*. Oxford: Oxford University Press.

Caulfield, Jon (1994) *City Form and Everyday Life: Toronto's Gentrification and Critical Social Practice*. Toronto: University of Toronto Press.

Cavell, Richard (2002) *McLuhan in Space: A Cultural Geography*. Toronto: University of Toronto Press.

Chambers, Iain (1990) *Border Dialogues: Journeys in Postmodernity*. London: Routledge.

Chaplin, J.P. (1975) *Dictionary of Psychology*. New York: Dell Publishing Co.

Charland, William A. (1990) *The Heart of the Global Village: Technology and the New Millennium*. London: SCM Press.

Chesterton, G.K. (1910) *What's Wrong with the World*. London: Cassell.

Chion, Michel (1994) *Audio-Vision: Sound on Screen*, ed. and trans. Claudia Gorbman. New York: Columbia University Press.

Coleridge, Samuel Taylor (1936) *Coleridge's Miscellaneous Criticism*, ed. Thomas Middleton Raysor. London: Constable.

Curtis, James M. (1978) *Culture as Polyphony: An Essay on the Nature of Paradigms*. Columbia: University of Missouri Press.

Curtis, James M. (1981) 'McLuhan: the aesthete as historian', *Journal of Communication*, 31 (3): 144–52.

Czitrom, Daniel (1982) *Media and the American Mind: From Morse to McLuhan*. Chapel Hill, NC: University of North Carolina Press.

Debord, Guy (1983) *Society of the Spectacle*. Detroit: Black and Red

Debray, Régis (1996) *Media Manifestos: On the Technological Transmission of Cultural Forms*, trans. Eric Rauth. London: Verso.

De Grazia, Sebastian (1964) *Of Time, Work and Leisure*. Garden City, NY: Doubleday.

Deleuze, Gilles and Guattari, Félix (1983) *Anti-Oedipus: Capitalism and Schizophrenia*, trans. Robert Hurley, Mark Seem and Helen R. Lane. Minneapolis: University of Minnesota Press.

Descartes, Réné (1954) *Descartes: Philosophical Writings*. London: Nelson.

Dickens, Charles (1949) *Oliver Twist*. London: Oxford University Press.

Eco, Umberto (1986) *Travels in Hyperreality*. London: Harcourt Brace Jovanovich.

Eikhenbaum, Boris (1974–5) 'Problems in film stylistics', *Screen*, 15 (4): 23–29.

Einstein, Elizabeth (1979) *The Printing Press as Agent of Change*. Cambridge: Cambridge University Press.

Eisenstein, Sergei (1949a) 'Dickens, Griffith and the film today', in *Film Form: Essays in Film Theory*, trans. Jay Leyda. New York: Harcourt Brace Jovanovich Inc.

Eisenstein, Sergei (1949b) 'A dialectical approach to film form', in *Film Form: Essays in Film Theory*, trans. Jay Leyda. New York: Harcourt Brace Jovanovich Inc.

Eisenstein, Sergei (1969a) *The Film Sense*, trans. and ed. Jay Leyda. New York: Harcourt, Brace and World.

Eisenstein, Sergei (1969b) *Selected Essays*. London: Faber and Faber.

Eliade, Mircea (1961) *The Sacred and the Profane: The Nature of Religion*. New York: Harper and Row.

Eliot, T.S. (1950) *Selected Essays*. New York: Harcourt Brace & Co.

Eliot, T.S. (1955) *The Use of Poetry and the Use of Criticism*. New York: Barnes & Noble.

Empson, William (1965) *Seven Types of Ambiguity*. Harmondsworth: Penguin.

Febvre, Lucien and Martin, Henri-Jean (1997) *The Coming of the Book: The Impact of Printing 1450–1800*, trans. David Gerard. London: Verso.

Fekete, John (1978) *The Critical Twilight: Explorations in the Ideology of Anglo-American Literary Theory from Eliot to McLuhan*. London: Routledge & Kegan Paul.

Fekete, John (1982) 'Massage in the mass age: remembering the McLuhan matrix', *Canadian Journal of Political and Social Theory*, 6 (3): 50–66.

Ferguson, Marjorie (1991) 'Marshall McLuhan revisited: 1960s Zeitgeist victim or pioneer postmodernist?', *Media, Culture and Society*, 13: 71–90.

Finklestein, Sidney (1968) *Sense and Nonsense of McLuhan*. New York: International Publishers.

Fitzgerald, Judith (2001) *Marshall McLuhan: Wise Guy*. Montreal: XYZ Publishers.

Flew, Anthony (1984) *A Dictionary of Philosophy*. New York: St Martin's Press.

Foster, Hal (2002) *Design and Crime and Other Diatribes*. London: Verso.

Foucault, Michel (1971) *The Order of Things*. New York: Patheon Books.

Foucault, Michel (1980) 'Two lectures', in Colin Gordon (ed./trans), *Power/ Knowledge: Selected Interviews and Other Writings*. New York: Patheon Books.

Foucault, Michel (1995) *Discipline and Punish: The Birth of the Prison*, trans. Alan Sheridan, 2nd edn. New York: Vintage Books.

Freud, Sigmund (1961) *Beyond the Pleasure Principle*, ed. James Strachey. New York: Norton.

Freud, Sigmund (1999) *The Interpretation of Dreams*, trans. Joyce Crick. Oxford: Oxford University Press.

Genosko, Gary (2001) *McLuhan and Baudrillard: The Masters of Implosion*. London: Sage.

Giedion, Siegfried (1967) *Space, Time and Architecture: The Growth of a New Tradition*, 5th edn. Cambridge, MA: Harvard University Press.

Giedion, Siegfried (1970) *Mechanization Takes Command: A Contribution to Anonymous History*. New York: Oxford University Press.

Gilmore, Myron (1959) 'The Renaissance conception of the lessons of history', in William Werkmeister (ed.), *Facets of the Renaissance*. New York: Harper and Row.

Gombrich, Ernst (1960) *Art and Illusion*. New York: Pantheon.

Gordon, Terrence W. (1997) *Marshall McLuhan: Escape into Understanding: A Biography*. New York: Basic Books.

Grosswiler, Paul (1998) *Method is the Message: Re-thinking McLuhan through Critical Theory*. Montréal, New York: Black Rose Books.

Habermas, Jurgen (1989) *The Structural Transformation of the Public Sphere: An Inquiry into a Category of Bourgeois Society*. Cambridge: MIT Press.

Hall, Stuart, with Laurence Grossberg (1996) 'On postmodernism and articulation: an interview with Stuart Hall', in David Morley and Kuan-Hsing Chen (eds), *Stuart Hall: Critical Dialogues in Cultural Studies*. London: Routledge, pp. 131–50.

Heidegger, Martin (1977) *The Question Concerning Technology and Other Essays*, trans. William Lovitt. New York: Garland Publishing.

Heyer, Paul (1989) 'Probing the legacy: McLuhan's communications history twenty-five years after', *Canadian Journal of Communication*, 14 (Winter): 30–45.

Heyer, Paul (2003) *Harold Innis*. Maryland: The Rowan and Littlefield Publishing Group.

Horrocks, Chris (2000) *Marshall McLuhan and Virtuality*. Cambridge: Icon Books.

Innis, Harold (1950) *Empire and Communications*. Toronto: University of Toronto Press.

Innis, Harold (1951) *The Bias of Communication*. Toronto: University of Toronto Press.

Innis, Harold (1956) *Essays in Canadian Economic History*. Toronto: University of Toronto Press.

Innis, Harold (1970) *The Fur Trade in Canada: An Introduction to Canadian Economic History*. Toronto: University of Toronto Press.

Jameson, Fredric (1981) *The Political Unconscious: Narrative as a Socially Symbolic Act*. Ithaca, NY: Cornell University Press.

Jeffrey, Liss (1989) 'The heat and the light: towards a reassessment of the contribution of H. Marshall McLuhan', *Canadian Journal of Communcation* 14 (Winter): 1–29.

Jung, Carl (1977) 'Foreword', in *The I Ching or Book of Changes*, trans. Richard Wilhelm, rendered into English by Cary F. Baynes. Princeton, NJ: Princeton University Press, pp. xxi–xxxix.

Koestler, Arthur (1961) *The Sleepwalkers: A History of Man's Changing Vision of the Universe*. London: Hutchinson.

Kroker, Arthur (1984) *Technology and the Canadian Mind: Innis, McLuhan, Grant*. Montreal: New World Perspectives.

Leavis, F.R. (1930) *Mass Civilization and Minority Culture*. Cambridge: Minority Press.

Leavis, F.R. ([1936] 1949) *Revaluation: Tradition and Development in English Poetry*. London: Chatto and Windus.

Leavis, F.R. and Thompson, Denys (1933) *Culture and Environment: The Training of Critical Awareness*. London: Chatto and Windus.

Lee, Dorothy (1959) *Freedom and Culture*. Englewood Cliffs, NJ: Prentice Hall.

Lee, Dorothy (1976) *Valuing the Self: What We Can Learn from Other Cultures*. Prospect Heights, IL: Waveland Press.

Lewis, C.S. (1967) *The Allegory of Love: A Study in Medieval Tradition*. London: Oxford University Press.

Lewis, Wyndham (1928) *Time and Western Man*. New York: Harcourt Brace.

Lewis, Wyndham ([1932] 1973) *Doom of Youth*. New York: Haskell House.

Lukács, Georg (1972) *Studies in European Realism*, trans. Edith Bone. London: Merlin Press.

Manovitch, Lev (1999) 'Avant-garde as software', in Stephen Kovats (ed.), *Ostranenie*. Frankfurt: Campus Verlag.

Manovich, Lev (2001) *The Language of New Media*. Cambridge, MA: MIT Press.

Marchand, Phillip (1989) *Marshall McLuhan: The Medium and the Messenger*. New York: Ticknor & Fields.

Massey, Doreen (1994) *Space, Place and Gender*. Minneapolis: University of Minnesota Press.

Masuda, Yeneji (1981) *The Information Society as Post-Industrial Society*. Bathesda: World Future Society.

McCallum, Pamela (1989) 'Walter Benjamin and Marshall McLuhan: theories of history', *Signature* (Summer): 71–89.

McNamara, Eugene (ed.) (1969) *The Interior Landscape: The Literary Criticism of Marshall McLuhan*. New York: McGraw-Hill.

Merleau-Ponty, Maurice (1973) *The Prose of the World*, trans. John O'Neill and ed. Claude Lefort. Evanston, IL: Northwestern University Press.

Miller, Jonathan (1971) *Marshall McLuhan*. New York: Viking Press.

Monk, Ray (1991) *Ludwig Wittgenstein: The Duty of Genius*. London: Vintage.

Mumford, Lewis (1961) *The City in History: Its Origins, its Transformations, and Its Prospects*. New York: Harcourt, Brace and World.

Mumford, Lewis (1963) *Technics and Civilization*. New York: Harcourt, Brace and World.

Nevitt, Barrington and McLuhan, Maurice (1994) *Who Was Marshall McLuhan?: Exploring a Mosaic of Impressions*, ed. Frank Zingrone, Wayne Constantineau and Eric McLuhan. Toronto: Stoddart.

Norden, Eric ([1969] 1995) 'Playboy interview: Marshall McLuhan' (*Playboy*, March), in Eric McLuhan and Frank Zingrone (eds), *Essential McLuhan*. Toronto: Anansi Press, pp. 233–69.

Ogden, C.K. et al. (1923) *The Meaning of Meaning: A Study of the Influence of Language upon Thought and the Science of Symbolism*. London: Kegan Paul, Trench, Trubner.

Ong, Walter (1981) 'McLuhan as teacher: the future is a thing of the past', *Journal of Communication*, 31 (3): 129–35.

Patterson, Graeme (1990) *History of Communications: Harold Innis, Marshall McLuhan, and the Interpretation of History*. Toronto: University of Toronto Press.

Pope, Alexander (1963) *The Dunciad*, ed. James Sutherland, 3rd edn. London: Methuen.

Porter, John (1984) 'Artists discovering film in post-war Toronto', *Vanguard*, 13: 5–6.

Rabelais, François (1974) *Pantagruel*. Paris: Gallimard.

Ransom, John Crowe (1941) *The New Criticism*. Norfolk, CT: New Directions.

Richards, I.A. (1925) *Principles of Literary Criticism*. London: Kegan Paul, Trench, Trubner.

Richards, I.A. (1950) *Coleridge on Imagination*. London: Routledge & Kegan Paul.

Richards, I.A. (1962) *Practical Criticism: A Study of Literary Judgement*. New York: Harcourt, Brace and World.

Roberts, Donald F. and Ulla G. Foelr. (2004) *Kids and Media in America*. Cambridge: Cambridge University Press.

Robertson, Gigi (1989) *Canadian Journal of Communications* 14 (Winter): i–ii.

Robins, Kevin and Frank Webster (1990) 'Broadcasting politics: communications and consumption' in Manuel Alvarado and John Thompson (eds), *The Media Reader*. London: BFI.

Rosenthal, Raymond (1968) *McLuhan: Pro and Con*. Baltimore, MD: Penguin.

Ross, Andrew (1965) 'High priest of pop culture', *Maclean's*, 78 (131): 42–3.

Ross, Andrew (1989) *No Respect: Intellectuals and Popular Culture*. New York: Routledge.

Samson, Anne (1992) *F.R. Leavis*. Toronto: University of Toronto Press.

Satre, Jean-Paul (1956, 1988) *Being and Nothingness*. Trans. Ruth Nehad. New York: Paragon Books.

Sassen, Saskia (2001) *The Global City: New York, London, Tokyo*. Princeton, NJ: Princeton University Press.

Shelley, Percy Bysshe ([1821] 1891) *A Defence of Poetry*, ed. Albert S. Cook. Boston: Ginn.

Smith, Michael Peter (2001) *Transnational Urbanism: Locating Globalization*. Oxford: Blackwell Publishers.

Spivak, Chakravorty Gayatri (1999) *Death of a Discipline*. New York: Columbia University Press.

Spivak, Gayatri Chakravorty (1999). *A Critique of Post-Colonial Reason: Toward a History of the Vanishing Present*. Cambridge Mass.: Harvard University Press.

Stamps, Judith (1990) 'The bias of theory: a critique of Pamela McCallum's "Walter Benjamin and Marshall McLuhan: Theories of history"', *Signature* 3 (Summer): 44–62.

Stamps, Judith (1995) *Unthinking Modernity: Innis, McLuhan and the Frankfurt School*. Montreal: McGill-Queen's University Press.

Stearn, Gerald E. (ed.) (1967) *McLuhan: Hot and Cool: A Critical Symposium with a Rebuttal by McLuhan*. New York: Dial Press.

Steiner, George (1967) 'As for Blake, McLuhan is his successor over and over again', in Gerald Stearn (ed.), *McLuhan: Hot and Cool*. New York: Signet Books.

Stengers, Isabelle (2000) *The Invention of Modern Science*, trans. Daniel W. Smith. Minneapolis: University of Minnesota Press.

Stevenson, Nick (1995) *Understanding Media Cultures: Social Theory and Mass Communication*. London: Sage.

Theall, Donald F. (1971) *The Medium is the Rear-View Mirror: Understanding McLuhan*. Montreal: McGill-Queen's University Press.

Theall, Donald F. (2001) *The Virtual Marshall McLuhan*. Montreal: McGill-Queen's University Press.

Thompson, Denys (ed.) (1932–53) *Scrutiny*. Cambridge: Deighton Bell, May 1932–October 1953.

Tomlinson, John (1991) *Cultural Imperialism*. Baltimore: The Johns Hopkins University Press.

Tomlinson, John (1999) *Globalization and Culture*. Chicago: University of Chicago Press.

Turrow, Joseph (1989) *Playing Doctor: Television, Storytelling and Medical Power*. New York: Oxford University Press.

Ulmer, Gregory (1985) *Applied Grammatology: Post(e)-Pedagogy from Jacques Derrida to Joseph Beuys*. Baltimore, MD: Johns Hopkins University Press.

Vico, Giambattista (1984) *The New Science of Giambattista Vico*, trans. Thomas Goddard Bergin and Max Harold Fisch. Ithaca, NY: Cornell University Press.

Von Békésy, Georg (1960) *Experiments in Hearing*, trans. E.G. Wever. New York: McGraw-Hill.

Wees, William C. (1972) *Vorticism and the English Avant-Garde*. Toronto: University of Toronto Press.

Whittaker, Edmund T. (1948) *Space and Spirit; Theories of the Universe and the Arguments for the Existence of God*. Hinsdale, IL: H. Regnery Co.

Willemen, Paul (1981) 'Cinematic discourse: the problem of inner speech', *Screen*, 22 (3): 54–69.

Williams, Raymond (1974) *Television, Technology and Cultural Form*. New York: Schocken Books.

Williams, Raymond (1989) *The Politics of Modernism*. London: Verso.

Willmott, Glenn (1996) *McLuhan, or Modernism in Reverse*. Toronto: University of Toronto Press.

Winston, Brian (1990) 'How are media born?', in John Dowling et al. (eds), *Questioning the Media*. London: Sage.

Wittgenstein, Ludwig ([1975] 2001) *Tractatus*, trans. D.F. Pears and B.F. McGuinness. London: Routledge.

Wolfflin, Heinrich (1905, 1950) *Principles of Art History: The Problem of the Development of Style in Later Art*, trans. M.D. Hottinger. New York: Dover Books.

Index